The Book of Daily Prayer

The Book of Daily Prayer

Morning and Evening, 1998

Kim Martin Sadler

Editor

United Church Press
Cleveland, Ohio

United Church Press, Cleveland, Ohio 44115
© 1997 by United Church Press

Biblical quotations are from the New Revised Standard Version of the Bible, © 1989
by the Division of Christian Education of the National Council of the Churches
of Christ in the U.S.A., and are used by permission

02 01 00 99 98 97   5 4 3 2 1

Library of Congress Cataloging-in-Publication Data

The book of daily prayer : morning and evening, 1998 / Kim Martin Sadler, editor.
p. cm.
ISBN 0-8298-1161-3 (alk. paper)
1. Prayers. 2. Devotional calendars. I. Sadler, Kim Martin.
BV 245.B586   1997
248'.8—dc20   95-51065
CIP

Contents

Introduction

The Book of Daily Prayer 1998 follows the success of last year's premiere edition. Those who have used this devotional guide every day can bear testimony to the renewal and revitalization of spirit they have experienced. Some have described the book as an "awesome" tool for prayerful reflection on the biblical text.

If you are using *The Book of Daily Prayer* as a personal devotional guide, begin by reading the Scripture passage for the day, followed by the opening prayer. The meditative prayer can be read aloud or silently. The intercessory prayers follow; here you are invited to lift up personal concerns and pray for others.

In some instances, the contributors have followed the intercessory prayers with words of encouragement, while others invite you to pray the Prayer of Our Savior. End with the closing prayer and repeat for evening devotions.

For those who are using the resource in a group setting, one person can read the Scripture verses aloud and another lead the group in the prayers. The meditative prayer may be said in unison. Each person may be invited to share in the intercessory prayers, followed by the words of encouragement or Prayer of Our Savior, which may be recited by the entire group. The group may end by joining in the closing prayer.

However you approach your daily devotions, we hope you will discover *The Book of Daily Prayer* to be an invaluable resource and will be inspired to use it year after year.

May God bless you.

THURSDAY, JANUARY 1
(Read Luke 2:41–52)

(Morning)
Loving God, I want to meet this day
knowing that you are with me
even though I may be unaware of your presence.

(Evening)
Loving God, throughout the day
you have been with me,
offering guidance and direction.

Eternal God, how often it is that we become disturbed by the celebration of our traditions and neglect your mission and purpose for our lives. Embrace us, O God, to find our way to your house, where we will find strength, hope, joy, and love.

(Morning)
Help me, O God, to seek your guidance and direction for this day.
(Prayers of Intercession)

(Evening)
O God, I thank you for the blessings of today
and for your abiding presence.
(Prayers of Intercession)

In the house of God there is joy.
(Pray the Prayer of Our Savior.)

(Morning)
Now, O God, lead me as I strive
to live for you. Amen.

(Evening)
As I take my rest, grant me your
peace that passes all understanding.
Amen.

FRIDAY, JANUARY 2
(Read 1 Samuel 2:18–20)

(Morning)
Eternal God, remind me
how precious are the little ones who love you.

(Evening)
Eternal God, I give you praise
for each child I have encountered this day.

O God of all people, through your servant Samuel, you have shown us that children can find a place in your service. Help us always to be open to the ministries that our children render in your church.

(Morning)
Bless, O God, each child who seeks your presence in his or her life.
(Prayers of Intercession)

(Evening)
Divine Parent, nurture each child who is in need of your tender care.
(Prayers of Intercession)

The innocence of children is the gift of God.
(Pray the Prayer of Our Savior.)

(Morning)
Dear God, let me be a blessing to a child this day. Amen.

(Evening)
O God, this night I pray for children who are hungry and homeless, that they may find rest in you. Amen.

SATURDAY, JANUARY 3
(Read Psalms 1 and 8)

(Morning)
Gracious God, I praise you for your goodness,
your mercy, and your love.

(Evening)
Gracious God, this day you have
shown me once again that you are worthy of praise.

You have taught us, O God, through the psalmist that all people should give praise to your name. Help me this day to find new ways to give you thanks and praise.

(Morning)
I give you praise this day, eternal God, because you are worthy.
(Prayers of Intercession)

(Evening)
O God of love, help me always to give you praise.
(Prayers of Intercession)

When the praises go up the blessings come down.
(Pray the Prayer of Our Savior.)

(Morning)
O God, may I this day give you the praise that is due to your name. Amen.

(Evening)
I praise you, loving God, that you watch over me even while I sleep. Amen.

12

SUNDAY, JANUARY 4
(Read Colossians 3:12–17)

(Morning)
O God, this morning as I adorn myself with garments of cloth,
may I also put on love.

(Evening)
O God, today I have tried to act as one of your chosen.

O God, the apostle Paul has taught us the importance of wearing a garment of righteousness. Keep us mindful of who we are and whose we are as we strive to live a life pleasing in your sight.

(Morning)
This day, dear God, let me walk in a way that is pleasing to you.
(Prayers of Intercession)

(Evening)
If I have failed to be what you wanted me to be this day,
forgive me, eternal God.
(Prayers of Intercession)

Christians need to dress for spiritual success.
(Pray the Prayer of Our Savior.)

(Morning)	(Evening)
Wonderful God, may my deportment this day be a blessing to others. Amen.	As I find my evening rest, may I find comfort in your providential care. Amen.

MONDAY, JANUARY 5
(Read Isaiah 43:1–4)

(Morning)
Holy One, I give you thanks for calling me by name
and guarding me with your love.

(Evening)
Holy One, I offer you praise for the ways your love
and care have sustained me this day.

I listen to the words you spoke to the fearful people of Israel, O God. The
sound is reassuring. Your people had been in exile so long that the dis-ease
of being forced to live in a foreign land had given way to habits of comfort
and routine. But now it was time to return home, to give up what had become known, to begin again. When I am afraid, do not let me become overwhelmed. Let me hear you when you tell me that I am precious in your
sight and that you love me.

(Morning)
Open me to new possibilities, O God.
(Prayers of Intercession)

(Evening)
Remind me of your steadfast love, O God.
(Prayers of Intercession)

With love for you and all creation, I pray.
(Pray the Prayer of Our Savior.)

(Morning)	(Evening)
Use me this day as a sign of your love.	Help me to recall your saving grace
Amen.	evident in the movement of the Spirit
	this day. Amen.

TUESDAY, JANUARY 6
(Read Isaiah 43:5–7)

(Morning)
Saving God, help me this day to navigate through perilous waters
and find joy in your sure promise of salvation.

(Evening)
Saving God, may I find my rest and strength in you,
gentled to sleep by your comforting presence.

When I think about what it means to be formed by you, O God, and created for your glory, I am startled by the intimacy that this implies. When I create something, I struggle to give it my essence, my joy, my love. When I form something, I strive to give it shape, care, intensity. To think that you would give this to me in the act of creating and forming me is almost too much to comprehend. But you say these words to me, and your word is true. Help me to trust in this relationship with you.

(Morning)
Stir in me compassion for the world you love.
(Prayers of Intercession)

(Evening)
Form me, O God, into one who is not overwhelmed by my fears.
(Prayers of Intercession)

Trusting your promises, I pray.
(Pray the Prayer of Our Savior.)

(Morning)
Spur me to compassionate acts this day, that I may find joy in service. Amen.

(Evening)
Quiet any restlessness within me this night, that I may awake attuned to your way. Amen.

WEDNESDAY, JANUARY 7
(Read Psalm 29:1–6)

(Morning)
O God, I begin this day confident of your sustaining presence.

(Evening)
O God, I rest from the labors of this day in the assurance of your gracious love.

Amidst the many competing sounds of life, your voice, Holy One, speaks to me. Will I be listening? Or will everyday distractions lure me to a place of inattentive wandering, of worshiping idols instead of you? Deter my misdirected attention when voices other than yours beckon. Help me to focus on you. Your voice is clear, like the clap of thunder. Your voice is sure, making my heart pulse with delight at the sound. Help me to profess your glory and strength. Keep me safe in you.

(Morning)
May the signs of your strength and majesty encourage me
to trust your power in the world.
(Prayers of Intercession)

(Evening)
Break open in me with lightning force
the desire to make known to you the prayers of my heart.
(Prayers of Intercession)

In awe and wonder, I pray.
(Pray the Prayer of Our Savior.)

(Morning)
God of glory, your voice calls the dawn into being. May I rise to this new day in hopeful anticipation of all that is before me to experience. Amen.

(Evening)
God of glory, your voice calls the night to enfold the day with darkness. May I rest in the splendor of your presence this night to dream new dreams. Amen.

THURSDAY, JANUARY 8
(Read Psalm 29:1–2, 7–11)

(Morning)
Majestic One, with joy I await your leading this day.

(Evening)
Majestic One, with weariness I surrender to you the tumult of this day.

Storms can be frightening: bright flashes of light, roars of thunder, winds that howl. The very thought leaves me feeling tense and uneasy. Like the storms in my life, they rage beyond my control, playing havoc with settled routines and entrenched ideas. And there you are, Creator, shaking my world with storms that shift the landscape of my habits and call me to praise you with a word: Glory! Help me to sense your majesty. Lead me to the place of peace that comes within the voice of the storm, that I might know your sheltering presence.

(Morning)
Shake the complacency from my heart with an invitation
to remember the needs of others.
(Prayers of Intercession)

(Evening)
Though storms may trouble my existence,
may I trust in your power over the whirling wind and mighty waters,
to bring life blessing and peace.
(Prayers of Intercession)

Ascribing glory to you, I pray.
(Pray the Prayer of Our Savior.)

(Morning)
May I live this day in faithful praise
of your name. Amen.

(Evening)
May I rest this night in your majestic
peace. Amen.

FRIDAY, JANUARY 9
(Read Luke 3:15–17)

(Morning)
Powerful Messiah, fill me with expectation this day.

(Evening)
Powerful Messiah, reassure my questioning heart this night.

Sometimes I feel so troubled by questions. They spin in my mind and heart, and I cannot seem to fend them off. Who are you, God? How do I know you? What are the signs? Where are you in my life? Having the questions without a hint to the answers leaves me feeling frustrated and alone. But you attend to questioning hearts; you send prophets and messengers to point to the way. Where are you pointing me, God? Let the chaff of my irritation at not having all the answers burn to ash. Fix in me a patient spirit to live the questions. Help me to look for your signs. Winnow my thoughts and claim the holy ones as rightfully yours. Gather me up, in your bountiful harvest, to nourish and serve a question-filled world.

(Morning)
Bring to my awareness in images of water and fire the powerful sweep of your gathering love. Inspire me to acts worthy of your name.
(Prayers of Intercession)

(Evening)
Let me not forget that you are the Messiah,
the Anointed One, who both loves and judges.
Forgive me when I question your authority in my life.
(Prayers of Intercession)

In humility, I pray.
(Pray the Prayer of Our Savior.)

(Morning)
Christ, help me to grow in my understanding of you as the one to whom I give my pledge of love and allegiance. Amen.

(Evening)
Christ, sift through the useless chaff of my sin and hold up for me the goodness you want me to live. Amen.

SATURDAY, JANUARY 10
(Read Luke 3:21–22)

(Morning)
O God, open me to the fluttering wings of your Spirit this day.

(Evening)
O God, as night embraces me, bring me to restfulness
by the murmuring voice of your Spirit.

After his baptism, while Jesus was praying, a wondrous thing happened. The heavens opened and the Holy Spirit alighted on him in the form of a dove. You, O God, proclaimed him your beloved child, with whom you were pleased. In this momentous event, prayer played a crucial part. Time and again, Jesus would withdraw to deserted places and pray. Time with you, O God, was critical to him. Is it so with me? What is it that draws me to prayer? What do I find when I seek you? What more do you want for our time together? In the deserted places, lead me to fresh insights.

(Morning)
Help me to be aware of the signs around me that reveal your love,
so that I might bring your good news to a world in need.
(Prayers of Intercession)

(Evening)
Set my heart and mind to the rhythms of your way,
calling me to greater faithfulness and love.
(Prayers of Intercession)

Touched by your Spirit, I pray.
(Pray the Prayer of Our Savior.)

(Morning)	(Evening)
In a mood of watchfulness, keep me yearning for the signs of your abiding Spirit this day. Amen.	In the stillness of this night, keep me searching for new ways to sense your closeness. Amen.

SUNDAY, JANUARY 11
(Read Acts 8:14–17)

(Morning)
Spirit of Truth, as this day begins, listen to my anxious heart
and draw me into your all-encompassing love.

(Evening)
Spirit of Truth, as this day comes to an end,
challenge my wandering mind to focus on you.

When the disciples heard that many in Samaria had accepted Jesus' message and had been baptized, they traveled there to pray for these believers. With the laying on of hands, Peter and John asked you, O God, to touch them with the Holy Spirit. How remarkable, Holy One, that your presence can be conveyed through the touch of another. But is it so surprising? Touch that is wanted, touch that conveys affirmation, touch that embodies all that is good, touch that is healing, is a mark of your love. Help me, O God, that I might be a bearer of your grace to all whom I touch.

(Morning)
Loving Spirit, nothing in all creation is beyond the depth and breadth of your love. Urge me on to ever-widening circles of inclusiveness in my love and concern for the world.
(Prayers of Intercession)

(Evening)
Renewing Spirit, help me to receive you with joy
and pray for creation with inspired love.
(Prayers of Intercession)

Fervently I pray.
(Pray the Prayer of Our Savior.)

(Morning)	(Evening)
Renew me, O God, in my commitment to creation and to all that is good. Amen.	Transform my casual concern for the world into a heartfelt passion for justice and inclusiveness. Amen.

MONDAY, JANUARY 12
(Read John 2:1–11)

(Morning)
Gracious God, you enliven my life and enrich my experience
with a mercy that is new every morning.
Give me grace to respond to your mercies with a grateful heart.

(Evening)
Gracious God, you have stretched out the heavens like a curtain; you have
ordered the change of the seasons and appointed the light to rule the day and
night. As I sleep, keep me safe from the snares of the evil one, and bring me and
all those I love to that perfect rest in you.

At the wedding feast in Cana, you were there, O God, in Christ! You did
not shrink from sharing your presence with us—even at a boisterous and
bawdy party! I learn from the presence of your Christ at this wedding party
that your loving concern for our well-being extends to all of human life, to
every human experience. You demonstrated at Cana that you are determined to redeem, to rescue, to enliven and enrich even my bawdy and boisterous moments! And when the party threatens to fail, your creative word
enlivens it again!

(Morning)
Condescending God, keep me aware today that you are with me in every
moment, not as judge or critic, but as companion.
(Prayers of Intercession)

(Evening)
Gracious God, you have enriched my life today in ways beyond my knowing.
Keep me conscious of your care in all I think and do and say,
in all those I meet, in everything I experience.
(Prayers of Intercession)

**Help me to see your glory and your good, O God, even in the bawdy and
boisterous, even in my moments of hilarity and frivolity.**

(Morning)	(Evening)
God of good times and of bad, help me to recognize your presence in those little moments of joy or exhila-ration which you have always en-trusted to those who believe. In Jesus' name. Amen.	I rest tonight confident in and grateful for your care, gracious God. I close my eyes in peace; let your holy angels keep me safe through all the hours of my helplessness. I pray in Jesus' name. Amen.

TUESDAY, JANUARY 13
(Read John 2:1–11)

(Morning)
God of all that is new, fresh, and unspoiled, I arise today in the confidence
that you have prepared another twenty-four hours pregnant with new possibility.
Help me to make the most of the opportunities to serve others
and to praise your goodness.

(Evening)
God of all that is new, fresh, and unspoiled, I praise you, as the labors and
loyalties of this day give way to the calm and quietude of rest. Charge your holy
angels to keep me in your care, and bring me fresh and enthusiastic to the
challenges and contentions of tomorrow.

God, you were present in Christ, at a simple village wedding! I marvel at
your presence here, and marvel more at your transforming power. At his
mother's urging, Jesus acted with authority and with grace to save the host
from embarrassment and his guests from diminished pleasure. Can I dare
to conclude that whenever, wherever human life is enriched, there is the in-
breaking of your reign?

(Morning)
Allow me the grace, loving God, to see your creative and redeeming hand at
work wherever human life or labor is enriched.
(Prayers of Intercession)

(Evening)
Ever-present God, the hours of night and day are both alike to you; the night
holds no terrors. Protect me through the time of my repose, and bring me safe
and refreshed to the hours of my waking.

In your light I will see light.

(Morning)
I commit myself today to offer all my
gifts and graces as potential signs of
the reign of God. May all I think, do,
and say become an advertisement for
your good, O God. Amen.

(Evening)
Guide me waking, O God, and guard
me sleeping, that awake I may watch
with Christ and asleep I may rest in
peace. Amen.

WEDNESDAY, JANUARY 14
(Read Isaiah 62:1–5)

(Morning)
God of all encouragement, you have told me through your prophet that you take delight in me. This promise from your prophet is enough. It will see me through this day and through all my days.

(Evening)
God of all encouragement, I offer to you, as an evening sacrifice, all my moments from the day now past. Accept them, in your mercy, as the homage of a humble heart. Use whatever is worthy there to the glory of your name and for the good of others.

"You shall be a crown of beauty in the hand of God. . . . As a bridegroom rejoices over the bride, so shall your God rejoice over you." At first hearing, I can scarcely believe these words from Israel's prophet. In my moments of depression or self-doubt, in my moments of shame, weakness, or inconstancy, I cannot imagine a God who loves me, who takes delight in me! Yet that is the assurance I hear from your Word, O Holy One of Israel. Keep this light always in my eye. Never let me lose the sense that you are Emmanuel: God-with-me, God-for-me. Keep me always aware of the promise that your last word to me will be the same as your first: not condemnation, but delight; not no, but yes.

(Morning)
Let me live today, great God, in the confidence in Christ that nothing will alter your perception of me as good, as worthy, as the object of your love, as the locus of your delight.
(Prayers of Intercession)

(Evening)
God of my good, I rest tonight in your care. I cast off my clothes.
I lie down to rest. And in the morning I will awaken and rise erect,
a figure of that resurrection life that you have promised in the victories of Jesus.
(Prayers of Intercession)

"You shall be called My Delight . . ."

(Morning)	(Evening)
I lift my head today, eyes bright with confidence in the sustaining love of a God who takes delight in me. Amen.	O God, in Christ you have declared that I am royalty from the day of my birth; from the womb before daybreak have you begotten me. Amen.

THURSDAY, JANUARY 15
(Read Psalm 36:5–10)

(Morning)
O loving God, because of Jesus, to you nothing human is alien.
I rise to face the day, even so, in the conviction that you do not abandon me;
your hand will sustain; your eye will guide;
your arm protect; and your love enfold.

(Evening)
O loving God, in your compassion, in my weakness and vulnerability,
keep me safe throughout the long night watch.
And when my final trial comes, keep me faithful.

I recall today, gracious God, that all through the generations you have been a light to those who are lost, a lamp to those who stumble, a tower of defense for those who fear, a well of water for those who thirst, a fountain of refreshment in a weary land. As you have led and supported your people of old, so lead and guide me. As you have fed and nourished your people of old, so feed and nurture me. As you have defended and vindicated your people of old, so save me in my time of trial.

(Morning)
Your love, O Sovereign, reaches to the heavens,
and your faithfulness to the clouds.
(Prayers of Intercession)

(Evening)
Keep me, O Sovereign, as the apple of your eye;
hide me in the shadow of your wings.
(Prayers of Intercession)

In your light we see light.

(Morning)
"The main thing is to keep the main thing the main thing," says a popular bumper sticker. I commit myself today to seek one thing, the will of God, and nothing else. Amen.

(Evening)
In righteousness I shall see you; when I awake, your presence will give me joy. Amen.

FRIDAY, JANUARY 16
(Read 1 Corinthians 12:1–11)

(Morning)
Generous and compassionate God, you have given me lavish gifts, pressed down, shaken together, running over. Today help me to make the most of what you have given me, to offer myself to your glory and to your people's good.

(Evening)
Generous and compassionate God, it was on a Friday afternoon that your Son Jesus yielded up his breath in death. Tonight I remember that my Christ shares even this with me: my journey into death. Protect me through the hours of my vulnerability, and bring me refreshed tomorrow to new life.

Today I recall that I am one member of a body whose head is Christ and whose tissues, limbs, and organs are my sisters and brothers in faith. I have been given my distinct and irreplaceable gifts; my brothers and sisters each have been given their own. Help me to recall my dependence on each brother and each sister in Christ. Help me to offer my gift as it is needed, willingly, for our common good.

(Morning)
Blessed be the God of Israel; you have come to your people and set them free.
(Prayers of Intercession)

(Evening)
It is good to give thanks to God, to sing praise to your name, O Most High; to herald your love in the morning, your truth at the close of the day.
(Prayers of Intercession)

To each is given the manifestation of the Spirit for the common good.

(Morning)
O God, open my lips, and my mouth shall declare your praise. Amen.

(Evening)
Stay with us, God, for it is evening and the day is almost over. Let your light scatter the gloom and illumine your church. Amen.

SATURDAY, JANUARY 17
(Read 1 Corinthians 12:1–11)

(Morning)
O Christ, through the night and into the morning, your broken body was laid in
Joseph's tomb. But after your crucifixion and before your resurrection,
you stormed the stronghold of the enemy and vanquished
the powers of hell itself, setting free all whom sin had bound.
Today, set me free from all that enslaves me.

(Evening)
O Christ, you have apportioned generous gifts to all.
Give me one thing more: a grateful heart.

I am sometimes guilty, O God, of a narrowness of vision that ignores my
brothers and sisters in Christ. The "priesthood of all believers" is a precious insight from the Reformation, but it must never be interpreted to
imply that faith is strictly a matter between me and you. The life of faith is
always a life that embraces me, you, and them—the sisters and brothers in
the household of faith. Help me always to remember that I need other people;
that I have come to faith through them; that I have access to you, great
God, through them, because of them. Keep me in solidarity with all who
believe. And give me grace to receive their gifts with gratitude.

(Morning)
As many as have been baptized into Christ have put on Christ.
Bring me with your saints to glory everlasting.
(Prayers of Intercession)

(Evening)
My soul proclaims the greatness of God; my spirit rejoices in God, my Savior.
(Prayers of Intercession)

Now there are varieties of gifts, but the same Spirit;
and there are varieties of services, but the same God.

(Morning)
May God Almighty bless me and direct
my days and my deeds in peace. Amen.

(Evening)
Let my prayer rise before you as
incense, the lifting up of my hands as
the evening sacrifice. Amen.

SUNDAY, JANUARY 18
(Read John 2:1–11)

(Morning)
O Creator God, today is Sunday, the new Sabbath. Your mercies are new every morning, and each day presents new opportunities, new possibilities, new beginnings. I give you thanks that your door is never closed but forever open.

(Evening)
O Creator God, I rest tonight in the confidence that your reign and rule have begun, in Christ. Awaken me refreshed tomorrow to take up once again my work with you as created co-creator.

You turned the water into wine, gracious Sovereign, at Cana's feast; you enlivened a village wedding; you rescued its host from a disastrous social situation; you nourished its guests. And you presented me with a vision of the fullness of the reign of God: human relationships restored; human life enriched, renewed, and rescued; human community completed and made whole. And in all of this, you revealed your glory. Allow me the privilege of helping you. Put me to work, this coming week, in just such tasks.

(Morning)
Keep me mindful, Creator God, of the importance of my role in serving your world, your people, as Christ served. I know that your reign comes indeed of itself, without my prayer. But remind me, today and always, that it may also come in me, through me, because of me.
(Prayers of Intercession)

(Evening)
Stay with me, God, for it is evening and the day is almost over.
(Prayers of Intercession)

**You nights and days, bless God; you sun and clouds, bless God.
We praise you and magnify you forever.**

(Morning)	(Evening)
I commit myself to share this week in Christ's work in the world and with all peoples. Amen.	Direct my thoughts, words, and deeds, gracious God. Purify my dreams, my fantasies, my longings, so that I may do only what is good. Amen.

MONDAY, JANUARY 19
(Read 1 Corinthians 12:12–26)

(Morning)
O God, I awoke with the post-holiday, midwinter, Monday morning blues.
Your Spirit meets my spirit at this early morning hour.
It awaits the dawn and speaks as I prepare to meet this day.

(Evening)
O God, thank you for working your good in the events of these days.
I rejoice in those that I was able to name, and I rest in your promise
for the good that my eyes could not see. Now I take my rest for the night.

I am not alone. God, your Word affirms my completeness and wholeness as I go to a world in which I, by the Spirit, am one with all persons baptized into the body of Christ. We, who form the body of Christ, are many. In this, my day is met with gladness. Thank you, Spirit of oneness who came to my loneliness before the day began. The same Spirit gives to all morning drink and nurture for the day's needs. God, I marvel at your wisdom. How interesting is your creating Spirit who seeks to bring all to new harmony.

(Morning)
Spirit Divine, ever creating; in the giving and in the receiving,
may a new earth be shaped. In the name of the Spirit of holiness I pray.
(Prayers of Intercession)

(Evening)
Forgive me, Spirit of holiness, for not always contributing to the new earth
begun by our Sovereign Christ, whose body I and others celebrated in communion. Fear robbed me of love's power. Grant to me another day for love's gain.
(Prayers of Intercession)

To each is given the manifestation of the Spirit for the common good.

(Morning)	(Evening)
I go forth into this day seeking the Spirit of God in the common good with joyful anticipation of my contribution to your new earth. Thank you, God, for including me in the body of Christ. In the name of Jesus I pray. Amen.	I accept your forgiveness of my sins for this day, and in that grace may I rest soundly. May I find new courage for the living of the body of Christ in the world that awaits me tomorrow. Spirit of all gifts, hear this prayer. Amen.

TUESDAY, JANUARY 20
(Read 1 Corinthians 12:27–31)

(Morning)
Dear God, I know I was baptized into the body of Christ. Help me to know who I am in that body and what gift the Spirit has given to me that I am to offer to my community of faith.

(Evening)
Dear God, one love came to me by your Spirit this day. I know my part in the body of Christ as ever changing and being renewed, like old cells in my body which die and are replaced by new ones.

Dear God, in this reading from Paul's letter to the Corinthians I am asked to seek the greater gifts and a more excellent way. Accept my prayer for the gift of healing. I want my congregation to be at peace with one another. Grant that my desire for peace will be the seed for the giving of the gift of healing. The passage says that some have deeds of power. God, accept my desire for my congregation to work together for the good of all of its members. Spirit of God, instruct me in the ways of your leadership as I claim my place within the body of Christ.

(Morning)
Spirit of God, empower me as a member of the body of Christ to live in unison and harmony with the other members of my congregation.
(Prayers of Intercession)

(Evening)
This day, accept my deeds of love as deeds of power for the coming of your new earth and the renewing of the congregation of which I am a member.
(Prayers of Intercession)

"Now you are the body of Christ and individually members of it."

(Morning)
God, I come to you. Awaken my desire to claim anew the power of Jesus Christ in my life. Show me today your most excellent way of living as one member amongst the many members of the body of Christ. Through Jesus my Savior I pray. Amen.

(Evening)
Jesus, again this day I have become aware that you are the way. Thank you for being my guide into new understandings and new relationships. By the healer named Jesus I pray. Amen.

WEDNESDAY, JANUARY 21
(Read Psalm 19:1–6)

(Morning)
Maker of all that exists, your early-morning sky speaks to me of how big you
are, and my heart sighs in amazement at your artistry.

(Evening)
Maker of all that exists, artist of my morning promise,
thank you for the beauty of this day. I looked up to you and found you faithful.

Maker of the heavens, in reading Psalm 19, I remember Dr. Preston Bradley's
closing words for each radio broadcast: "Keep looking up." I am looking
up to your artistic creation on this January early-morning sky. A gentle,
fragile, cool snowflake, innocent to a world of hardships, floats down, and
I connect. I listen as many flakes of your artistic hand, in union with one
another, find for themselves new power and strength as they fall in the
towns, cities, and countryside to rest. Today, I seek to gather in the company of others as one of many snowflakes seeking to tell your possibilities.

(Morning)
Creator God, how marvelous are your creative works.
Help me to know myself as one of your marvelous handiworks.
(Prayers of Intercession)

(Evening)
Creator God, I marvel at your handiwork. Help me to listen now as the moon
and stars speak to me of your gospel of justice for the whole of creation.
(Prayers of Intercession)

**"The heavens are telling the glory of God;
and the firmament proclaims God's handiwork."**

(Morning)
My God, today I need your shade of
power, for I fear that the day's experience may be as a sun's blinding rays
upon new snow. May the glory of
your heaven be known this day upon
your earth. Amen.

(Evening)
I asked my God, "I did wrong today.
Can you forgive me even this?" And
the God who painted the sky above
me heard my prayer and replied, "The
Word that spangled the stars into the
vast heaven can revive your soul. It is
my pleasure to do so." Amen.

THURSDAY, JANUARY 22
(Read Psalm 19:7–14)

(Morning)
Perfect God, praise be to your awesome management of life's activities when I trust in your truth and do not err in my day's journey. Direct me toward people and places where the purpose is to be a part of your reign.

(Evening)
Perfect God of order and good precepts, my hope is that your dominion is possible. May I be secure in this hope, and may I be courageous for the living out of this hope.

Dear God, when your promise and will for my life become my daily living, I am refreshed as the morning dew and see possibilities beyond my previous imagination. It is wonderful to know you with such awe. The right way becomes a joy and not a chore. Let me not be caught up by the negative energy of persons who are curt, contemptuous, and condescending. Let my thoughts and actions be congenial, cordial, and courteous, as a courageous person who holds the glory of your goodness in awe and reverence.

(Morning)
Instruct me in the wisdom of living by your decrees. Show me my errors, that I might rejoice in the knowledge of truth and know and obey your law.
(Prayers of Intercession)

(Evening)
God of all that is right and just, instruct me in my night's rest that my dreams may see the vision of a world in which courage overcomes fear, and courteous behavior overcomes contemptuous behavior.
(Prayers of Intercession)

"Let the words of my mouth and the meditation of my heart be acceptable to you, O God, my rock and my redeemer."

(Morning)	(Evening)
God, mentor me in a just way of living. As I look to Jesus as my example, come, Holy Spirit, and rekindle within me the fire of holy living, that my soul may be revived. By my salvation in Christ I pray. Amen.	I accept your forgiveness of my sins for this day, and in that grace may I rest soundly. May I find new courage for the living of the body of Christ in the world that awaits me tomorrow. Spirit of all gifts, hear this prayer. Amen.

FRIDAY, JANUARY 23
(Read Luke 4:14–21)

(Morning)
Spirit of the living God, come unto me and anoint me for the living of this day.

(Evening)
Spirit of the living God, unto you I entrust this day's activities and my spoken word. I pray that you found favor with me. May my deeds lead to the release of persons who are bound by oppression.

God of my Sunday praise and worship, with great joy we shared what you had given to us, the "others." A burst of joy, a sharing explosion, beginning from your community of faith in worship. It was good to be in your house. Thanks be to you, great and wondrous God.

(Morning)
Loving God, grant unto me victory from my own sins and self-respect
to face my oppressors.
(Prayers of Intercession)

(Evening)
God, it was good to be in your company this day. Now watch over me as I sleep, that I may again walk with you tomorrow.
(Prayers of Intercession)

Today, may your holy Word be fulfilled in my living out my discipleship.

(Morning)
Spirit of the living God, assist me in claiming my own freedom, that I might be witness to your release of others. I pray for those who are in prison, either by their own free will or by the oppressive will of others. Renew your Spirit upon this, your child, I pray in Jesus' name. Amen.

(Evening)
May this year be the year of your favor, I pray. For I witnessed this day people unaware of your goodwill, poor people, and people oppressed and in captivity. May I be in your favor, my gracious God, so that your reign will come quickly. In Jesus' name I pray. Amen.

SATURDAY, JANUARY 24
(Read Nehemiah 8:1–3, 5–6)

(Morning)
O God, that I might come to love your Word with hearing ears and bent knees, in prayer from dawn till noon. May this worship root me to stir the earth with actions of love into the beauty of the night.

(Evening)
O God, I come now to rest. Your Word this day was true and your presence sufficient for life's events.

The story of Ezra reading Moses' law book to the descendants of Abraham returning from Exile reminds me of returning home for a family gathering. All of us gathered around the old family album retelling the stories. The elders shared stories of people and places that I knew as my heritage, stories I would hear and retell when I became the elder. We, like Ezra, had moments of joy and sorrow as we shared together our present and our past; we sang. When someone called, "It's ready," we blessed you, our God, as the most senior among us offered grace before the meal.

(Morning)
Holy God, may your Word instruct me and guide me to know my past as a part of my present.
(Prayers of Intercession)

(Evening)
I spent the day listening to your Word, holy God, and I discovered moments of praise and moments of worship with others.
(Prayers of Intercession)

My holy God, I will seek to understand your Word for the workplace, for the play place, and for places even within your church place.

(Morning)
Although a busy day awaits me, I pray that I may take time to hear your Word, my God, and to name the event as time with you. For Jesus' church on earth I pray. Amen.

(Evening)
Parent God, your child came to you in pride, and you showed me my shame. By your Spirit, I received knowledge of myself and wisdom for a new life. Thanks be to you, parent God. Amen.

SUNDAY, JANUARY 25
(Read Nehemiah 8:8–10)

(Morning)
God, may I understand and find sense in the reading and
the hearing of your Word today.

(Evening)
God, I end the day in thanksgiving, for your Word has filled me and
I understood much.

My God, even as the people of Israel returned to you in worship, may my presence with my church family be a holy time of worship. I also weep tears of sadness, for when I hear your holy Word I am in want of your holiness. Turn my weeping into joy and grant unto me and all within your church strength for the renewing of our day. May I, as one among the worshiping people who feast upon your Word, receive strength to spend my afternoon and night sharing my food with the hungry people of my town in in a spirit of joy.

(Morning)
God who feeds the hungry, feed me from your cup of holy peace, that I may this
day be to others a messenger of your peace.
(Prayers of Intercession)

(Evening)
Forgive me, God, for falling short of your holiness. I took little risk in sharing
with my neighbor in need.
(Prayers of Intercession)

"This day is holy to God; do not mourn or weep."

(Morning)
Dear God, as I go this day to eat and drink at your place of worship with my brothers and sisters, may our dining together give strength to follow your will. And may we provide also for those who are without provision. I pray in Jesus' name. Amen.

(Evening)
To be honest with you, God, is work. It leaves me tired. May I now sleep by your grace to awaken tomorrow to claim the new day with new grace. In the name of Jesus my Savior, I pray. Amen.

34

MONDAY, JANUARY 26
(Read Luke 3:15–17)

(Morning)
Almighty God, I thank you for the night, a time to rest. I thank you for the sun,
a lovely gift that brings life to earth. Help and guide me today, that I may bring
sunshine to others.

(Evening)
Almighty God, thank you for this wonderful day and for being there when I
needed you most.

Thank you, Jesus, for baptizing me with the Holy Spirit. I know that I am
not worthy to untie your sandals. Forgive me. As John the Baptist prophesied about your coming, spare my soul when the time comes. I beg you to
come into my heart, that I may share the fire you have given me.

(Morning)
I feel refreshed as I awaken. God, thank you for the time to rest. Help me to
realize the wonderful gifts that I take for granted. As the sun's rays touch my
skin, remind me of your love for humankind.
(Prayers of Intercession)

(Evening)
God, you gave me this wonderful day as a gift. Thank you. As I rest my weary
soul, come and bless me with your Holy Spirit.
(Prayers of Intercession)

God, I now pray.
(Pray the Prayer of Our Savior.)

(Morning)	(Evening)
With the gift of your Holy Spirit, I will enjoy this day. Amen.	God, may you grant peace to those who are weary tonight. Amen.

TUESDAY, JANUARY 27
(Read Luke 3:15–17)

(Morning)
God, as I awaken from sleep and begin this day, be with me as
I face new challenges.

(Evening)
God, thank you for all the challenges that you have given me. I survived
because of your Holy Spirit. As I cast my soul to you, grant me peace.

God, John prophesied about the coming of your Child. He described the
Redeemer as a tool for judgment, "a winnowing fork," who would clear
the earth and gather your people for the coming of your realm. We face
many challenges in life. But with your love as a shield, we can survive.
Guide me.

(Morning)
I trust my day to you, God. As a Christian, may I be righteous and prepared for
another day.
(Prayers of Intercession)

(Evening)
God, as I remember today's challenges, remind me to be strong and ready for
what tomorrow will bring.
(Prayers of Intercession)

God, I now pray.
(Pray the Prayer of Our Savior.)

(Morning)	(Evening)
With the Holy Spirit as my shield, I am ready to face today's challenges. Amen.	God, may you grant peace to those who are weary tonight. Amen.

WEDNESDAY, JANUARY 28
(Read Psalm 29:1–2)

(Morning)
God of glory and strength, good morning. Thank you for another day as I greet my neighbors with love and care.

(Evening)
God of glory and strength, tonight I am thankful and grateful. Allow me to rest in your love and care.

As I meditate on the psalms, I know that the psalmist wants to convey to us that we need to give ourselves totally to you. Whenever we need you, we call you. We should only worship you in holy magnificence.

(Morning)
O God, bestow upon my humble self the strength I need to face the future.
(Prayers of Intercession)

(Evening)
O God, forgive me if I have not extended your love and care to my neighbor.
(Prayers of Intercession)

God, I pray.
(Pray the Prayer of Our Savior.)

(Morning)
As your servant, empower me now as I show the world your glory and strength. Amen.

(Evening)
God, thank you. I consign myself to your love and care. Bless the needy and the poor. Amen.

THURSDAY, JANUARY 29
(Read Acts 8:14–17)

(Morning)
God, once again I thank you for the chance to rest. I awaken to another day full
of your gift—life. Thank you.

(Evening)
God, grant me your love and keep me safe as I rest.

As I meditate on today's reading, I see that Peter and John had to lay hands
on the people of Samaria so that they could receive your Holy Spirit. God,
we take for granted so many things in this world. Most of us forget that we
don't need someone to lay hands on us to receive your Spirit. Through faith
and baptism, it is ours. Thank you.

(Morning)
God, with the Holy Spirit in my soul, help me to show your love to those
who are in need this day.
(Prayers of Intercession)

(Evening)
Another day is almost over, God. Thank you for the love you gave me.
(Prayers of Intercession)

I now pray.
(Pray the Prayer of Our Savior.)

(Morning)	(Evening)
Heavenly Mother and Father God, be with me as I face another day. Amen.	God, our loving Creator, thank you for being with me today. Amen.

FRIDAY, JANUARY 30
(Read Psalm 29:3–11)

(Morning)
God, open my eyes to your mighty powers. Thank you for this beautiful
morning. I love you.

(Evening)
God, I recall the might of your power today. I am glad that you are
always with me.

I know that your voice thunders when I hear thunder. I know that your
power is mighty when I see lightning. I know that your strength is powerful as I experience earthquakes. And I know that you show your compassion and control over your creation. God, give me strength and peace as I
enjoy your creation and your gift of life.

(Morning)
God, talk with me throughout the day. Let me feel your might through
conversations today.
(Prayers of Intercession)

(Evening)
Today, God, I witnessed the greatness of your power. I am happy that you
are ever present.
(Prayers of Intercession)

God, thank you for your strength and peace. I now pray.
(Pray the Prayer of Our Savior.)

(Morning)
God, let me experience your voice
through your creation. Amen.

(Evening)
As I sleep, bless me with peace, so that
when I wake tomorrow I can love you
more. Amen.

SATURDAY, JANUARY 31
(Read Isaiah 43:1–7)

(Morning)
God of forgiveness and strength, good morning. Thank you for another day to greet my neighbors in love and care.

(Evening)
God of forgiveness and strength, allow me to rest in your love and care.

As I meditate on the writings of Isaiah, I see more of the Savior's power. I might go through deep waters and trouble, but Jesus will be with me. I might go through rivers of hardship, but Jesus will not let me drown. There is only one Savior. Through Jesus there is a way, there is truth, and there is eternal life.

(Morning)
God, bestow upon your humble servant the strength I need to face the future.
(Prayers of Intercession)

(Evening)
God, forgive me if I did not show love and care to my neighbors.
(Prayers of Intercession)

I worship you, God, in holy splendor as I pray.
(Pray the Prayer of Our Savior.)

(Morning)
As your servant, empower me as I share your glory and strength with the world. Amen.

(Evening)
God, thank you. I consign myself to your love and care. Thank you for saving me. Amen.

SUNDAY, FEBRUARY 1
(Read Luke 3:21–22)

(Morning)
Dear Father and Mother God, as I open my eyes to a new day, may I extend my grateful appreciation for your love during this past week.

(Evening)
Dear Father and Mother God, thank you for caring for us who are sinners. As I rest my weary self, I surrender to you once again.

Thank you, God, for baptizing me with the Holy Spirit. Open the heavens to me, Mother and Father God. Let your Spirit journey with me and guide me. Thank you, Creator, for your many gifts.

(Morning)
I feel refreshed as I awaken. Thank you for the time of rest.
As I begin another day, give me the chance to please you.
(Prayers of Intercession)

(Evening)
God, you who gave me this wonderful day as a gift, thank you.
Bless me today with your Holy Spirit.
(Prayers of Intercession)

As I say the words that you taught your disciples, I now pray.
(Pray the Prayer of Our Savior.)

(Morning)
With the gift of your Holy Spirit, I will enjoy yet another marvelous day. Amen.

(Evening)
God, may you grant peace to those who are weary tonight. Amen.

MONDAY, FEBRUARY 2
(Read Psalm 138)

(Morning)
God of words and deeds, I begin this new day praising your love and faithfulness. Truly your glory is great and greatly to be praised.

(Evening)
God of words and deeds, keep my praise from reflecting only the words and
experiences of others. May my praise spring from my own knowledge of you
acting in your world.

The psalmist begins with a personal burst of praise which is rooted in a
particular experience of your activity, dear God. You answered a call for
rescue; you gave the psalmist boldness and courage in the face of the anger
of enemies. In light of such a personal experience, how else could one
respond! As I reflect on my personal experience of your activity, may I,
like the psalmist, burst forth in praise.

(Morning)
God who acts, hear me as I give you praise for those specific moments
when you transformed my life.
(Prayers of Intercession)

(Evening)
God who acts, hear me as I pray for family and friends and the rulers of the
earth. May all praise you, recognizing your hand at work in moments
of transformation.
(Prayers of Intercession)

**In the midst of all the words and phrases that can be used to praise God,
the psalmist calls me to root praise in my personal experience
of God's activity.**

(Morning)
May all that I do today prompt me to
praise you, O God. Amen.

(Evening)
I end this day knowing that you will
continue to act for transformation in
my life and in your world. Truly your
glory is great and greatly to be praised.
Amen.

TUESDAY, FEBRUARY 3
(Read Isaiah 6:1–8)

(Morning)
High and Holy One, empower my life as I begin this day. Frame each moment
with the knowledge that your glory fills the whole earth.

(Evening)
High and Holy One, thank you for those moments in this day when your
presence made the ordinary extraordinary, when the sense of your call to me
was heightened and renewed.

The world is full of claims to the spectacular: spectacular special effects in
movies, the spectacular nature of space travel. So many are these claims
that the spectacular can lose its power to move us, to draw us into a reality
greater than our own. In the vision of Isaiah, your awesome presence is
revealed. May the depth of the extraordinary flow over my being and per-
meate my living throughout the day.

(Morning)
God of the extraordinary, make me mindful of the signs of your majesty and
glory which fill the world around me.
(Prayers of Intercession)

(Evening)
God of the extraordinary, I hear you calling me to see my life within the frame-
work of your glory. Help me to name how I might continue to live that calling
more completely.
(Prayers of Intercession)

Thank you for the forgiveness and renewal that are part of my life of faith.

(Morning)
I commit myself to looking for signs
of your spectacular presence in the
world around me. Amen.

(Evening)
Affirmed by the signs of your presence
today, let me greet tomorrow's newness with a continuing sense of your
greatness in the ordinary moments.
Amen.

WEDNESDAY, FEBRUARY 4
(Read Isaiah 6:9–13)

(Morning)
Calling and empowering God, as I begin this day, remind me of my call to ministry in your world. May I know throughout my waking hours your power and holiness which were present to Isaiah.

(Evening)
Calling and empowering God, thank you for reminding me that my call to ministry is centered in you. I do not do it alone.

As a result of his experience in the temple, Isaiah must have felt ready to take on the world. God, he did not have to wait long for the unveiling of your commission to him. How disappointing it must have been to learn that it would commit him to a people who would neither listen nor respond. There would be no glory or adulation; instead, his call would demand faithfulness and perseverance in the face of a lifetime of seeming failure.

(Morning)
Before I engage the world around me, center me, O God, as I name before you those people and situations that will demand faithfulness and perseverance today.
(Prayers of Intercession)

(Evening)
What I have been a part of today, O God, I now commend to your care. I ask for forgiveness where I have failed and a sense of peace in all things.
(Prayers of Intercession)

Isaiah remained God's faithful messenger for almost forty years.

(Morning)
I commit myself to ministry knowing that failure and success will be part of this day. Amen.

(Evening)
May I awaken to a new day reconfirmed in my all, ready to commit myself once again to ministry in your world. Amen.

THURSDAY, FEBRUARY 5
(Read Luke 5:1–5)

(Morning)
Calling God, your call to recommit myself comes anew every morning. Especially when I experience a sense of futility, you call me. May this new day find me faithful in my response.

(Evening)
Calling God, thank you for those moments in this day when your call broke through my discouragement.

Sometimes in life, O God, a sense of futility is very strong. Peter's reluctance is easy to understand. He had been out all night and caught nothing, and then he was asked to go out again—out into even deeper water, where the storms could be intense. Why would there be fish now when last night had been such a failure? Peter must have seen only storms, more empty nets, and wasted effort. Yet he went.

(Morning)
God, I begin this day mindful that you expect me to look for new possibilities, particularly in the midst of discouragement. Hear me as I dream those possibilities into reality.
(Prayers of Intercession)

(Evening)
God, you ask me to risk in spite of discouragement. Hear me as I bring to you those things that might render me unwilling to respond to your call.
(Prayers of Intercession)

Peter went back out even though there was no indication that he would be more successful than he had been the night before.

(Morning)
This day I commit myself to risk, especially where it might seem most fruitless. Amen.

(Evening)
I look forward to a new morning which will call me to things unimagined. Amen.

FRIDAY, FEBRUARY 6
(Read Luke 5:5–11)

(Morning)
God of hope, I thank you for moments when hope springs to life,
nurtured by every endeavor.

(Evening)
God of hope, speak to me words of forgiveness, acceptance, and commission
which allow me to end this day in hope.

God, Peter had spent the whole night fishing, catching nothing. Your child
Jesus called him to go out again, and the result was beyond Peter's imagination—a catch so large that the nets began to break; a catch so large that
another boat was filled and both began to sink. Confronted by the miraculous, Peter was aware of his own insignificance, and, like your servant
Isaiah, he needed to hear words of forgiveness, acceptance, commission.

(Morning)
Hope-inspiring God, in the face of your miraculous presence, I am conscious of
my need for forgiveness. Hear me as I bring before you those things that prevent
hope from springing to life within me.
(Prayers of Intercession)

(Evening)
Hope-inspiring God, hear my prayer for signs of hope where there seems
to be no hope.
(Prayers of Intercession)

**Hear Jesus' assurance to Peter in this way: "Don't be afraid.
From now on you will draw people into the net of God's loving care.
You will draw them into new hope."**

(Morning)
This day, as I launch into deeper
waters, I commit all I do and say to
your care. Amen.

(Evening)
I end this day in thanksgiving,
mindful of those moments in which
hope sprang to life within me. Amen.

SATURDAY, FEBRUARY 7
(Read 1 Corinthians 15:1–11)

(Morning)
God of good news, I am mindful of what has been passed on to me by generations of faithful people. May I live this day thankful for those essential matters.

(Evening)
God of good news, I thank you for that great cloud of witnesses who have confessed the faith before me.

God, when the Corinthians tried to live the gospel faithfully a diversity of viewpoints emerged, a diversity which strained their unity in your gospel. In responding to this diversity, Paul repeats a very early creedal statement: that your Child, Christ, died for our sins, that he was buried, was raised, and appeared to believers. This, says Paul, is the common ground of all who believe in and preach Christ.

(Morning)
God of unity and diversity, I am conscious of those places here and throughout the world where minds are closed to any truth but their own.
For them, hear my prayer.
(Prayers of Intercession)

(Evening)
God of unity and diversity, hear my prayer for those who live the good news in peaceful places. Hear my prayer for those whose faith demands great sacrifice.
(Prayers of Intercession)

To live faithfully, the balance between unity and diversity is part of our calling as people of the good news.

(Morning)
May I be faithful in living and speaking your gospel. May I be clear about its authority and particularity in my life. Amen.

(Evening)
I end this day thankful for the communion of faithful people who continue to enrich my life of faith. Amen.

SUNDAY, FEBRUARY 8
(Read Psalm 138)

(Morning)
Loving and enduring God, I begin secure in the knowledge that you have a
purpose for me. This day, may I add my song to the hymns of others
who also have sung your praise.

(Evening)
Loving and enduring God, keep praise ever present in my life.

Loving God, the psalmist is leading the community of the faithful to celebrate your presence in their midst at that very moment. The message is
not a litany of your past actions but an act of worship, calling forth celebration, dancing, and singing. In that moment of praise their world is
changed. May this same call to celebrate, to dance, to sing, to embrace a
new world, be my response as I praise you within my community of faith.

(Morning)
God who is present now, hear me as I name your activity in my life. May I
know afresh your call to celebrate all you created me to be.
(Prayers of Intercession)

(Evening)
I bring before you all whom you have created, praying that they may be drawn
into praise for your enduring love.
(Prayers of Intercession)

The psalmist declares God's endless love and purpose for all creation.

(Morning)
May each moment of today be a fresh
opportunity to praise you.
Amen.

(Evening)
Day in and day out may my living
know celebration and hope. In my
faith may I be faithful. Amen.

MONDAY, FEBRUARY 9
(Read Jeremiah 17:5–10)

(Morning)
God, you have granted me another Monday; for that I am grateful. Today I ask that you rescue me from my illusion that I can be made safe by my talents, my friends, my possessions. Today let me place my trust in you and you alone.

(Evening)
God, as the day ends, help me to remember how it felt to live a day in which I placed my trust in you alone.

God, with you it is always one way or the other: either cursed or blessed; either "trust in mere mortals" or "trust in you." But I much prefer the middle ground: the world of "both/and," not "either/or." I want to trust in my talents, my friends, and my wealth. I want to put off trusting you until there is no alternative. And then I want you to be available when I am ready for you. I want you to be my safety net. But you don't work that way. You refuse to make it easy for me. If I want to face life's turmoil without anxiety, if I want to live a fruitful life, you insist that I trust you instead of anyone or anything else. Well, if that's the way you want it . . .

(Morning)
I want to be a shade tree, O God, under whose green leaves a dusty traveler can find a moment of relief. Let me bear fruit for my neighbors.
(Prayers of Intercession)

(Evening)
Let me remember, God, how it felt to be a nurturer of others today. Help me to savor the sweet taste of those moments in which I really, truly lived love. And help me repeat them again and again.
(Prayers of Intercession)

"Believe that you have it, and you have it." —Erasmus

(Morning)
With you as my companion, God, I am ready to face the day—even this day. Amen.

(Evening)
Tonight, let me dream a New Jerusalem. Tomorrow, let me carry in my heart a lingering hint of its beauty. Amen.

TUESDAY, FEBRUARY 10
(Read Luke 6:17–19)

(Morning)
Creator of mornings, you have gifted me with another day. As all days, it breaks upon me as a mystery to be unraveled, a present to be unwrapped. Help me maintain my enthusiasm for your gift through each passing moment.

(Evening)
Creator of evenings, thank you for the mountains and valleys of this day. Thank you for supporting and guiding me.

What a beautiful image! Your Child, Jesus, came down and stood on a level place with a multitude of people. And there, in their midst, he gave them what they had come for—healing. God, I feel that story was written just for me. Like that multitude, I don't live on the mountaintop. I live on a "level place," amid the trivialities of everyday life. And also, like that multitude, I am troubled by "diseases" and "unclean spirits." I seek healing in this "level place," and lo, there is Jesus! He has come to me where I am. And he has given me just what I needed. Praise be to you, almighty God!

(Morning)
As healing power flowed from Jesus, so let your power flow through me this day. Let me serve as a conduit of your peace to those who are troubled, a channel of your healing to those who are broken, a river of your strength for those who are weak.
(Prayers of Intercession)

(Evening)
I thank you, God, for the opportunity to have been of service to my neighbors today. Yet I know I have fallen short. Forgive my failures, my insensitivity, and my cowardice. With your help, I'll do better tomorrow.
(Prayers of Intercession)

"Faith is the parent of charity." —Jeremy Taylor

(Morning)
With you as my companion, God, I am ready to face the day—even this day. Amen.

(Evening)
Tonight, let me dream a New Jerusalem. Tomorrow, let me carry in my heart a lingering hint of its wonder. Amen.

WEDNESDAY, FEBRUARY 11
(Read Luke 6:17–23)

(Morning)
God, blessed be this day which you have made. And blessed be those who are granted the enjoyment of this day. Be with me, God, as I live it.

(Evening)
God, this has been a blessed day. Not a perfect day, but a day that was blessed by your touch. Thank you for being a part of my life today.

God, when Jesus was among us, he made us aware that your ways are not our ways. We tell the poor, "Get a job." You grant them what they need and say, "No charge." We tell the hungry, "Make do with what you have." You fill their plates. We tell the depressed, "Snap out of it." You make them laugh. Though it is hard, God, we ask that we be taught to bless those whom you bless. We ask that we may learn to bless the poor, the hungry, those who weep, and those who are hated. And we ask that we give our blessings with our hearts and hands, and not with words alone.

(Morning)
Jesus, turn my face toward the poor, that I might see myself in their eyes; toward the hungry, that I might feel their need as my own; toward those who weep, that I might hear in their cries my own sadness; and toward those who are hated, that I might taste the bitterness of their plight.
(Prayers of Intercession)

(Evening)
Rejoice with me, God. For in my heart I have seen the hungry filled; the tearful laugh; the hated leap for joy; the poor enfolded in your realm. It has been a wonderful day!
(Prayers of Intercession)

"In the harsh face of life, faith can read a bracing gospel."
—Robert Louis Stevenson

(Morning)
With you as my companion, God, I am ready to face the day—even this day. Amen.

(Evening)
Tonight, let me dream a New Jerusalem. Tomorrow, let me carry in my heart a lingering hint of its glory. Amen.

THURSDAY, FEBRUARY 12
(Read Luke 6:17–26)

(Morning)
Thank you, God, for the promise of this morning. As I go forth to meet the day,
I pray that you will protect me from myself. Lead me into temptation and then
safely out again, for the blade must pass through fire to be hardened.

(Evening)
Thank you, God. I felt strengthened. At times I felt comforted. At times I felt
urged forward. Was that you?

What am I to do, God? My life, the life you have given me, is a good life.
And this very life makes me the object of your judgment. You say "woe" to
my good reputation, my happiness, my comfort, my security. What am I to
do? Like the rich young man, I grieve at your hard words. Would you have
me sell all that I have and give the money to the poor? Would you have me
cover myself in ashes and spend my days in mourning? Would you have
me cultivate the hatred of my neighbors? What am I to do? I will do the
only thing I can do. I will seek your grace. I must trust you to show me how
I can move from judgment to grace, from "woe" to "blessed." Your will be
done.

(Morning)
Righteous Judge, you have spoken strong and fearful words to those, like me,
who have been granted much in this life. Show me a path
through your judgment.
(Prayers of Intercession)

(Evening)
Thanks be to God for the Word which shakes us to our foundations and
for the grace which rebuilds us.
(Prayers of Intercession)

"Faith is the antiseptic of the soul." —Walt Whitman

(Morning)	(Evening)
With you as my companion, God, I am ready to face the day—even this day. Amen.	Tonight, let me dream a New Jerusalem. Tomorrow, let me carry in my heart a lingering hint of its peace. Amen.

FRIDAY, FEBRUARY 13
(Read Psalm 1)

(Morning)
I thank you, God, for Friday. May this Friday be more than the beginning of another weekend. May this Friday be a real celebration—a celebration of the beauty of creation and the glory of living.

(Evening)
I thank you, God. The sun has set. The day is over. I am ready to make peace with my day.

The psalmist urges me to "delight" in the law. What a strange and wonderful idea! And how alien to my nature! For I rebel against restraint. Like humans throughout all of history, I prefer to be free to establish my own rules, plot my own course, determine my own fate. The psalmist knows better than I that my way is the way of chaff—buffeted here and there by fleeting gusts of wind. It is much better to be a tree planted by the waters: free to grow, free to yield fruit, free to prosper. God, help me to cultivate a taste for the law. Teach me to savor the freedom that comes from being anchored in your path.

(Morning)
God, the "wicked" are not so different from me. I pray for them and their reformation with the same fervor with which I pray for myself. Grant all your creatures access to the path of righteousness, the path of life.
(Prayers of Intercession)

(Evening)
Righteous One, I thank you that you have placed me on the way of the righteous, that you have planted me by streams of water.
(Prayers of Intercession)

"Faith is not a thing which one 'loses,' we merely cease to shape our lives by it." —Georges Bernanos

(Morning)
With you as my companion, God, I am ready to face the day—even this day. Amen.

(Evening)
Tonight, let me dream a New Jerusalem. Tomorrow, let me carry in my heart a lingering hint of its energy. Amen.

SATURDAY, FEBRUARY 15
(Read 1 Corinthians 15:12–19)

(Morning)
God of fresh beginnings, I am about to face another day. Give me the grace to turn away from the past and its burdens. Keep my face toward the future. Keep my heart filled with hope.

(Evening)
God of fresh beginnings, today when I felt ready to give up, you were there. When I felt angry and resentful, you were there. When I turned to you, you met me. Thank you, persevering Spirit.

In all creation, there is nothing so wondrous as the human mind. A creature of quicksilver, the mind is at one moment stubborn and self-confident, malleable and insecure at the next; at one moment compassionate, and at the next cruel; at one moment brave, and at the next cowardly. So it is, God, with my faith in you. At one moment I vibrate with awareness of your reality. And then, in the next, I fear that my sense of your presence is but a delusion. I oscillate between faith and doubt with bewildering frequency. Is there any way to end this dance of faith and doubt? Or must I learn to like the music?

(Morning)
Pity the doubter, Faithful One, for doubts come to human beings
as wind comes to the prairie.
(Prayers of Intercession)

(Evening)
I have held on to you, God, through another day. Or have you held on to me?
(Prayers of Intercession)

"Not to have faith is not a personal fault, it is a misfortune."
—Etienne Gilson

(Morning)
With you as my companion, God, I am ready to face the day—even this day. Amen.

(Evening)
Tonight, let me dream a New Jerusalem. Tomorrow, let me carry in my heart a lingering hint of its nearness. Amen.

SUNDAY, FEBRUARY 14
(Read 1 Corinthians 15:12–20)

(Morning)
Risen One, at last it is Sunday, the day of resurrection. I ask you, God, to make the church's ancient proclamation, "Christ is risen," a reality in my life today.

(Evening)
Risen One, you have been my companion today just as you were a companion to your disciples. Thank you for the gift of your presence.

How can I doubt the resurrection when I witness the green shoots of a crocus bursting forth from a bank of snow? when I taste the sweetness of just-picked corn? How can I doubt the resurrection when I hear the startled wail of a newborn baby? when I see the sparkle in a child's eyes at Christmas? How can I doubt the resurrection when I know alcoholics and drug addicts who have returned to life? when I have felt the healing touch of love? How can I doubt the resurrection when I recall the martyrs who were empowered to die with grace? when I remember the saints who were emboldened to live with power? I am glad that I have been overcome by a God who turns death to life!

(Morning)
If death can be defeated, then there is no misfortune that cannot be overcome, no situation that cannot be turned around, no human being who cannot be redeemed. Life-renewing God, help me contribute to your work of resurrection.
(Prayers of Intercession)

(Evening)
As another day ends, I thank you, God, for the renewal of my life which you have granted me today. And I pray that you will continue your work of resurrection in me tomorrow.
(Prayers of Intercession)

"The state of faith allows no mention of impossibility." —Tertullian

(Morning)
With you as my companion, God, I am ready to face the day—even this day. Amen.

(Evening)
Tonight, let me dream a New Jerusalem. Tomorrow, let me carry in my heart a lingering hint of its reality. Amen.

MONDAY, FEBRUARY 16
(Read Luke 9:28–36)

(Morning)
Dearest God, what mountain will I encounter on this new day of your creation?

(Evening)
Dearest God, for the strength in my body and spirit to climb your mountain,
I am grateful.

Whenever I see a mountain, I think of you, O God. Throughout the Bible story, you have chosen a mountain to reveal yourself and to allow us to experience you. Moses knew your awesome presence as thunder and lightning, fire and cloud. Elijah knew you as a "small still voice." Jesus knew you as a parent. We, too, experience you.

(Morning)
Let all the earth bear witness to your everlasting presence, O God.
(Prayers of Intercession)

(Evening)
O mighty God, grant me rest this night so that I may continue my journey
toward you tomorrow.
(Prayers of Intercession)

"I have been to the mountaintop." —Martin Luther King Jr.

(Morning)
Open my ears, that I may hear Jesus and know your presence. Amen.

(Evening)
Enable me, O God, to greet the new sun with new ears. Amen.

TUESDAY, FEBRUARY 17
(Read Luke 9:37–43)

(Morning)
Dearest God, open my heart and soul to greater faith.

(Evening)
Dearest God, forgive me if I have not been faithful.

Remind us always, O God, that you are not merely a "mountaintop experi-ence." We know that as soon as Jesus came down from experiencing your presence on the mountain, he made that experience real by healing a child, by transforming a life. Help us to know, O God, that our experience of you must lead to transformed lives—our own lives and the lives of our people.

(Morning)
Keep me from taking your presence for granted, O God.
(Prayers of Intercession)

(Evening)
Forgive me, O God, if I have remained untransformed by your presence.
(Prayers of Intercession)

"And we . . . are being transformed into God's likeness."

(Morning)
God, just for today, help me not to be afraid of your presence. Amen.

(Evening)
You have touched me, O God. I am grateful. Amen.

WEDNESDAY, FEBRUARY 18
(Read Exodus 34:29–35)

(Morning)
Dearest God, let the radiance of your love engulf me.

(Evening)
Dearest God, forgive me if I have not shared your light this day.

For those who know you not, the light of your love is blinding and, hence, can be terrifying. We have all known the terror of the unknown. When Moses first witnessed your light, he was afraid. He did not know of your great love. But you welcomed him into your holy presence. You invited him to a sacred relationship. You taught him not to be afraid. You taught him to trust. We know that we can remove the veil of our fear with you, O loving God.

(Morning)
Draw me near to the mystery of your presence, O God.
(Prayers of Intercession)

(Evening)
Eternal One, I close my eyes knowing that the radiance of your love
is never extinguished.
(Prayers of Intercession)

**"This little light of mine, I'm gonna let it shine.
Let it shine, let it shine, let it shine!"**

(Morning)
O God, give me the courage to share the light of your world today and always. Amen.

(Evening)
O Eternal Light, surround me always in the halo of your love through this night and into the new dawn. Amen.

THURSDAY, FEBRUARY 19
(Read Psalm 99:1–5)

(Morning)
Dearest God, I am like a young poet, eager to compose my words and deeds in accordance with your will.

(Evening)
Dearest God, thank you for the inspiration of your leadership.

God, we live in uncertain times. Long-held givens and absolutes are no more. Dominant paradigms of thinking and being are radically shifting. How are we to lead and be led in such a time as this? We turn to you, O God, in confusion and fear. You are sovereign. You are exalted. You are holy. You love justice. You establish equity. You are holy. Help us to lead and be led into your holiness. Make us holy, as you are holy.

(Morning)
Lead me, O God, by what is holy in your eyes.
(Prayers of Intercession)

(Evening)
Forgive me, O God, if my words and acts have not been holy in your eyes.
(Prayers of Intercession)

**"But let justice roll down like a river,
righteousness like a never ending stream."**

(Morning)
Let not my steps falter as I follow your lead, O God. Amen.

(Evening)
Let me never tire of following you, O God. Amen.

FRIDAY, FEBRUARY 20
(Read Psalm 99:6–9)

(Morning)
Dearest God, I await your call on this new day.

(Evening)
Dearest God, you have answered.

God, there are times when your awesomeness can be so intimidating that you seem almost unreachable. And yet, the Bible is filled with stories of persons who called out to you: Abraham, Moses, Hannah, Jesus. Each time you answered. "They called on God and God answered them." The Bible is a testimony that you are a reachable God.

(Morning)
With my first awakened breath, I reach for you, O God.
(Prayers of Intercession)

(Evening)
Even in sleep, I reach for you, O God.
(Prayers of Intercession)

"Before they call, I will answer; while they are still sleeping, I will hear."

(Morning)
Eternal Presence, my body reaches out for you; my soul awaits your voice. Amen.

(Evening)
All is quiet. God, let your voice be heard. Amen.

SATURDAY, FEBRUARY 21
(Read 2 Corinthians 3:12–18)

(Morning)
Dearest God, set me free in your Spirit.

(Evening)
Dearest God, if I have used my freedom for only my personal gain, forgive me.

Teach us, O God, about freedom. Teach us the freedom of leaving the suffocation of sin and entering the breath of your Spirit. Teach us the freedom of letting go our materialism and receiving priceless life. Teach us the freedom of risking our individualism to join the circle of your family and make it complete. Teach us, God, about freedom.

(Morning)
Remind us, O God, that there is no freedom outside of community.
(Prayers of Intercession)

(Evening)
I rest my faith in the freedom of your love, O God.
(Prayers of Intercession)

"Freedom is never free."

(Morning)
Free me, O God, to be all that you want me to be. Amen.

(Evening)
I rest freely in your presence, tonight and always, O God. Amen.

SUNDAY, FEBRUARY 22
(Read 2 Corinthians 4:1–2)

(Morning)
Dearest God, embolden me to embrace your truth.

(Evening)
Dearest God, forgive me if I have wavered from your truth.

How easy it is to be honest and truthful, open and vulnerable, with you, O God. It is easy to offer my heart to you. If only this were all that was required of your love, of your ministry. But the good news of Jesus Christ was never meant for just one and one alone; it was meant for all your children. So grant us courage, O God, to be honest and truthful, open and vulnerable, one child of God to another. Grant us courage to give our hearts to one another, so that you are made known for all the world to see.

(Morning)
Let me not be afraid to risk all for your glory, O God.
(Prayers of Intercession)

(Evening)
I thank you for the courage you have given me today to be the child that you wanted me to be, O God.
(Prayers of Intercession)

"These are the things you are to do: speak the truth to each other."

(Morning)
God of truth, how eager I am to seek you. Amen.

(Evening)
O God, I pray that my actions and words have pleased you this day. Amen.

MONDAY, FEBRUARY 23
(Read Luke 4:1–4)

(Morning)
Great and gracious God who never abandons us in times of testing, help me now to recognize and confess where I am most vulnerable to evil's crafty lures of temptation. May your abundant grace help me to measure up to the tests and challenges you want me to face today.

(Evening)
Great and gracious God, I truly thank you for traveling beside me during today's ups and downs. Forgive me for times when I may have stumbled. Thank you for times when your grace enabled me to be steadfast.

I realize that Jesus refused to turn the hard rock of tough survival into quick and easy "fast food," and I wonder, O God, how I can ever have what it takes to reject the easy way out. Help me to hang in there and make those difficult decisions which, with your blessings, can make a vital difference.

(Morning)
Guide me during my contacts today with these persons regarding crucial issues and concerns.
(Prayers of Intercession)

(Evening)
Tonight I pray on behalf of special persons who, like me, need your blessing in facing life's challenges.
(Prayers of Intercession)

**Instead of the world's easily available "junk food,"
the bread and the wine of your spirit are well worth waiting for
and will always be on the table when needed.**

(Morning)
When life seems difficult today, may I turn to your Child, Jesus, who is ever ready to share his bread and his cup to nourish my spirit in times of testing.
Amen.

(Evening)
Refresh me this night with the cup of your overflowing peace which will give me joyful confidence to face whatever tomorrow brings my way.
Amen.

TUESDAY, FEBRUARY 24
(Read Luke 4:5–8)

(Morning)
Holy God, who alone is worthy of worship and adoration, help me to turn away from evil's shrewd sales pitch, making false priorities hard to resist. Rekindle the flickering light of my fickle devotion into a reliable flame of joyful and steadfast commitment to you.

(Evening)
Holy God, I thank you for guiding me whenever it has been difficult to recognize clearly what is truly holy or cleverly seductive. Forgive me if at any time I became sidetracked by the attraction of something that only brought out the worst in me. Help me sort out my life's priorities and make a fresh start tomorrow with greater wisdom and courage.

God, I know that Jesus refused to accept evil's glamour of "go for the gold" but did accept your demands for the highest and best. I can even recall when I have been tempted to settle for life's mediocre "goodies" instead of holding out for the best that you would give me. Help me, O God, to follow your narrow, difficult pathway, regardless of how sweet life in the "fast lane" always seems to be.

(Morning)
Give me what it takes in these tempting situations to choose what you want instead of settling for less.
(Prayers of Intercession)

(Evening)
Tonight I pray on behalf of special persons who, like me, are confronted with tempting choices.
(Prayers of Intercession)

**God's most difficult path makes us "slow down and live,"
in contrast to life in the "fast lane" headed hell-bent for a deadly collision.**

(Morning)	(Evening)
With so many wolves disguised as sheep wherever I go, help me to hear and follow the voice of the Good Shepherd today. Amen.	Use this night's rest, O God, to hush all the voices clamoring for my attention and to fine-tune my spirit to your wavelength. Amen.

WEDNESDAY, FEBRUARY 25
(Read Luke 4:9–13)

(Morning)
Almighty God, who protects and rescues your children from peril, help me to reject temptation. May I never take your love for granted but always seek your approval and guidance before I take action.

(Evening)
Almighty God, I thank you for seeking to get me back on track whenever I have strayed off course. Continue to help me choose between genuine and ill-advised risks.

I consider how Jesus refused to take the challenge of evil's "bungee jump." I am ashamed of the ways I expect you, Savior God, to bail me out whenever I get myself out on a limb—without ever having asked for your guidance ahead of time. Make me more committed, O God, to keep in touch with you, especially in regard to those life concerns when I might assume it isn't necessary to bother you.

(Morning)
Help me today to avoid taking foolish chances in risky situations.
(Prayers of Intercession)

(Evening)
Tonight I pray on behalf of special persons who, like me, can go off the deep end.
(Prayers of Intercession)

God is ever ready to help me find answers to frustrating or baffling situations even when I am tempted to jump to conclusions without turning to God first.

(Morning)
Today let me stop trying your patience and instead try responding to your patient efforts to steer me straight. Amen.

(Evening)
Forgive me for being difficult. Give me grace, wisdom, and patience to stay in close partnership with you. Amen.

THURSDAY, FEBRUARY 26
(Read Deuteronomy 26:1–11)

(Morning)
Gracious God, who has blessed me abundantly. May my talents and resources be offered first to you before I consider my own wants and needs. Keep me aware of past generations whose struggles have given me a worthy example to follow.

(Evening)
Gracious God, who calls me to give you my very best, thank you for the opportunities to try to make a vital difference in the lives of others. Help me to know the best ways to expend my time and energy for your sake.

Just as the people of Israel needed to be reminded of the hardships of slave labor in Egypt, so we, too, O God, need to be reminded of whoever in our own past had to endure sweatshop working conditions. In these troubled times of corporate downsizing and layoffs of highly gifted people, show us, O God, how to find the most fruitful outlets for our talents.

(Morning)
Show me the difference between what is good, better, and best in situations when I will be called to serve you today.
(Prayers of Intercession)

(Evening)
Tonight I pray on behalf of special persons who, like me, may wonder what is the best way to give you first priority in the use of our gifts.
(Prayers of Intercession)

When we seek first to learn what God wants abundantly from us, we understand more clearly what God has given abundantly to us.

(Morning)
Help me joyfully to put your "first things first" today. Amen.

(Evening)
Forgive me whenever I failed to make your priorities first and foremost, and continue to help me make a vital difference. Amen.

FRIDAY, FEBRUARY 27
(Read Psalm 91:1–2)

(Morning)
Great Protector, I thank you that when life seems overwhelming and perplexing, my troubled heart can find peace within the shelter of your steadfast care. Today, be my refuge, so that I can face life squarely, drawing upon your strength to sustain my spirit.

(Evening)
Great protector, I thank you for watching over me today and helping me to thrive and survive, in spite of my life's baffling twists and turns. Tonight let me come closer to you and know your reassurance that you are truly in charge.

Teach me, O God, how to take refuge in you when the storms of life overtake me. Instead of running away from life's challenges, help me to face them and move forward through them until, with your protection, I reach the calm and quiet place at the very center of the storm, where your peace can be found.

(Morning)
I need your protection today if a storm breaks loose in these situations.
(Prayers of Intercession)

(Evening)
Tonight I pray for these special persons who, like me, need your help to safely ride out the storms in our lives.
(Prayers of Intercession)

As our refuge and shelter, God provides only the very best to see us through life's very worst.

(Morning)
Today when I face life, let me know, O God, that shelter is at hand when I need it. Amen.

(Evening)
Let me take refuge tonight within the embrace of your loving care and discover once again how great is your love. Amen.

SATURDAY, FEBRUARY 28
(Read Psalm 91:9–16)

(Morning)
Savior God, you have promised that I can put my trust in the available power of your salvation. How glad I am that you will surely answer when I call upon you, knowing that your vigilant eye is ever on me and even the littlest sparrow.

(Evening)
Savior God, I thank you for being there when I needed you today. Help me to be gratefully aware of the ways in which you step in quickly at my time of need. Because your grace has brought me safely through all my toils and troubles, help me to face the future with greater confidence that you won't quit on me and that your grace will someday lead me safely to your eternal home.

Today's reading from the Psalms makes it clear, O God, that you want to establish and maintain a lifelong covenant, reassuring me that you will indeed deliver and protect me and fill my life with deepest satisfaction and fulfillment. Help me as a covenant partner to follow your pathway, keeping the door of my heart open to you, so that nothing can hinder you from keeping your promise of salvation to me.

(Morning)
Here is what is happening today when I will want to count upon your protection and deliverance.
(Prayers of Intercession)

(Evening)
Tonight I pray for these special persons who, like me, will need your quick hand to rescue them if trouble breaks loose.
(Prayers of Intercession)

Confessing our weakness opens the door for God to send us abundant strength.

(Morning)
May this day give me the satisfaction of living in close partnership with you. Amen.

(Evening)
May your peace bring reassurance that I am safe in your hands at all times. Amen.

SUNDAY, MARCH 1
(Read Romans 10:8b–13)

(Morning)
Gracious God, who through Jesus has offered salvation to all, sometimes I am afraid to believe that you truly love me just as I am. Help me to know the peace of your presence and the embrace of your love which will never forsake me.

(Evening)
Gracious God, it seems incredible that simply a heartfelt prayer, "I want Jesus as my Savior," is enough for me to grasp your outstretched hand. Thank you for continuing to reach out to me, even when I find it hard to believe how simple it is to respond to you.

So much, O God, depends upon whether I can believe that Jesus really was raised from the dead. Whenever I find myself doubting the Easter miracle of resurrection, I find myself controlled by a fear that takes all the joy out of life. Help me, Savior God, to meet the risen Christ extending a hand to me and inviting me on the journey each day.

(Morning)
God, here are situations in my life which make it hard for me sometimes to feel close to you and to Jesus.
(Prayers of Intercession)

(Evening)
Tonight I pray for these special persons who, like me, at times are whistling softly a song of faith in the spirit of anxious doubt instead of singing joyfully a hallelujah chorus with robust confidence in the risen Christ.
(Prayers of Intercession)

The risen Christ is someone I can know now on earth and not just later in heaven.

(Morning)
Precious Savior, take my hand today so I know you are real. Amen.

(Evening)
God, tonight make it simple for me to know the presence of you and Jesus at my bedside. Amen.

MONDAY, MARCH 2
(Read Luke 13:31–35)

(Morning)
God, as I wake to another day of life, with your help I will face whatever will come my way. I give you thanks because I know you will be with me.

(Evening)
God, thank you for helping me through another day of life and all that I faced. I give you thanks because you were there.

Loving God, we see Jesus facing great danger in life for simply living out the ministry to which you called him. With the Pharisees' threats against him and with Herod's desire to kill him, my Savior, your Child, faced death because of his teaching, preaching, and healing. Unlike Jesus, we do not face death as the obstacle to living out our ministries.

(Morning)
Help me, God, to recognize the obstacles I face as I live out
my Christian beliefs.
(Prayers of Intercession)

(Evening)
I have made it through another day seeking to see more clearly my obstacles.
Recognizing my obstacles, I thank you for the energy to live my beliefs and
to perform my ministries.
(Prayers of Intercession)

As Christ taught me, I pray.
(Pray the Prayer of Our Savior.)

(Morning)
Heavenly Creator, I put myself in your hands today. Teach me the obedience and perseverance I need to follow the example of Jesus. Amen.

(Evening)
Loving God, thank you for your presence today in my life. As I retire for the evening, give me the rest I need to wake tomorrow with the energy and strength to live out your will in my life. Amen.

TUESDAY, MARCH 3
(Read Genesis 15:1–12, 17–18)

(Morning)
Loving God, I am grateful for another day of life.
Help me to show my gratitude to you.

(Evening)
Loving God, thank you for receiving the gratitude I have shown you today.

God, Abram was your faithful servant. There where times when he did not understand what you asked or talked about. Even though you declared that Abram's heir would inherit the lands, he had no children and therefore did not understand this prophecy. Nevertheless, he gave you thanks and praise without hesitation. For what do we not understand that you are asking us to give thanks?

(Morning)
Even if I do not think I should be grateful, today I will seek to find something for which I can express my thanks to you, O God.
(Prayers of Intercession)

(Evening)
In every situation, I am looking for blessings for which to be thankful.
God, help me find the blessings that I had not considered before.
(Prayers of Intercession)

Humbly I pray.
(Pray the Prayer of Our Savior.)

(Morning)
Loving God, help me to find the ways in which you want me to express my thankfulness to you, even when I do not understand the situation. Amen.

(Evening)
Gracious God, as the day passes, I am warmed with the list of items I have discovered. Thank you for your love and giving. Amen.

WEDNESDAY, MARCH 4
(Read Genesis 15:1–12, 17–18)

(Morning)
Gracious and loving God, as I rise today, help me give thanks for the blessings you have given me.

(Evening)
Gracious and loving God, thank you once again for all the blessings you have given me today. Help me to rejoice in the opportunity to rest in the security of your love.

God, I have always been amazed by the biblical stories in which your grace was revealed somehow through a dream. Abram had a revelation during a dream. Once again it was during sleep that you blessed one of your children. Sometimes in our waking hours we worry and pray without ceasing over problems and situations that we cannot control. But when we lay our heads down to rest in your hands, we will be refreshed and made ready to face a new day.

(Morning)
God, knowing that I will face many questions for which I will not have answers, I pray that you will be with me in these situations.
(Prayers of Intercession)

(Evening)
Thank you, God, for giving me the wisdom to figure out when I need to let go of the situations I can no longer control, and for making me know that your loving arms will carry me forward into a restful night's sleep.
(Prayers of Intercession)

Confidently I pray.
(Pray the Prayer of Our Savior.)

(Morning)
Send me off, O loving God, with the assurance that you will stand by my side this day. Amen.

(Evening)
Almighty God, thank you for the insight you blessed me with today. Now I ask you to help me reach a deep, peaceful sleep, so that perhaps within that time of rest you will bless me again. Amen.

THURSDAY, MARCH 5
(Read Psalm 27)

(Morning)
God, you are "my light and my salvation; whom shall I fear?" Even in my times of trials and tribulation, whom shall I fear if I have you?

(Evening)
Finally, God, as this day comes to an end, the light of your salvation still shines. Of whom should I be afraid?

There are times when we face life's trials and tribulations. We forget the words of the psalmist reminding us that you are always with us and that, therefore, we have no reason to fear. God, one of your greatest gifts to us is other human beings, though sometimes it is in these relationships that we find trials and tribulations. But like the psalmist, I can proclaim, "Whom shall I fear if I trust in you."

(Morning)
"I believe that I shall see the goodness of God in the land of the living. Wait for God, be strong, and let your heart take courage; wait for God."
(Prayers of Intercession)

(Evening)
"I believe that I shall see the goodness of God in the land of the living. Wait for God, be strong, and let your heart take courage; wait for God."
(Prayers of Intercession)

As Christ prayed, I pray.
(Pray the Prayer of Our Savior.)

(Morning)
Be with me, O God, as I encounter all those relationships that represent any type of trial in my life. Help me to trust in you; then I will fear no longer. Amen.

(Evening)
Thank you, God, for giving me the strength to love others through trying times. It is through sharing your love with everyone in my life that I receive your blessings. Amen.

FRIDAY, MARCH 6
(Read Psalm 27)

(Morning)
Creator God, as the new day rises, so shines the light of your salvation.
Of whom should I be afraid?

(Evening)
Creator God, as this day comes to an end, your light of salvation still shines.
Of whom should I be afraid?

It is painfully true that the trials and tribulations we suffer when we are in discord with others hurt us and can bring great sadness. It is through our own personal relationship with you, Savior God, that we gain the inner strength to cling to you. When we are close to you, we can live, fearing no one or nothing because you are with us.

(Morning)
I embark on another day seeking to draw nearer to you for
inner strength and courage.
(Prayers of Intercession)

(Evening)
I celebrate your steadfastness today. As I drew near to you,
you were always present.
(Prayers of Intercession)

In God's peace I pray.
(Pray the Prayer of Our Savior.)

(Morning)
God, I will be strong, and my heart
will take courage in you. Amen.

(Evening)
God, I will be strong, and my heart
will take courage in you. Amen.

SATURDAY, MARCH 7
(Read Philippians 3:17–4:1)

(Morning)
O God, thank you for the time you granted me last night to rest my soul
in your arms.

(Evening)
O God, today I rejoice in you. Thank you for giving me courage to stand firm
with you. I am comforted by your mercy which is present when I have failed.

God, there are times when the greatest difficulty in being a Christian is
trying to follow Christ's example. Sometimes we like to forget that we are
Christians, especially when we are forced to be humble or to give someone
else the upper hand. Paul instructs the church at Philippi, "We must stand
firm in God." Paul calls the church to remember that we are citizens of
heaven and not of earth.

(Morning)
Help me today, God, to look to my Savior Jesus Christ as a model for how I am
to live my Christian life.
(Prayers of Intercession)

(Evening)
I celebrate the life and resurrection of our Savior Jesus Christ, whose life I am
inspired by and humbly fall short of.
(Prayers of Intercession)

Humbly I pray.
(Pray the Prayer of Our Savior.)

(Morning)	(Evening)
Go with me now, God, as I embrace the living of this day. Be with me, Jesus, as I seek to walk closer to you. Fill me, Holy Spirit, with the courage to live out my faith today. Amen.	As I retire to a time of restful blessing, O God, inspire me this night to be more like our Savior. Amen.

SUNDAY, MARCH 8
(Read Luke 9:28–34)

(Morning)
God, be with me as I rise to a new day.

(Evening)
God, thank you for helping me incline my ear in search of your voice.

Merciful God, we can find many distractions to keep us from concentrating and listening to your voice in our lives. You told Peter and his companions not to be distracted by building noble dwellings. At times we, too, get so distracted by our activities that we miss hearing your voice in our lives. Who knows? We may be missing something very important.

(Morning)
Grace me, O God, with the discipline to seek your voice throughout this day.
(Prayers of Intercession)

(Evening)
As the clutter of the day filled my world, thank you, God, for breaking through with your voice.
(Prayers of Intercession)

With praise I pray.
(Pray the Prayer of Our Savior.)

(Morning)
Be with me now, God, as I go forward with my day. Help me to seek your voice where I would otherwise not seek it. Help me to hear when you are blessing me. Amen.

(Evening)
I now seek your love as I rest, God. Refresh my soul. Fill me during this time, so that tomorrow I can be even closer to your presence in my life. Amen.

MONDAY, MARCH 9
(Read Isaiah 55:1–5)

(Morning)
God, I arise today in the power of the Trinity, and I bind myself to the truth of
the Unity, the strong truth of the Creator.

(Evening)
God, I seek the One who made the stars; who turns deep shadows into morning,
who dims day into the night.

God, where are the waters that will satisfy my thirst? Where is the food
that will fill my emptiness? Where is the delight? Where is the glory? The
delight begins with the thirst. The glory begins with the hunger. I listen to
you, Holy One, and I eat. I listen, that I may live.

(Morning)
With all my heart and all my mind, I pray to you, Sovereign Christ.
(Prayers of Intercession)

(Evening)
Jesus, remember me when you come into your reign, and teach me how to pray.
(Prayers of Intercession)

Listen, everyone who thirsts: Come to the waters.
(Pray the Prayer of Our Savior.)

(Morning)
Praise to you, O gentle Christ, that
you have raised me from the night,
from shadows of the deepest night to
the kindly light of day. Amen.

(Evening)
Christ with me sleeping, Christ with
me waking, Christ with me watching
through the night until the dawn.
Amen.

TUESDAY, MARCH 10
(Read Isaiah 55:6–9)

(Morning)
God, I arise today in the power of Christ, and I bind myself to Christ's compassion with the strength of Christ's dominion.

(Evening)
God, I will bless you who gives me counsel. My heart teaches me, night after night. You are always before me. Because you are at my side, I shall not fall.

You say you are near, but why does the way that leads to you seem so long? The truth is that I do not want to leave this dry and empty place. I hate the hunger and the thirst, but I cannot leave them. Help me to forsake my way and find your way. God, have mercy.

(Morning)
Trusting in your mercy, I bow my heart to you, gentle Christ.
(Prayers of Intercession)

(Evening)
Seek me, God, that I may seek you; call me, God, that I may call you.
(Prayers of Intercession)

Return to God, that God may have mercy on you.
(Pray the Prayer of Our Savior.)

(Morning)
Bless the sight that goes to my eyes; the sound that goes to my ears; the taste that goes to my mouth; the note that goes to my song; the desire that seeks my living soul; the Three who seek my heart; and the One who seeks my heart. Amen.

(Evening)
O Being of wonders, shielding me with might. O Being of stars and story, surrounding me this night. Amen.

WEDNESDAY, MARCH 11
(Read Psalm 63:1–4)

(Morning)
O God, I arise today in the strength of earth and heaven, and I bind myself to
the shadows of night with the brilliance of sun, the stillness of water with the
speed of fire, the sleep of snow with the wakefulness of flowers,
and the stability of rock with the energy of storms.

(Evening)
O God, yours is the day, yours also the night; you established the moon and the
sun. You fixed the boundaries of the earth; you made both summer and winter.

God, even here in this weary land, I can see into your sanctuary. My flesh
is weak, but you have shown me your power and glory. Your love is better
than life, and so I will lift up my hands.

(Morning)
O God, you are my God, I seek you.
(Prayers of Intercession)

(Evening)
I will lift up my hands and call upon your name.
(Prayers of Intercession)

**My soul thirsts for you; my flesh faints for you, as in a dry and
weary land where there is no water.**
(Pray the Prayer of Our Savior.)

(Morning)
O Sovereign of moon and sun,
O Ruler of belovèd stars, in you we
live and move and have our being,
O merciful God of life. Amen.

(Evening)
In your name, O Jesus, who died and
rose, I lie down to sleep. Watch over
my sleeping. Hold me in your hand.
Amen.

THURSDAY, MARCH 12
(Read Psalm 63:5–8)

(Morning)
God, as I arise today, I bind myself to your power to strengthen me, your Word to teach me, your eye to watch over me, your hand to raise me, your arms to hold me, your way to guide me.

(Evening)
God, my mouth praises you with joyful lips when I think of you on my bed and meditate on you in the watches of the night.

O feast that satisfies my soul, O wings that shelter me, O strong hand that holds me, O God: You are my God. I seek you.

(Morning)
Protect me in the shadow of your wings, O God, and hear my prayer.
(Prayers of Intercession)

(Evening)
Hold me with your hand, O God, and hear my prayer.
(Prayers of Intercession)

My soul is satisfied as with a rich feast.
(Pray the Prayer of Our Savior.)

(Morning)
Be with me through each day. Be with me through the night. Be with us night and day. Be with us day and night. Amen.

(Evening)
Guide my waking, Holy One, and guard my sleeping, that awake I may watch with Christ and asleep I may rest in peace. Amen.

FRIDAY, MARCH 13
(Read 1 Corinthians 10:1–13)

(Morning)
God, Christ is with me, Christ before me; Christ behind me, Christ within me;
Christ beneath me, Christ above me; Christ in my looking, Christ in my hearing;
Christ in my lying down, Christ in my rising up.

(Evening)
God, if I say, "Surely the shadows will cover me, and the light around me turn
to night," to you, even the night is filled with light; night is bright as the day,
for shadows and light to you are both alike.

How many times have you satisfied my hungers, and how many times have
I forgotten I was ever hungry? How many times have I turned away from
you? How many times have I tried to go it alone, and how many times have
I failed? O my rock, save me from the times of trial.

(Morning)
Sovereign Jesus Christ, Child of the living God, have mercy on me.
(Prayers of Intercession)

(Evening)
I pray to you, O Christ, that this evening may be holy, good, and peaceful.
(Prayers of Intercession)

So if you think you are on the mountaintop, watch out that you do not fall.
(Pray the Prayer of Our Savior.)

(Morning)
Lift from me, O God, my pain; lift
from me, O God, my fear; lift from
me, O God, my empty pride, and
flood my soul with light. Amen.

(Evening)
Bless for me, God, the moon above
me. Bless for me, God, the earth
beneath me. Bless for me, God, the
ones who love me, and bless my
neighbors near and far. Amen.

SATURDAY, MARCH 14
(Read Luke 13:1–9)

(Morning)
God, Christ in the heart of everyone who thinks of me; Christ in the mouth of
everyone who speaks to me; Christ in every eye that sees me;
Christ in every ear that hears me.

(Evening)
God, Jesus said, "I am the light of the world: Whoever follows me
will not walk in night, but will have the light of life."

I am sometimes so aware of my own hungers that I forget that others hunger too. I want my life to be a feast for them. But Jesus, I am barren, and I am running out of time. I have nothing to give. Tend my soul, Jesus. Help me grow. Help me repent and live. Help me bear fruit worthy of your love.

(Morning)
Jesus, you forgive all who turn to you: Christ have mercy.
(Prayers of Intercession)

(Evening)
Jesus, you lived and died to reconcile sinners to God: Christ have mercy.
(Prayers of Intercession)

**The owner said to the gardener, "If the tree bears fruit next year,
well and good; but if not, you can cut it down."**
(Pray the Prayer of Our Savior.)

(Morning)
Jesus, you are the joy of joyful things. You are the light of the shining sun. You are the door that opens. You are the love of all lovely desires. Amen.

(Evening)
Jesus, you are the glow of the setting sun. You are stillness in the night. You are the surprising star. You are the dark wisdom of dreams. Amen.

SUNDAY, MARCH 15
(Read Luke 13:10–17)

(Morning)
Creator God, I arise today in the power of the Trinity, and I bind myself to the
truth of the Unity, the strong truth of you, the Maker of all.

(Evening)
Creator God, it is not ourselves we proclaim; we proclaim Christ Jesus as
Sovereign, and ourselves as your servants, for Jesus' sake. For you who said,
"Out of the night let light shine," have caused your light to shine within us,
to give the light of revelation—-the revelation of your glory
in the face of Jesus Christ.

Through my thirst, through all my hungers, through my emptiness, through
my falling, through the sin that binds me and pulls me down, you come to
me. You touch and set me free. Now I can praise you. And those who try to
limit your love are ashamed.

(Morning)
Jesus, your healing hands touch our deepest wounds: Christ, have mercy.
(Prayers of Intercession)

(Evening)
With trust in your boundless mercy, I pray to you, O gentle Christ.
(Prayers of Intercession)

**When Jesus laid his hands on her, immediately she stood up straight and
began praising God.**
(Pray the Prayer of Our Savior.)

(Morning)
Jesus Christ our Savior has come, and
the Spirit of truth has come, and the
Sovereign of Sovereigns has come, to
raise you from the night, the Three in
One have come, to raise you
from the night. Amen.

(Evening)
O God, shade are you in the heat.
Shelter are you in the cold. Eyes are
you to the unseeing. Hands are you to
the fallen. Island are you in the storm.
Guiding star are you in the night.
Amen.

MONDAY, MARCH 16
(Read Joshua 5:9–12)

(Morning)
Bread of Heaven, I awake with an insatiable hunger for you.
Feed me until I want no more.

(Evening)
Bread of Heaven, I have feasted from the bounty you have provided from
many sources today.

How good it is to be reminded that you care for the needs of your people.
You promised that those who would follow your direction, trust your providence, and keep the faith would live in houses they did not build and eat
from vines and fields they did not plant. Like us, they did not believe your
covenant. At many points they felt you had forgotten them: The Red Sea
seemed uncrossable; the wilderness seemed unbearable; the water was un-
drinkable; and what would all these people eat? And you rained down manna,
the food of angels, for mere mortals to eat their fill! Generous One, help
me to remember today how well you continue to supply our needs!

(Morning)
Many people are hungry today. Some desire physical food, others emotional
food, and many need spiritual food. Feed us today.
(Prayers of Intercession)

(Evening)
Today I have encountered many folks who needed a taste of you.
(Prayers of Intercession)

I live in a house I did not build. I eat from vines I did not plant!

(Morning)
Help me to pass the Bread! Amen.

(Evening)
I have tasted of your goodness all this
day! Amen.

TUESDAY, MARCH 17
(Read Psalms 32:1–5)

(Morning)
Eternal Morning Light, what a gift to awake to the amazing grace you supply.

(Evening)
Eternal Evening Light, what a joy to approach a night of sweet sleep in you.

Divine Advocate, you know how much I like to hide my imperfections. Heaven forbid I call them sin. I can so easily see the wrong that others do, but I always seem to find good reason for whatever I do. It's not like I'm a really bad person, yet when I refuse to "fess up" and come clean before you, my very silence speaks to my spirit. I find myself moaning, groaning, and sighing all day long, for my sin is ever before me. How good to open up before you and to acknowledge my sin which is hidden before others but is as bright as the morning sun in your sight. It is so freeing to be forgiven.

(Morning)
Hidden sin keeps us from intimacy with you.
Turn your spotlight upon us and know us in every way. Shine upon . . .
(Prayers of Intercession)

(Evening)
Your inward search and my outward confession have allowed my soul to be in flight today. For those who cannot fly, I pray.
(Prayers of Intercession)

Confession bring forgiveness. Forgiveness brings joy.

(Morning)
Today, let my Christian talk match my Christian walk! Amen.

(Evening)
How good it feels to acknowledge my sin, confess my wrong, and receive your forgiveness. Now, I rest in you. Amen.

WEDNESDAY, MARCH 18
(Read Luke 15:1–3)

(Morning)
O Host of sinners, I appreciate your bidding to this new day! You have been
watchful over me all the night and now call me to fresh hospitality within your
loving care. How can I say thanks?

(Evening)
O Host of sinners, all day long, I have been wrapped in your providence.
All day long, my lips have spoken your praise.
Your abundant love is overwhelming. How can I say thanks?

So often I have wandered far away from you. Your commandments seem
so strict, your covenant so binding, and your way so straight and narrow. I
want to do what I want to do. I want to chart my own course. I want to
follow the path that I design. I never want to hear "No!" or "Wait!" These
words grate on my reserve nerve! But I always find that my way leads to
self-destructive people, places, and positions. When I try to do my own
thing, I fall flat on my face and end up in some gutter-type situation. Then
I call for your help. You are always welcoming in your embrace! How can
I say thanks?

(Morning)
There are many seemingly attractive pigpens in our world today.
I pray for those who are trapped in them.
(Prayers of Intercession)

(Evening)
I have encountered many who are struggling to find their way home.
I remember them before you.
(Prayers of Intercession)

**When I fall, let it always be on my back. For when I look up,
I can see your loving face.**

(Morning)
Help me not to be wasteful with the
abundant blessings of spiritual gifts
you have invested in me today. Amen.

(Evening)
O Star of Direction, guide me in my
sleep so that your way is plain when I
awake to face tomorrow. Amen.

THURSDAY, MARCH 19
(Read Luke 15:11–20)

(Morning)
Bringer of Beauty, how I appreciate the gift of this new day. Help me to take
beauty and creativity into every place I go. Let me remember that I am a gift to
my siblings everywhere.

(Evening)
Bringer of Beauty, it was an awesome day! I continued to remember your love
toward me. It allowed me to remember to be kinder and gentler
with my sisters and brothers. I thank you for the gift of memory.

Sibling rivalry is such a demonic trick. It makes sisters and brothers act
hateful, spiteful, and mean toward one another. We operate out of a men-
tality of scarce love. We don't believe that our parents have enough love
for all the children in the family, so we scheme, lie, and manipulate in
order to snatch a few precious crumbs of parental attention. How awesome
it is to recognize and remember that you have more than enough love for
every one of your children. You are an Equal Opportunity Parent! Help me
always to remember this essential fact.

(Morning)
I remember times when I have been jealous of sisters and brothers.
Today I can be generous with my love and remember them before you.
(Prayers of Intercession)

(Evening)
Many times this day, I have noticed siblings who experience a lack of love.
I hold them in my heart.
(Prayers of Intercession)

There is no shortage in the love God has for any one of us!

(Morning)	(Evening)
Let me be an instrument of divine love everywhere I go, to everyone I meet. Amen.	Precious Parent, today I tried to model you. Rock me now in the cradle of your love and let the night's rest be a sweet lullaby. Amen.

FRIDAY, MARCH 20
(Read Luke 15:20–25)

(Morning)
Searching and celebrating Savior, thanks for looking out for me and watching
over me all the night long. The light of your love awakens me,
and I look with joy toward this new day.

(Evening)
Searching and celebrating Savior, how wonderful to have been wrapped in your
care this day. It's so good to be at home in you.

We give our lives to Christ and forget how to party! We get dour of face
and lose our jubilant spirits. It's rich to read about a God who throws a
party whenever a lost child finds the way home! Standing there, waiting,
watching, and wanting for this child to return to the abundance is the God
of many chances! "Get out the best steaks; order the best clothes; and bring
the most fabulous diamond ring, for my wandering child has come home!
Hire a band and send engraved invitations to the entire community. It's
party time!"

(Morning)
God of new beginnings, help me to celebrate this day.
I lift those who refuse to party with you.
(Prayers of Intercession)

(Evening)
I saw many today who don't know that you are awaiting them.
Receive now my prayers for . . .
(Prayers of Intercession)

God is ready to throw a party in my honor!

(Morning)	(Evening)
Music-making God, let the melodies	Let the angelic choir whisper chants
from heaven rain down on me today!	of praise as I rest in the delight of
Amen.	your amazing love. Amen.

SATURDAY, MARCH 21
(Read Luke 15:26–32)

(Morning)
Lavishly generous God, you have called me from the slumber of the night to
join you in continuing the creation of your world. I respond with anticipation.

(Evening)
Lavishly generous God and worker of wonders, how you manage to keep the
world in order continues to amaze me. The sun has gone to sleep,
and the moon has come out to play. What can I say but thanks?

So often I am the oldest child, lost in the house of love. I can get so caught
up in what others are doing, achieving, and getting away with that I forget
how generous you are to me. I can whine with the best of them! I can talk
about those who are not doing all the wonderful, sacrificial things I do for
you, dear God! I get angry and resentful about what others are allowed to
do with ease and freedom. I hide my anger and hurt behind snide com-
ments and petty complaints. In your house, and still lost! What a shame!
Forgive me! Reclaim me! Adjust my attitude! Help me to see the many
blessings you provide me every day.

(Morning)
I pray for the oldest child who lives in me.
And I submit prayers on behalf of my siblings.
(Prayers of Intercession)

(Evening)
My attitude is one of gratitude.
I lift before you these dear to my heart and to you . . .
(Prayers of Intercession)

God is in the house. I don't want to be lost!

(Morning)
Help me to discover the many
storerooms filled with surprises
galore. Amen.

(Evening)
I have explored many facets of God's
great house today. The treasures from
my explorations bless me now with
sleep. Amen.

SUNDAY, MARCH 22
(Read 2 Corinthians 5:16–21)

(Morning)
Reconciling Redeemer, today is a gift from you.
Help me to be an instrument of your peace in the world.

(Evening)
Reconciling Redeemer, thank you for pouring into me what I was able to offer
unto others in your name today.

Ambassadors are very important people. They represent countries, nations, and people. They are selected from wide pools of candidates because they have proven themselves to be of high character, decent morals, and upstanding judgment. When they speak, they speak for their nation's highest elected officials. When they are in public, they stand for the best their country has to offer. It is the same with Christians. We represent the Christ of Calvary, the Creator of the universe. The local church is our training ground, and the Word of God is our text. How well are we representing heaven?

(Morning)
Let yesterday's resentments fade as the night. Hear my prayers for . . .
(Prayers of Intercession)

(Evening)
I have walked the earth as you today. I have seen the needs of your people.
Hear now my prayers for . . .
(Prayers of Intercession)

I am God's ambassador. I am the minister of reconciliation!

(Morning)
Let peace be upon the earth. Let peace
begin with me. Amen.

(Evening)
Gently I have touched many today.
Gently now let rest and refreshment
bathe my spirit with your shalom!
Amen.

MONDAY, MARCH 23
(Read John 12:1–8)

(Morning)
Renewing God, thank you for the refreshment and renewal of last night's rest and for the new possibilities of the day ahead to share your generosity.

(Evening)
Renewing God, thank you for your graciousness, generosity, mercy, and guiding hand this day.

God, both Martha and Mary have lessons to teach us. Martha exhibits faithful service day in and day out. Mary displays an amazing gift and spirit of generosity. One should give and not count the cost and give without the need for recognition. The whole creation will then be filled with a new fragrance. One person's act of generosity is often the inspiration for another's act of generosity.

(Morning)
Throughout this day, O God, may the examples of Martha and Mary and their gifts of quiet service and sincere generosity inspire me.
(Prayers of Intercession)

(Evening)
O God, omnipotent and omniscient, thank you for the day's interactions and work. Where I have failed, forgive me. Where I have tried to act according to your Word and will, confirm and strengthen me.
(Prayers of Intercession)

Jesus awakens extravagance in us and inspires us to generosity.

(Morning)
This day, O God, will offer me new situations and encounters of which I am not yet aware. But whatever the day brings, may I comport myself with faithful service and a gracious spirit. Amen.

(Evening)
To you, all-encompassing God who knows me by name, I entrust all my interactions and activities of this day with the prayer that you use me as a vessel of your love and hope. Amen.

TUESDAY, MARCH 24
(Read Isaiah 43:16–17)

(Morning)
O God, be my guide this day. Be my sight. Be my strength. Be my path. Be my deliverer. Help me to see you at work in history and in my own life.

(Evening)
O God, thank you for acts of deliverance for your people throughout history and for me in the here and now.

The community of faith lives between memory and hope. God, we remember your mighty acts in history in order to live in the present and future with hope and confidence. You are a God of deliverance, one who frees and liberates us from bondage, oppression, and everything that prevents us from experiencing life in all its fullness. I am indeed thankful that through your Child, Jesus Christ, I can be delivered and set free.

(Morning)
For what you have done, are doing, and continue to do, thank you. Remind us of your mighty acts which give us confidence and hope for today and tomorrow.
(Prayers of Intercession)

(Evening)
Comforting God, thank you for the assurance that there is a path through the mighty waters, and that there is a way through every problem.
(Prayers of Intercession)

**When Jesus blessed the bread and the wine, he said,
"Do this in remembrance of me."
This remembrance sparks confidence and hope.**

(Morning)
May I follow your path this day, O God, and may I be a pathfinder to others seeking the way. Amen.

(Evening)
Holy, holy, holy is the God of hosts. The whole creation is full of your glory and majesty. May I rest this night filled with this song of praise. Amen.

WEDNESDAY, MARCH 25
(Read Isaiah 43:18–21)

(Morning)
O God, who guides your children home from exile, thank you for bringing me home to you and for all the peace and promise of that gift born of your providence and grace.

(Evening)
O God, my heart is filled with song, for you have done a new thing in restoring and redeeming your people. Thank you for the assurance that if anyone is in Christ, he or she is a new creation.

The poet and prophet Isaiah encouraged his people with the vision of faith. He enabled them to see through the eyes of faith that there was a way through the wilderness and that there were rivers in the desert. The Israelites needed that message. We need it, too. We are seeking a new and better way and thirsting for rivers in the desert. God, you who made yourself known through patriarchs, prophets, apostles, and martyrs, and above all through Jesus Christ, continue to make yourself known to your people.

(Morning)
For the new things you have in store for me this day, O God, thank you.
(Prayers of Intercession)

(Evening)
O Holy One, who provided a way for me this day and who also satisfied my thirst, I praise your holy name.
(Prayers of Intercession)

May the church be that community which provides a way home to the heart of God, and may it share living water with a thirsty world.

(Morning)
May this time of prayer and praise lead me to the One who said, "Those who drink of the water that I will give them will never be thirsty." Amen.

(Evening)
Dwell within me this evening, loving God. Stay within my heart. Fill me with hope. Grant me your peace which passes all human understanding, through Jesus Christ our Savior. Amen.

THURSDAY, MARCH 26
(Read Psalm 126:1–3)

(Morning)
Loving God, my tongue is filled with shouts of joy because you have restored me to health and wholeness. You have done great things for me, and I rejoice.

(Evening)
Loving God, may the calm of the evening, the brilliance of the stars, and the restorative power of sleep refresh me for the challenges and opportunities of tomorrow.

May I live this day in a spirit of doxology, with words of praise and an attitude of praise. With such an attitude, the day will go more smoothly. It will guide my speech and help me in setting my priorities. It will help me to see your hand in all that I do. This centering in praise is a foundational principle for wholesome living. Sing a doxology. Live one, too!

(Morning)
Your mercy flows like living water, your benevolence stretches to the ends of the earth, your steadfast love endures forever. Thanks be to you, O God!
(Prayers of Intercession)

(Evening)
All-encompassing God, you fill our days with your presence and watch over our nights with your care. May I fall asleep with praise in my heart.
(Prayers of Intercession)

"Bless God, O my soul, and all that is within me, bless God's holy name . . . and do not forget all God's benefits."

(Morning)
May my mind stay on you this day, O God, Creator, Redeemer, Sustainer, Eternal Parent, Child, and Spirit. Amen.

(Evening)
Thanksgiving is on my lips and in my heart for all of your manifold blessings, both material and spiritual, bountiful God. May thoughts of praise sanctify my rest, through Jesus Christ my Savior. Amen.

FRIDAY, MARCH 27
(Read Psalm 126:4–6)

(Morning)
Creator God, instruct me with your wisdom and guide me with your counsel this day. Help me to ponder the paradoxes of the faith, that tears turn into shouts of joy, despair turns into hope, death turns into life.

(Evening)
Creator God, may what I have planted this day bring forth a harvest that will be an offering of praise to you.

God, you restore our dreams, heal our hurts, and satisfy our needs. As you encouraged the Israelites through the prophets, judges, poets, and seers with the promise of restoration, so you encourage us on our pilgrimage. The divine seeds of hope and promise that your Spirit scatters in our souls will bring forth a harvest of peace and well-being. And even in our trials we will sense your presence, enabling us to be victors in the midst of strife.

(Morning)
I acknowledge you, O Sovereign One, as my rock and my fortress.
Thank you for hearing me when I implore your mercy and
for granting me your gift of grace.
(Prayers of Intercession)

(Evening)
Your faithfulness spans generations and nations, almighty and everlasting God.
You are our guide and stay. Hear our songs of praise.
(Prayers of Intercession)

**May I help the wisdom and the insight of the
Scriptures come alive to a troubled world, so that the life-changing
truths therein provide foundation stones for abundant living.**

(Morning)
O God, our hope and our salvation, we are not left to ourselves but have the assurance of your love which redeems and restores. May my life this day be a testimony to your love. Amen.

(Evening)
Faith, hope, and love endure. The harvest is secure. I rest in these assurances, O God, and am at peace, through Jesus Christ, who is the hope of the world and the anchor of my soul. Amen.

SATURDAY, MARCH 28
(Read Philippians 3:4b–11)

(Morning)
Redeeming God, thank you for loving me, not for what I do or achieve
but simply because I am your creation, your child.

(Evening)
Redeeming God, forgive me if I define myself through doing rather than
through being. Let me define myself as one created in your image and as one
for whom Christ died.

The Liberty Bell of the Christian faith is the biblical insight that we are
made right with you, O God, through faith. Knowing this, believing this,
internalizing this gives me an experience of liberation and deliverance as
well as a sense of well-being and power. Salvation is not dependent upon
what I do, but upon what you have done for me in Christ. Now I am at
peace to share in Christ's sufferings and to know the full depth of the power
of the resurrection. Alleluia!

(Morning)
God of wisdom, help me to ponder the words of Jesus: "Do not
think that I have come to abolish the law or the prophets; I have come not to
abolish but to fulfill."
(Prayers of Intercession)

(Evening)
Thank you, O God, for the Word which became flesh and dwelt among us, who
suffered death for our redemption, and who set us free from the bonds of
sin and death. Alleluia!
(Prayers of Intercession)

**May I share in Christ's sufferings to experience
the depth and power of the resurrection.**

(Morning)
My heart overflows with thanksgiving
to you, O holy God, for the gift of
Christ and for knowing Jesus as Savior,
friend, Alpha and Omega. May the love
that is in him abide in my heart, and
may I serve him on the streets where
I live. Amen.

(Evening)
Let your peace, O God, come down
upon my soul. As the night lengthens
and sleep beckons, I rest in the
knowledge that your abundant and
amazing love has set me free and
made me whole, through Jesus Christ,
my Savior, who makes all things new.
Amen.

SUNDAY, MARCH 29
(Read Philippians 3:12–14)

(Morning)
O God, this day illumine me with your Word and set before me a clear path that
I may follow all the day long.

(Evening)
O God, thank you for your child, Christ Jesus, and for laying hold of me. May I
be able to say, "It is not I who live, but you who lives through me."

God, the United Church of Christ Statement of Faith declares: "God saves
us from aimlessness and sin." Aimlessness is missing the mark. We miss
the mark when we do not have our eyes and lives focused clearly on Jesus,
who is the pioneer and perfecter of our faith. With Jesus in clear sight, we
will not wander from the way; or if we do, we will be called back to it.
Recall the words of Jesus: "Strive first for the dominion of God and God's
righteousness, and all these things will be given to you as well."

(Morning)
You who hold me in the hollow of your hand, help me to press on toward the
goal for the prize of your heavenly call in Christ Jesus.
(Prayers of Intercession)

(Evening)
Sovereign God, I praise you that you have saved me from aimlessness by setting
before me a goal that leads to life in all its fullness.
(Prayers of Intercession)

Goal setting, clear focus, priorities based on holy guidance:
These all help to make the day richer and fuller.

(Morning)
May I be a channel of your love to
others this day, O God. May others
see in me one who has the clear
purpose in life of making known your
love in Christ. Amen.

(Evening)
O God of peace, thank you for the
day's work and for the goal that you
set before me to keep your plan and
purpose in focus. Amen.

MONDAY, MARCH 30
(Read Philippians 2:5–8)

(Morning)
Loving God, thank you for Jesus, who came to earth to fully share our humanity. Thank you, too, for his complete obedience to you. May I this day be filled and live in his spirit.

(Evening)
Loving God, thank you for this day and the knowledge that Jesus lived his earthly life as one of us and understands the joys as well as the frustrations I have known.

As I read the second chapter of Paul's letter to the church at Philippi, it makes me exceedingly thankful to know I am seeking to follow the One who came to earth just as I came to earth, as a mortal human being. How comforting it is to know that your child Jesus was subjected to all the temptations, all the frustrations, all the joys and sorrow that I face. May I be as humble, caring, and loving as Jesus was. May I also remember that Jesus did not come as an exalted ruler claiming equality with you, Creator, Father and Mother of the universe, but as a lowly servant. Imprint his story and suffering on my heart.

(Morning)
As a new day dawns, help me to be aware of all Jesus has done for me.
(Prayers of Intercession)

(Evening)
Divine Spirit, whose presence has been with me this day, accept those things in which I have exhibited the mind and way of Jesus. Forgive me when I have not acted as Jesus would have acted.
(Prayers of Intercession)

**Thank you for your gift of Jesus Christ, whose life was lived
to show me how to act, think, and live.**

(Morning)
Help me to live today in a manner pleasing to you. Amen.

(Evening)
Tomorrow may I more closely mirror the earthly life of Jesus. Amen.

TUESDAY, MARCH 31
(Read Philippians 2:8–11)

(Morning)
Eternal and everlasting God, thank you for exalting Jesus and making him
Sovereign for me and for all who would follow him.

(Evening)
Eternal and everlasting God, thank you for Jesus, who set an example for living
and for the men and women who have followed in Christ's steps.

I live in a world which, more often than not, does not recognize Jesus as
Sovereign. Thanks be to you, loving Creator, for exalting Jesus and making him Sovereign God with you, Divine Being. I remember and am thankful for those through the ages who not only believed in the Messiah and
confessed Jesus as Savior, but also went to their deaths rather than deny
Christ. Above all, thank you for Jesus, who has become my Savior and
Sovereign and lives with you, God, above all others in heaven on earth,
and who loves me.

(Morning)
May the radiance, joy, and caring which the Christ brings be manifest
in me this day.
(Prayers of Intercession)

(Evening)
Ever-loving God, accept those deeds and words with which I have exhibited the
mind of Jesus today, and forgive me when I have failed to be a vessel
of Christ's love.
(Prayers of Intercession)

**Thank you, divine and holy God, for the life of Jesus,
who was exalted by you and who is the Christ.**

(Morning)	(Evening)
Spirit of the living God, guide me this day. Amen.	Dear God, grant unto me peaceful rest this night, and may my tongue ever confess that Jesus is the Christ, sent into the world and exalted by you. Amen.

WEDNESDAY, APRIL 1
(Read Isaiah 50:4–5a)

(Morning)
God, morning by morning, you awaken me to live each day joyfully and with courage. You have created me to bring glory and honor to you, to bless and be a blessing to all with whom I come in contact.

(Evening)
God, thank you for the day just over. Thank you for my tongue and the ability to express my thoughts; thank you for my ears to listen to others.

How wonderful it is to realize anew that you, Eternal One, have created me with a tongue to speak words of kindness, caring, and love, especially to those who find life difficult and wearisome. I remember, too, that some of your children have entered this world without the ability to hear. Grant me, loving God and Creator, the ability to show compassion to such individuals. Grant me the grace to show true love and help to all those who are differently abled, as did Jesus. Above all, O God, enable me to listen for your voice speaking to me, and may I then have the willingness to carry out your will.

(Morning)
May I begin the day knowing when to use my tongue to speak and when to use my ears to listen.
(Prayers of Intercession)

(Evening)
Ever-present God, whose love has embraced me this day, grant me a night of rest and renewal. Accept any kind and helpful thought I have expressed. Forgive, O merciful God, when I have failed to hear others speak.
(Prayers of Intercession)

Thank you for a tongue to speak and ears to listen.

(Morning)
I commit myself to being a good servant of your gifts of speech and hearing to listen this day. Amen.

(Evening)
Help me, Divine One, tomorrow to be a better steward of all my senses, especially my speech and hearing, that Jesus may be seen in me, Amen.

THURSDAY, APRIL 2
(Read Isaiah 50:6–9a)

(Morning)
Holy God, you are always with me. Thank you for the day before me. Thank you, too, for the knowledge that no matter what this day brings—happiness or disappointments—you are present.

(Evening)
Holy God, I have been sustained today by knowing that you are near. Thank you.

Some of us never have been subjected to physical persecution or verbal insults. Yet I know that the prophets who lived hundreds of years prior to Jesus were persecuted for the stands they took. As we move toward Holy Week, I am grateful for the stand taken by the early Christian martyrs, "in spite of dungeon, fire, and sword." Most of all, I remember and praise your name for Jesus, who, although completely innocent, went to the cross knowing that it was your will. Enable me to be as true a disciple of Jesus as was Jesus to you, holy God.

(Morning)
Ever-loving God, help me to be a good servant of Christ,
as Christ was the perfect servant to you.
(Prayers of Intercession)

(Evening)
For you, O God, have been with me and helped me this day.
Praise be to you. If I have been silent rather than vocal in the face of insults
against the Christian way of life, forgive me. Gracious God,
help me to be a better steward of your gifts tomorrow.
(Prayers of Intercession)

Thanks be to God for the perfect model set by Jesus.

(Morning)
May my love and commitment to
Christ be genuine. Amen.

(Evening)
May my resolve to grow spiritually
increase each day I live. Amen.

FRIDAY, APRIL 3
(Read Psalm 118:12, 19–29)

(Morning)
Thank you, gracious God, for you are good and your love will endure forever.
Thanks be to you for another day of life. May I rejoice and be glad for it.

(Evening)
Thank you, gracious God, for the day that just has passed. Help me to remember
your constant and steadfast love.

I exist in a world which knows both good and evil. May your Spirit, O
God, always be with me, that I may face each hour and enter the gates of
righteousness and truth rather than those of evil and falsehood. Grant that I
may so live that others may know that my life is built on the cornerstone of
Jesus Christ. Thank you, God, for sending Jesus into the world to give us a
perfect pattern for living. Your love for me and for every human life will
never come to an end. Blessing, glory, and honor be unto you.

(Morning)
God, as I begin a new day, may I live in joyful celebration that I am your child.
(Prayers of Intercession)

(Evening)
I give you thanks, O God most high, for light which you have shed upon my
path. Thanks be to you, O God, for your steadfast love which will
endure forever.
(Prayers of Intercession)

Thank you for the gift of life and for each moment of the day.

(Morning)
Help me to be a good follower of Jesus
the Christ this day. Amen.

(Evening)
May I remember tomorrow, more than
I have today, to give thanks at all
times for your steadfast and
enduring love. Amen.

SATURDAY, APRIL 4

(Read Luke 19:28–40)

(Morning)
Everlasting and almighty God, thanks be to you for Jesus Christ. As I live this day, may I emulate the courage that Jesus exhibited as he entered Jerusalem, fully aware of the hostility he would meet.

(Evening)
Everlasting and almighty God, thank you for Jesus who came and lived among us, setting a perfect example of the way to live.

I thank you, God, that Jesus knew as he entered Jerusalem that the rulers and chief elders would certainly put him to death. Thank you, too, Holy One, that knowing the signs of the day, Jesus believed it was your will that he go to Jerusalem and was obedient. I doubt I would have had such courage. When being a Christian becomes difficult or unpopular, grant me courage, O gracious God—a portion of the courage of Jesus—when life for me becomes difficult and it would be easier to turn and run away. Grant me strength and unwavering faith to follow in Jesus' footsteps at all times.

(Morning)
Help me, almighty God, to live this day with the boldness and the caring of Jesus, our Savior.
(Prayers of Intercession)

(Evening)
Thank you, merciful God, for your presence and guidance this day. Now grant me rest this night, that I may awake more determined to be a better disciple.
(Prayers of Intercession)

Thanks be to you, holy God, for Jesus and his complete obedience to you.

(Morning)	(Evening)
I promise, O God, insofar as I am able, to be as obedient a follower of Jesus as he was of you. Amen.	May I more closely follow Jesus tomorrow with obedience and steadfastness. Amen.

SUNDAY, APRIL 5
(Read Luke 19:28–40)

(Morning)
Great God, new every morning is your mercy. On this Palm Sunday, may my heart sing for joy as I remember the entry of Jesus into the Holy City.

(Evening)
Great God, thank you for the pageantry and wonder of this day.

As I read and ponder the events of Palm Sunday, I praise you with the multitude of disciples who have blessed you joyfully throughout the ages for all the deeds of Jesus. Enable me to remember, holy God, that Jesus did not enter Jerusalem as an exalted ruler, riding on a mighty horse, but deliberately entered the city riding on a lowly colt, a sign of peace. O God, I implore you to help me realize anew that Christ never will force his way into my heart, but comes only as I humble myself and invite him in. Come, Jesus, the Chosen One of God, and live and reign within me.

(Morning)
Spirit of love, Spirit of truth, guide and direct my way this day. May I feel you once again as the all-embracing power that you are.
(Prayers of Intercession)

(Evening)
Accept my gratitude this night, blessed God, for the awe of today. If I have failed to glean the full impact of this holy day and this Holy Week ahead, speak afresh to my heart.
(Prayers of Intercession)

All glory and honor for the rich spiritual gifts of this day.
Jesus Christ has come anew as a lamb into my heart.

(Morning)
Enable me to find you once more in a fresh way, my God and Sovereign. Amen.

(Evening)
Because of this day, may I seek you and attempt to be a better Christian steward tomorrow. And now, grant me a night of peaceful rest, I pray. Amen.

MONDAY, APRIL 6
(Read John 20:1–18)

(Morning)
O God, help me today as I rise to seek Christ early in my day.

(Evening)
O God, this day I have met many challenges.
Your presence has enabled me to be victorious.

O loving God, it is the empty tomb that reminds us of your resurrection power. Help us to continue to seek you in all times and places and to know that we, too, may share in your resurrection.

(Morning)
God, this day guide my feet as I walk in the assurance of your strength.
(Prayers of Intercession)

(Evening)
Throughout this day, loving God, your love has been my help and hope.
(Prayers of Intercession)

You can overcome any obstacles.

(Morning)
O God, may I this day tell others that you live. Amen.

(Evening)
O blessed God, this night I rest in you, knowing that you live for me. Amen.

TUESDAY, APRIL 7
(Read Acts 10:34–43)

(Morning)
Merciful God, help me this day to hear the good news afresh and
to strive to be a witness for you.

(Evening)
Merciful God, this day, I have tried to be a witness for you.

O eternal God, you indeed are God of all. Help me to allow you to reign in
every area of my life so that you may be glorified in all I do.

(Morning)
O God, throughout this day, continue to reveal yourself to me through the
spoken word.
(Prayers of Intercession)

(Evening)
Today, Creator God, I have seen you working in all things.
(Prayers of Intercession)

"Make me a witness for you, O God."

(Morning)
Help me, wonderful God, to be an
effective witness for you. Amen.

(Evening)
O God, may I sleep through the night
knowing that I have tried to share
your Word. Amen.

WEDNESDAY, APRIL 8
(Read Isaiah 65:17–25)

(Morning)
Dear God, I thank you for the newness of this day and the fresh opportunity to serve in your vineyard.

(Evening)
Dear God, this evening I reflect on the glimpses of your glorious creation that I have seen today.

O God, through your prophet Isaiah, you promised us a world where peace would abide and hope endure. Help us, Divine Teacher, to be the instrument through which this world may be created. Use us to do your perfect will.

(Morning)
O God, let me focus my attention on those who need an answer from you.
(Prayers of Intercession)

(Evening)
Precious and eternal God, you have moved in mighty ways. I bring to you now those whom I have encountered today.
(Prayers of Intercession)

The peace of Christ is beyond our understanding.

(Morning)
O God, today let me go into a new world of possibilities for you. Amen.

(Evening)
O God, may I find rest and strength for tomorrow's journey. Amen.

THURSDAY, APRIL 9
(Read Psalm 118:1–2)

(Morning)
Creator God, thank you for this day and for your enduring love.

(Evening)
Creator God, your love has been as real to me as my very being.

O God, you are great and deserving of thanks. When I think of your goodness, I am always overwhelmed by how undeserving I am of all you do. Help me, God, to spread your goodness everywhere I go, so that others may see you in me.

(Morning)
I ask now, O God, for your presence in the lives of others.
(Prayers of Intercession)

(Evening)
For all the goodness I have experienced through your people this day,
I give thanks.
(Prayers of Intercession)

"God is good, all the time."

(Morning)	(Evening)
Bless me this day to be a blessing to someone else. Amen.	As I recline for this evening's repose, let me rest in your goodness. Amen.

FRIDAY, APRIL 10
(Read Psalm 118:14–25)

(Morning)
Precious God, be a source of strength for the work of this day.

(Evening)
Precious God, your strong hand has upheld me valiantly this day.

Eternal God, I praise you that the rejected one has become the cornerstone of our faith. Enable me, O God, to enter your gates of righteousness and to dwell therein.

(Morning)
O God, I praise you for your salvation and pray for all who need you.
(Prayers of Intercession)

(Evening)
Now, O God, help me to rejoice and be glad in all that you have done this day.
(Prayers of Intercession)

God answers prayer.

(Morning)
I go to this new day with your peace and joy in my heart, dear God. Amen.

(Evening)
O God, I give you thanks and praise for all the marvelous works that you accomplished this day. Amen.

SATURDAY, APRIL 11
(Read 1 Corinthians 15:19–26)

(Morning)
Loving God, I rejoice this day that I labor for an eternal reward prepared
by your hand.

(Evening)
Loving God, this evening I celebrate the resurrection power that has been my
source of strength today.

Powerful God, you raised your Child, Jesus Christ, from death to life. And
by this, you promise us that we also will be raised. Help me to live in the
assurance of your ability to bring renewal in the midst of despair and hope
in the midst of sorrow.

(Morning)
God, I offer up to you now all those who need a
resurrection experience within their lives.
(Prayers of Intercession)

(Evening)
Wonderful God, for all whose lives represent your renewing presence,
I give you thanks.
(Prayers of Intercession)

Rise up, O church of God!

(Morning)
I give thanks to you that I am resurrected daily in Christ. Amen.

(Evening)
I thank you, God, that in my disappointments there is always hope for
tomorrow in you. Amen.

SUNDAY, APRIL 12
(Read Luke 24:1–12)

(Morning)
Dear God, like the women at the empty tomb, may I run and tell the good news of your resurrection this day.

(Evening)
Dear God, I thank you that this day has been a celebration of your resurrection from death to life.

God, help me always to handle your truth with fear and trembling. May I never discount a word that comes to me from you, regardless of the source. May I always be amazed by your mighty acts of greatness.

(Morning)
God, I offer to you those who need your renewing touch.
(Prayers of Intercession)

(Evening)
Today, O God, I have touched many lives. For each one, I offer a special prayer.
(Prayers of Intercession)

Christ is risen indeed!

(Morning)
May this day be a day of new life in you, merciful God. Amen.

(Evening)
Precious God, may I rest my hope in you this night and be restored through sleep. Amen.

MONDAY, APRIL 13
(Read John 20:19–23)

(Morning)
God of history, I thank you for the immense gift that your perfect love has given me through Jesus Christ, my Savior; the hope of eternal life that I share in the resurrection; and the gift of the Holy Spirit, who sustains and guides me.

(Evening)
God of history, thank you for sustaining and guiding me during this day through your great Spirit.

O God, how wonderful it is to know that you are always with me! Your gracious presence is real in my life. I have no fear, since you are my support and my friend. Thank you, loving God, for all the goodness of your hand, allow me to distinguish the voice of your Spirit from all other voices, and grant me the strength to follow you.

(Morning)
Guide me, so that I may feel and see your companionship during this day.
(Prayers of Intercession)

(Evening)
God of history, transcendent and immanent, bless my rest tonight, so that my morning may be as fruitful tomorrow as it was today. For you are the glory.
I praise you, O God!
(Prayers of Intercession)

Humbly I pray.
(Pray the Prayer of Our Savior.)

(Morning)
To be your witness is my desire; may your Spirit guide me forever. Amen.

(Evening)
May this night equip me, so that tomorrow and during the rest of my life I will be able to discern what you want me to do. Amen.

TUESDAY, APRIL 14
(Read John 20:24–29)

(Morning)
O gracious God, I give you thanks for all the wonders you have revealed to me, especially the gift of faith. I am redeemed.

(Evening)
O gracious God, my Father and my Mother, though I cannot see you, nor touch you, I know that you are close. In my heart and my mind, I can feel your love. You care for me as you guard me through each day and night.

As I continue to live in an era where the things of value and importance are those that can be bought, I reflect on the life and teachings of Jesus Christ. Jesus taught us a new world order, an order where the dispossessed will be the owners of the promised land and those who have nothing will live the abundant life. Thank you, my God, for your gift of faith and for hope which enables us to see you with the eyes of our heart.

(Morning)
Please grant me the blessing to see your face in everyone I encounter today, and let me see their differences as gifts to enrich and make me a better human being.
(Prayers of Intercession)

(Evening)
Transcendent and immanent God, grant me and those who surround me a peaceful rest. Forgive me when I have sinned against my neighbor, because I have sinned against you.
(Prayers of Intercession)

As my Savior Christ taught, I pray.
(Pray the Prayer of Our Savior.)

(Morning)
Thank you for making me aware of your presence as I serve my neighbor. Amen.

(Evening)
May I look at the new day with excitement and praise you for the gift of love in Jesus Christ. Amen.

WEDNESDAY, APRIL 15
(Read Acts 5:27–32)

(Morning)
God of mercy, God of love, God of justice, who lives close to me and close to the ones I love most, thank you for your Word which always nurtures me. It challenges me to become a better witness in this world.

(Evening)
God of mercy, God of love, God of justice, I pray for discernment, so that I will always choose your way and follow Jesus until my last day in this world.

I live in a world that forces me to make choices and decisions regarding politics, religion, and moral issues. Sometimes these choices are difficult; many times, they jeopardize my values and my faith. But I know I am your child and your disciple. Thank you, God. You have given me the intelligence and the courage to choose what is right and to follow you.

(Morning)
May the decisions I make today speak about my faith in Jesus Christ and make me a better human being.
(Prayers of Intercession)

(Evening)
Dear God, while I sleep, let your Spirit embrace and empower me to be your witness in the midst of the powers that neglect your presence.
(Prayers of Intercession)

Boldly I pray.
(Pray the Prayer of Our Savior.)

(Morning)
I commit myself to make decisions grounded in the faith of Jesus Christ. Amen.

(Evening)
If there is just one reason to live, may it be to do your will. Amen.

THURSDAY, APRIL 16
(Read Psalm 118:14–20)

(Morning)
God of my salvation, I do not have enough words to express my gratitude for all
that you have done for me and through me! I know that you sustain me with
your hand. My crises are small because you are with me and
you have given me the victory.

(Evening)
God of my salvation, my spirit rejoices in you! You have come to me in ways
that I never expected. Yet I am not surprised, because you are the almighty God,
who has opened the gates of righteousness giving me a new life.

Creator God, whose mercy and love are beyond my human comprehension, I know that your arms are always open for me and for every human
being on earth. Your love is so unlimited that you have forgiven my sins,
and now I sing a new song, a song of victory and joy.

(Morning)
O God, today I pray that I will smile a new smile, the smile of joy and victory
which is my testimony of what you have done in me and for me.
(Prayers of Intercession)

(Evening)
God of victory, may my rest during this night give me new strength
to continue to be the new person you have created.
(Prayers of Intercession)

In victory I pray.
(Pray the Prayer of Our Savior.)

(Morning)
Righteousness is a virtue I will
always want to exhibit. May your
help be there for me. Amen.

(Evening)
Daily, may my life praise you for all
your love and sustenance. Amen.

FRIDAY, APRIL 17
(Read Psalm 118:21–25)

(Morning)
Thank you, dear God, because your ears are never closed to the claims of those who follow you! Thank you, O God, because you have heard my words and have answered my prayers.

(Evening)
Thank you, dear God. There is nothing I have that you have not provided. Wonderful God, even during the silent night you are working to give me what I need.

When I look at the heavens during the night, contemplating the beautiful darkness, the moon and stars, I have no choice but to praise you with my mind, my spirit, and my body. When I walk during the day and I contemplate the sun, sky, oceans, mountains, and rivers, I have no choice but to praise you, my God. I exclaim with the psalmist, "This is the day that God has made; let us rejoice and be glad in it."

(Morning)
God of my joy, hear my prayers for those who are close to my heart, and be you their joy and gladness.
(Prayers of Intercession)

(Evening)
God of my joy, hear my prayers for the ones who are less close to my heart, and be you their joy and gladness.
(Prayers of Intercession)

With joy in my heart, I pray.
(Pray the Prayer of Our Savior.)

(Morning)
To know you, my God, is to know what a real friend is. Thank you, O God. Amen.

(Evening)
May my voice be always open to praise you and to speak about your doings. Amen.

SATURDAY, APRIL 18
(Read Psalm 118:26–29)

(Morning)
O God, I give you thanks. Your love has taught me to love and to see others as my special neighbors. I praise you, God!

(Evening)
O God, I praise you because your love has changed my life; your goodness has brought goodness into my life. I praise you, God!

God, who is the One who comes in your name? The One who is righteous, and tame? Who is the One who does justice and is an instrument of liberation and peace to those who are bound by prejudice, selfishness, and arrogance? O God of goodness, liberate me!

(Morning)
O God, give me the strength and the wisdom to do justice in your name and to bring peace during this day.
(Prayers of Intercession)

(Evening)
O God, forgive me if during this day I did not come in your name. If I have been weak to do justice and peace, may this night prepare me to come in your name.
(Prayers of Intercession)

In righteousness I pray.
(Pray the Prayer of Our Savior.)

| (Morning) | (Evening) |
| I commit myself to come in your name, O God, as you empower me to become. Amen. | Give me the strength to be good and righteous as you help me, O God. Amen. |

SUNDAY, APRIL 19
(Read Revelation 5:4–8)

(Morning)
God of all ages, I praise you and I extol you for giving me eternal life in Jesus, the slaughtered lamb whose victory on the cross has facilitated my way to you.

(Evening)
God of all ages, I give you thanks because in Jesus I have assurance of salvation, life, and resurrection.

God,as I read this text, I reflect on the meaning of your Child Jesus' death on the cross. I ask myself how would it be if Jesus had not become the slaughtered lamb. To me, Jesus' name means life—the open door to bring your dominion to this world. It is the hope for people of all races, genders, cultures, ages, sexual orientations, classes, and abilities to be one in you. Thank you, God, for Jesus, your incarnate Word.

(Morning)
May my actions today show the hope of living in a better world.
(Prayers of Intercession)

(Evening)
May my night, O God, be blessed, so that tomorrow I will be your instrument to those I meet and those in need of hope.
(Prayers of Intercession)

As Jesus taught the disciples, I pray.
(Pray the Prayer of Our Savior.)

(Morning)	(Evening)
I want to serve you, O God. Equip me to do so. Amen.	May my lifestyle show that Jesus, the slaughtered lamb, is the center of my life. Amen.

MONDAY, APRIL 20
(Read Psalm 30)

(Morning)
God, where there is illness in the world today,
send promises of healing and hope.

(Evening)
God, give rest to all those who are weary from spending the day
struggling with aches and pains.

Illness brings a fascinating mixture of memories, energy, weariness, longing, and hope. It sometimes brings mental and physical aches that seem overwhelming. However, you, O God, have not forsaken the psalmist. The prayer uttered is one of thanks, proclaiming your might and watchfulness to all generations. When we think of this, we marvel at your endless love and caring.

(Morning)
As I begin this day, I pray for those who are ill.
(Prayers of Intercession)

(Evening)
As I reach day's end, I remember those who spent this day
working to alleviate suffering.
(Prayers of Intercession)

God is gracious. God is merciful. God is forever.

(Morning)
Haunt me this day with the needs of
the aching world. Amen.

(Evening)
Fill me with gratitude for the wisdom
and skill of all who heal. Amen.

TUESDAY, APRIL 21
(Read Acts 9:1–6)

(Morning)
Colorful Creator God, as each new day is born of your making,
help me make something new of this day.

(Evening)
Colorful Creator God, as the setting sun spreads a canopy of hues over the
earth, let your brilliance overcome all chaos.

God, you always make a connection between creating and the truth, between creation and what is right. All around us we see things being created to cover up or erase the truth. Saul worked to cover up and erase your truth until he journeyed to Damascus. It was here that he began to speak your truth and declare what is right.

(Morning)
Let the artist in me emerge this day to be an expression of you,
O God, the Great Creator.
(Prayers of Intercession)

(Evening)
Whatever I have done this day, let that which is truthful remain. Forgive me all
that may have contributed to chaos.
(Prayers of Intercession)

I was created in God's image, to be a creator.

(Morning)
Let me wake up this morning with my
mind on you, Creator God. Amen.

(Evening)
God, let me relax in the evening
hours, so that I may bask in the glory
of your creation. Amen.

WEDNESDAY, APRIL 22
(Read Acts 9:7–20)

(Morning)
Indwelling God, as the sun penetrates earth once again, fill me with the warmth
of your being and the power of your love.

(Evening)
Indwelling God, as the moon and stars envelop the earth, surround me with
gentle affirmations of sustaining care.

God, everything on earth and everything in those mysterious heavens is
called upon to give you praise. You chose Saul to be your instrument of
truth and praise. We, too, must give you praise and declare the glory of
Jesus Christ. We are in awe of you and give you praise because you have
called us forth and your loving Spirit is deep within our very being.

(Morning)
Even if the day brings fire, hail, snow, frost, or stormy winds,
God, let me see your glory in their midst.
(Prayers of Intercession)

(Evening)
As most creatures settle quietly into the night,
may your peace descend upon the universe and on all I love.
(Prayers of Intercession)

In Jesus Christ all the fullness of God was pleased to dwell.

(Morning)
Indwelling God, abide with me in
every passing hour of this day. Amen.

(Evening)
Indwelling God, abide with me as the
evening gracefully arrives. Amen.

THURSDAY, APRIL 23
(Read John 21:1–8)

(Morning)
God, as this day unfolds, wrap me in the security of your loving arms,
so that I may face any strain or care in the comfort of your love.

(Evening)
God, even as I seek your forgiveness, I rejoice in the knowledge that
we are reconciled and that you overlook our offenses.

God, how often our seeking is fruitless until we seek guidance from you.
Our labors are often futile and our meanderings pointless until we hear
your Word and follow your directions. Help us, like the fishermen, to cast
our nets on the right side of the ship.

(Morning)
Loving God, someone may need my embrace and forgiveness today.
Free me to be the giver of that love.
(Prayers of Intercession)

(Evening)
Underneath me are the everlasting and ever-forgiving arms.
Let me know no shame in leaning on them.
(Prayers of Intercession)

Blessedness and peace are mine, as I lean on the everlasting arms.

(Morning)
God, share your gentle comfort with all
who need to feel love today. Amen.

(Evening)
God, hug every hungry, cold, and
despairing person in your arms this
night and use my arms as an exten-
sion of your caring. Amen.

FRIDAY, APRIL 24
(Read John 21:9–19)

(Morning)
Eager God, fill me with anticipation for this day. May its newness be an opportunity for me to find something fresh and fulfilling in what I must do.

(Evening)
Eager God, even though the energy of the day may still be
very much with me, grant me the renewal that comes in rest,
that I might be refreshed in the morning.

God, we give you thanks and praise. When our souls are hungry, you feed us with the bread of life. Help us to see that our nourishment must come from you. Grant that each time we share food and companionship, we might experience anew the early-morning banquet which you prepared for your disciples.

(Morning)
In a society where abundance is so often seen as the accumulation of wealth, let us pray for abundance of justice.
(Prayers of Intercession)

(Evening)
In a world where hunger, disease, falsehood, and unkindness are so prevalent, let us pray for the abundance that Jesus embodied.
(Prayers of Intercession)

God, anoint my head with oil; my cup overflows.

(Morning)
Eager God, whatever my age, show
me the wisdom of your Child Jesus.
Amen.

(Evening)
Eager God, thank you for all that was
good, creative, and fulfilling today.
Amen.

SATURDAY, APRIL 25
(Read Revelation 5:11–12)

(Morning)
God of the saints, give us the assurance in the coming day
that your care and concern are never-ending.

(Evening)
God of the saints, give us the assurance at the end of our days
that we are still precious in your sight.

Merciful God, you have given to us the greatest gift of all by sacrificing your Child for our sake. Help us to recognize our own unworthiness and, in so doing, to reflect upon your divine goodness.

(Morning)
Strengthen my resolve, my faith, my limbs,
and my courage to walk with the saints this day.
(Prayers of Intercession)

(Evening)
In the quiet of the day's end, help me bring to mind all those whose saintliness
has touched my life.
(Prayers of Intercession)

The saints lived not only in the past. Their company is vast today.

(Morning)
Today, let me know that I am surrounded by a great cloud of your witnesses. Amen.

(Evening)
Tonight, let me know that I am surrounded by a great cloud of your witnesses. Amen.

SUNDAY, APRIL 26
(Read Revelation 5:13–14)

(Morning)
Strong God, the day is full and the demands may seem more than I can manage.
Help me know the strength that comes when I share my day with you.

(Evening)
Strong God, in your wisdom, you created the seventh day for rest.
Let me find strength by resting with you this night.

Eternal God, the vision that you gave to John on the Isle of Patmos is still a source of mystery and awe to your people. As we focus our thoughts on the end times, allow us to remain steadfast in the pursuit of your vision for this world today.

(Morning)
God, let your power overshadow me this day
to remind me that nothing is impossible.
(Prayers of Intercession)

(Evening)
God, let me know that I have found favor with you,
even if the day has been filled with impossibilities.
(Prayers of Intercession)

God has nurtured us yesterday and today.
God will nurture us in all our tomorrows.

(Morning)
Mother God, give me the assurance of
your presence each hour of this day.
Amen.

(Evening)
Father God, enfold me with your
loving forgiveness as I seek strength
in rest. Amen.

MONDAY, APRIL 27
(Read Psalm 23)

(Morning)
Dearest God, creator of this new day and this new week of life, thank you for
being my shepherd and for guarding my path. Lead me in right paths today, that
my life may give glory to you.

(Evening)
Dearest God, creator of this new day and this new week of life, thank you for
being my shepherd and for guarding my path.

Today I will live in the promise that you are my shepherd. In my life I have
known green pastures; I have also known valleys of death and times when
I have stood weak-kneed in the presence of my enemies. Today I choose to
feast at the table you set before me in the presence of my enemies—depression, disease, conflicted relationships, disorder in society. I will feast
on whatever you provide. I will feast in thankfulness for who you are and
who I am to you.

(Morning)
May I begin this day mindful of all the ways you seek to shepherd me.
(Prayers of Intercession)

(Evening)
Good Shepherd, you have led me so lovingly through this day, being present in
times of peace as well as in times of danger. Lead me just a little further to the
green pastures of renewing sleep.
(Prayers of Intercession)

Thank you for all the ways your care was made evident to me this day.

(Morning)
Today I choose to follow the Good
Shepherd in the paths that lead to a
full life. Amen.

(Evening)
Tonight I will sleep in peace, trusting
that the Shepherd's eye is upon me.
May I rise in the morning, renewed to
walk with you through another day
of life. Amen.

TUESDAY, APRIL 28
(Read Psalm 23 and John 10:22–30)

(Morning)
Messiah, thank you for revealing yourself to me in so many wondrous ways.
Allow me the grace to see you clearly this day. Allow me the grace to follow
where you lead.

(Evening)
Messiah, thank you for revealing yourself to me in so many wondrous ways.

"How long will you keep us in suspense. If you are the Messiah tell us plainly." I am so like the religious leaders who rejected you. I want factual certainty. I am skeptical of the mystery unfolding all around me in your work. I am tempted to close my ears to the sound of your voice in creation. God, thank you for continuing to work in me and in the world, in spite of my doubts, in spite of my troubling disbelief. Thank you for calling to me until I recognize your voice. Thank you for gently prodding me until I willingly follow.

(Morning)
As I begin another day of life, I open my ears and my heart to the voice of the
Good Shepherd. I give myself to the unfolding mystery revealed only in
surrender to you, the one who calls my name.
(Prayers of Intercession)

(Evening)
Loving Shepherd, you have called me to follow you, to heed your voice
throughout this day. Forgive me for any times when I have refused to listen and
follow. Forgive me if I have in any way thwarted your will.
(Prayers of Intercession)

Thank you for all the ways you lead me through this, another day of life.

(Morning)
Today I commit myself to being aware of Christ, present and at work in the people and in all of creation around me. Amen.

(Evening)
Tonight, loving God, I rest in the mystery of your love for me. May this sleep renew my body, mind, and spirit in order that I might walk closer to you. Amen.

WEDNESDAY, APRIL 29
(Read Acts 9:36–43)

(Morning)
Creator God, giver of all life, thank you for the birth of another day. Open me to the power of the resurrection. Call me out of death to new life in the moments of this new day.

(Evening)
Creator God, giver of all life, thank you for this day of life, for calling me out of death to new life in the moments of this past day.

Ever-renewing God, in your love and power you raised Jesus from the dead and worked through Peter to bring life back to your servant Tabitha. I see your resurrecting power in my own life as well as in those around me. You empower me with resurrecting love, that I might be your hands, your feet, your voice, your eyes and ears in this earthly life. O great God, give me the courage to use the power of this love for the good of all.

(Morning)
May I begin this day aware of the power of the resurrection present in my own life and in those around me.
(Prayers of Intercession)

(Evening)
God of all life, you have empowered me this day with your love and grace, bringing new life to dead places and spaces in my life. Forgive me for the times when I have chosen death over life.
(Prayers of Intercession)

**Thank you for all the witnesses of new life
I have seen in all of creation this day.**

(Morning)	(Evening)
May I this day be a life-giver, breathing your Spirit into a weary soul. Amen.	I surrender myself to restful sleep in Christ, knowing that you will use it for the renewal of my body, mind, and spirit. Amen.

THURSDAY, APRIL 30
(Read Revelation 7:9–17)

(Morning)
Everlasting, ever-unfolding mystery, you who are both lamb and shepherd, I
bow before you at the beginning of another day. I open myself to life in you.

(Evening)
Everlasting, ever-unfolding mystery, you who are both lamb and shepherd, I
bow before you at the end of another day. I pray that I have brought blessings to
others and glory to you this day.

With great humility I join the vast multitude before your throne, a multitude so great that it cannot be counted, people from all tribes and lands, all
races and languages. I am one of the many who have known your saving
power, your loving ways. Today I ponder what it means to be a part of such
a diverse people united under one God. Grant me the wisdom to find and
accept my particular place in your people and plan.

(Morning)
May I begin this day mindful of the diversity and vast beauty
of your people, O God.
(Prayers of Intercession)

(Evening)
Sovereign One, forgive me for the times today when I have seen myself as too
high or too low, when I have isolated myself from the great multitude. Forgive
me for the times I have failed to give you the glory.
(Prayers of Intercession)

**Thank you for surrounding me with such a great multitude of believers,
people of all ages, races, and places.**

(Morning)	(Evening)
I commit myself this day to recogniz-ing your presence in those I perceive as being different from myself. Amen.	As I come to the end of another day, I thank you for your care and for the rest that you promise me this night and in eternity. Amen.

FRIDAY, MAY 1
(Read John 10:22–30 and Revelation 7:9–17)

(Morning)
Giver of eternal life, thank you for the gift of another day of life, a life that
holds the promise of eternity within it. Let me live this day
as the beginning of forever.

(Evening)
Giver of eternal life, thank you for the gift of another day of earthly life, a life
that holds the promise of eternity within it.

God, often I feel like one who has come through the "great ordeal"—beaten
down, worn out. So many things press upon me that I must admit there are
times when I am tempted to give up the faith, I feel like a "Christian-at-
risk." I know the promise, though. If I am one of Christ's sheep, "none will
snatch them out of my hand." All this is promised as long as I keep listening for the Shepherd's voice and following, even in difficult times—especially in difficult times.

(Morning)
May I live this day not in fear of being lost, but in confidence of having been
found in Christ. I am known to you and am safe in your hands.
(Prayers of Intercession)

(Evening)
Protective, loving God, whose Spirit has held me close this day, carry me now
to a night of peaceful rest. Forgive me for any times I have turned away from
your care and guidance.
(Prayers of Intercession)

**Thank you for holding me in your hands,
not only this day but for all of eternity.**

(Morning)	(Evening)
Today I commit myself to trusting the Good Shepherd with my entire life. Amen.	Tonight I rest in your strong, loving hands and commit my tomorrow to another day of service to you, my sisters, and my brothers. Amen.

SATURDAY, MAY 2
(Read Acts 9:36–43 and John 10:22–30)

(Morning)
God of all times, thank you for bringing me through another week.
Thank you for shepherding me. As I begin this day and end this week,
I praise you for your power, your wisdom, your protection.

(Evening)
God of all times, thank you for bringing me through another day and another
week of life. Thank you for shepherding me, for calling me to follow,
for calling me out of death to new life.

God of Tabitha and Peter, I give thanks for the stories of the early church,
which give hope and life to me this day. Remind me that what I do today is
important, that it has value. As the widows held close the clothing Tabitha
had made during her life, so might the works of my life have value to you.
Give me the grace to use the talents and resources I have been given for
your glory.

(Morning)
May I begin this day mindful of the talents and resources I have been given to
use for the building of your dominion and the care of all your creation.
(Prayers of Intercession)

(Evening)
As I come to the end of another day, forgive me, God, for any times I have
wasted or hoarded the gifts you have given me. Forgive me for not sharing.
(Prayers of Intercession)

**Thank you for the many and diverse gifts and abilities
you have given me and all your children.**

(Morning)
At the beginning of this new day, I
ask for the grace to share abundantly
all that I have been given. Amen.

(Evening)
At the end of another day, I am
reminded that whether asleep or awake
I belong to you, O God. Take my
worries and all my anxieties now and
let me rest secure in your loving arms.
Amen.

SUNDAY, MAY 3
(Read Psalm 23 and Acts 9:36–43)

(Morning)
Great God, lover of my soul, thank you for the beginning of this new day and
this new week. As I celebrate this holy day, restore and renew in me your
resurrecting power.

(Evening)
Great God, lover of my soul, thank you for the end of another day and
the beginning of another week.

Great God, thank you for continually amazing me with your love and your
power; for surprising me by bringing life to places and parts of my life I
thought were dead, especially to relationships, to causes, and to people I
had given up on. As I work with you this day for resurrection, remind me
of the promise found in Revelation: There will come a time when your
realm encompasses all of heaven and earth. Remind me as I work with
your plan for the coming of that great day.

(Morning)
May I begin this day aware of all the ways I need the resurrecting power of you,
O God, in my life. May I open myself to your power, so that I might be a
conduit of this life for others.
(Prayers of Intercession)

(Evening)
Renewing God, thank you for all the ways you have been present to me this day,
in times of death and resurrection, in times of struggle and of peace. Forgive me
for the times I refuse to be a part of your plan for new life, for life eternal.
(Prayers of Intercession)

**Thank you for the promise of a day when pain and death will be no longer.
Thank you for the promise of eternal life with you.**

(Morning)	(Evening)
Today I commit myself to looking for evidence of the in-breaking of your dominion all around me. Amen.	I now surrender myself to the peace of the night, asking for renewing rest, that I might wake in the morning for another day to serve you. Amen.

MONDAY, MAY 4
(Read Psalm 148)

(Morning)
E Kou Makou Makua iloko o Ka Lani, our heavenly God, for the songs of life, voices of birds and animals, wind, the sounds of children and other people, the gurgling of our waterways, the loving embrace of waves upon the shores, all praise you, gracious God. The sounds of praise reflect your majesty and glory, E Ke Akua (God).

(Evening)
E Kou Makou Makua iloko o Ka Lani, thank you for creation's sounds of praise all through the day and as we enter the night hours. May I also share in the night's praise of you, gracious God.

I hear creations' praise of their source, God. The praising sounds of birds, animals, people, streams, and waterfalls. Trees singing in the wind, waves embracing the shore. Even the sounds of technology have their own sounds of life and praise. I share in these varied songs of praise. I love you, God, and I lift my voice to praise you.

(Morning)
Source of my life, may my sounds today bring only praise to you and add to the praises from creation. Praise God.
(Prayers of Intercession)

(Evening)
Evening has come, the day has been spent praising you. Thank you for accepting sounds. May my praises be included with the praises throughout the night, for the world is truly yours, O Gracious One.
(Prayers of Intercession)

**The wondrous voices of the universe praise God—
I, too, lift my voice in praise to you.**

(Morning)
May my life be filled with praises to you, gracious God. Amen.

(Evening)
May all of the sounds of life praise you always. Amen.

TUESDAY, MAY 5
(Read Psalm 148 and Acts 11:1–8)

(Morning)
To you, the source of all creation, the Ha (breath) of all life, your glory is
revealed in the goodness of creation and all the universe.

(Evening)
To you, the source of all creation, I thank you for sharing with me the purity of
life. As I praise and reflect on this day, may I also prepare to share in the
specialness of the voices of praise throughout the night.

I am very much a part of the family of creation. Part of my responsibility is
to share in recognizing, honoring, and praising you, O God. It is a joy to
praise you; it is a joy to lift my voice with the other voices of creation,
praising you, the source of all life.

(Morning)
Praise God from whom all blessings flow, praise God all creatures here below,
praise God all you heavenly host, praise God.
(Prayers of Intercession)

(Evening)
May my sounds and actions of praise join the rest of the creation in praising
you, O God, incessantly.
(Prayers of Intercession)

**All of the universe praises God on earth and in the heavens—
and may my voice always be a part of this chorus.**

(Morning)
May my sounds of praise be as honest
and sincere as the sounds of creation
praising you. Amen.

(Evening)
May my sounds of praise continue
through the night. Amen.

WEDNESDAY, MAY 6
(Read Acts 11:1–9)

(Morning)
E Ke Akua Mauloa, eternal God, thank you for a new morning, cleansed with
the refreshing dew and the cooling breezes that remind me that each morning
brings a fresh day to start anew.

(Evening)
E Ke Akua Mauloa, thank you for your breath (Ha) in my being today. It allows
me to share as a special blessing of creation.

I live in a world that attempts to separate everything as good or bad, clean
or unclean. God, as I understand and confess that your breath gives creation its life energy, I also confess the total acceptance of your creation of
which I am part. Thank you for your Ha in me, for this is a blessed life,
filled with blessings.

(Morning)
Gracious God, may I be able to confess the wonderful blessings of all of
creation and your goodness.
(Prayers of Intercession)

(Evening)
E Ke Akua Mauloa, whose Ha fills me with all of the goodness
of creation and supports me as I share life with creation,
thank you for your Ha's cleansing power.
(Prayers of Intercession)

Thank you for the goodness of all parts of creation.

(Morning)	(Evening)
May your Ha in me and all of creation be in harmony throughout this day. Amen.	May your Ha continue to refresh all of creation throughout this night. Mahalo ia oe, E Ke Akua, thank you, God. Amen.

THURSDAY, MAY 7
(Read Acts 11:1–8 and Revelation 21:1–6)

(Morning)
Ever-present God, the Ha of our lives, thank you for the completeness of
creation and the continuing love that carries me over my shortcomings
to the lokahi of creation.

(Evening)
Ever-present God, thank you for your sustaining power this day. Thank you for
sharing in my empowerment to reach the potential to which you have called me.

Water is very essential for island folk. God, even more important is my
foundation based on your love and Ha. This reflection allows me to confess your presence from the ever-present beginning to the never-ending
completion of my life's journey. God, your Ha makes all things possible,
for you are my Mother, my Father, my lokahi with all of creation. I now
need to share this with others.

(Morning)
Good morning Mother, Father, Grandmother, Grandfather, all of my relations in
creation, how graciously all of you reflect our God. May I continue in my
journey of faith, leaning on you, the foundation of all life.
(Prayers of Intercession)

(Evening)
Gracious One, the foundation of my life, may I continue to build on your
blessings of life, your breath within me, throughout the coming night
of refreshment and re-creation.
(Prayers of Intercession)

**God is the foundation of my life. Let my life build
on the firm foundation to the glorious heights of serving
God, my Mother, Father, Grandmother, Grandfather.**

(Morning)
How firm a foundation it is to build on
your breath in me. Amen.

(Evening)
A firm foundation, the comforting
coolness and inspiration of your Ha,
strengthens the building of my life's
journey. Amen.

FRIDAY, MAY 8
(Read Revelation 21:1–6)

(Morning)
E Ke Akua Mauloa, you are the Alpha and the Omega in the foundation of my life's journey. You are also the water of life, Ka wai ola, refreshing and strengthening the growth of my life. I am thankful for you as the refreshment of my journey—always sustaining.

(Evening)
E Ke Akua Mauloa, through the heat of life's journey, the desert of aloneness, you, Ka wai ola, have carried me, one step at a time. Mahalo ia oe, E Ka wai ola.

As Pacific Islanders traveled between islands, their major concerns were a seaworthy canoe (foundation) and water. God, you are thus in my life as I paddle my canoe through life, refreshing myself on Ka wai ola.

(Morning)
On my journey today, may my canoe be seaworthy and the supply of Ka wai ola be refreshing and sustaining.
(Prayers of Intercession)

(Evening)
God, today's journey in your canoe, drinking Ka wai ola, has led me to this space in my journey. May Ka wai ola refresh me throughout the night and prepare me for another day of living.
(Prayers of Intercession)

Sail on, O my soul, with God as my canoe and Ka wai ola refreshing my life.

(Morning)
In my canoe, one paddle stroke at a time, refreshed by Ka wai ola, God, I will answer your call to witness faithfully. Amen.

(Evening)
Evening has come, the table is set with Ka wai ola to refresh and restrengthen for another day's journey. Amen.

SATURDAY, MAY 9
(Read Revelations 21:1–6 and John 13:31–35)

(Morning)
E Ka wai ola, you have shared with me the oneness and lokahi I have with all creation as I travel. Thank you for refreshing and restrengthening me.

(Evening)
The canoe has been filled with love, Ke Akua no Aloha, the God of love. Thank you for allowing me to share lokahi, my firm foundation, and you, wai ola, with others in our canoe. Together, with love, we travel on, supporting one another.

E Ka wai ola, I do not travel alone in the canoe. Continue to teach me how to love so that I can share your love with others.

(Morning)
God, may your love shared with others, in lokahi with creation, continue to strengthen me as I share a life of loving with others, in your name.
(Prayers of Intercession)

(Evening)
As I pause this evening, I share the refreshing love with others who have accompanied me. God, I pray that we will build together on you as our firm foundation and the fountain of love with no conditions.
(Prayers of Intercession)

**God, as my helm and navigator,
fills the journey with all accepting love,
accepting people for who and what they are.**

(Morning)
God, may your Aloha, love, be as refreshing and nourishing as your Ka wai ola. Continue to fill me. Amen.

(Evening)
God, may your love and water of life shelter and protect me as my body refreshes itself throughout the night. Amen.

SUNDAY, MAY 10
(Read John 13:31–35)

(Morning)
God, morning has broken and a new day lies before me. I thank you for filling me with your love, a love that I can share with all of creation.

(Evening)
God, the coolness and safe rest of the evening give me time to immerse myself in your love and the love of all of creation. Thank you for the safety of this foundation of living, E Ke Akua.

Sharing life built on love provides a place of safety, a place of rejoicing, a canoe filled with loving people all working toward the same goal. Working together, I am able to share all my potential with the rest of creation.

(Morning)
God, continue to allow me to be filled with your love, and may I be able to share this love with all I come into contact with during today's journey.
(Prayers of Intercession)

(Evening)
Thank you, God, for all the love I have been able to share throughout this day. I pray for your continued guidance.
(Prayers of Intercession)

**Loving is the adhesive that keeps my community of faith together.
This community is part of the foundation that God was, is, and will be.**

(Morning)
Love Divine, all love excelling fills all of my life and includes all of creation. Thank you, God. Amen.

(Evening)
Love keeps me open to all people and to all of creation. God, thank you for loving and teaching me to love. Amen.

MONDAY, MAY 11
(Read Acts 16:9–12)

(Morning)
Loving Guide, thank you for your gentle inspiration, by night and by day. You are always with me and with all you have created.

(Evening)
Loving Guide, I give myself to you. Help me to know that your will for me, as for all your loved ones, is only good.

Sender of dreams, I am thankful for your guidance, both in my sleep and in my waking. May I seek ever to be open to those whose needs you place upon my heart. May my response, like Paul's, be swift and trusting. Help me also to accept, humbly and gratefully, the loving care of others; to be as willing to be the "Macedonian" as to be "Paul," and to recognize you as the divine link in either situation. Even when my efforts seem futile, help me to remember that you called us only to be faithful. Success is your responsibility.

(Morning)
Loving Creator, please be my vision, moment by moment throughout this day.
(Prayers of Intercession)

(Evening)
Thank you for the opportunities this day has brought for both giving and receiving your help.
(Prayers of Intercession)

Thank you, God, that the giver and the receiver are equally precious to you.

(Morning)
Help me always to see and hear with my heart and not just with my eyes and ears. Amen.

(Evening)
Be with me as I relax into sleep, knowing that my dreams are safe with you. Amen.

TUESDAY, MAY 12
(Read Acts 16:13–15)

(Morning)
Loving Companion, let me find you both within the walls of my daily life and
by the river of rest and refreshment.

(Evening)
Loving Companion, bless the seeds that I have planted this day and those that
have been planted within my heart. Water them with your love.

Gatherer of the beloved community, I thank you for calling me to come
outside the gates of daily routine to a place of prayer by the river. Open my
heart to hear your voice in the water's ripples and the birds' songs, and to
join all creation in praising you. Help me also to hear your voice in the
words and actions of my sisters and brothers and to speak and show your
love to them.

(Morning)
Divine Listener, help me to hear, to speak, and to share, always aware that you
hold both speaker and listener in your love.
(Prayers of Intercession)

(Evening)
Loving God, you made this beautiful earth to be my home.
Help me to care for it, to share the home I've made,
and to accept graciously the hospitality of others.
(Prayers of Intercession)

Thank you for the places of prayer in my life.

(Morning)
Hospitality is a gift I can give,
whether or not I have a home. A
shared park bench, a quiet walk is a
valued blessing. Amen.

(Evening)
Thank you for your gift of healing
sleep and your peaceful presence
through the night. Amen.

WEDNESDAY, MAY 13
(Read Psalm 67:1–5)

(Morning)
Loving Creator, maker of mornings, I join with Moses, Paul, and David in
seeking your gracious and shining face. May I recognize it in the faces of those
I meet today.

(Evening)
Loving Creator, maker of evenings, today I have praised you. People everywhere know you and praise you, for in your way of love lies true happiness.

Wise guide of nations, how quickly the nations would follow you if only
they realized that you want them to be glad and sing for joy. I am one
person within a nation of people. Am I glad? Do I sing for joy? Are my
judgments equitable like yours? I am the only psalm many people will ever
read. Help me to be so joyful and fair in my dealings with my neighbors
that your countenance will shine through my smile and your graciousness,
through me, will bless others.

(Morning)
Every day is a new beginning. Help me to go forth clothed
in garments of praise.
(Prayers of Intercession)

(Evening)
Thank you for being with me through the challenges and blessings of this day
and every day.
(Prayers of Intercession)

Happy is the nation whose guide is God.

(Morning)	(Evening)
I want to follow your road map today.	Thank you for the realm of your
Thank you for the compass of your	Spirit, to which people of all nations
love and for walking beside me. Amen.	may belong. Amen.

THURSDAY, MAY 14
(Read Psalm 67:6–7)

(Morning)
Loving God, in the beginning, you created the heavens and the earth. Thank you for putting your creative Spirit within us.

(Evening)
Loving God, you looked upon what you made and saw its goodness. Help us to see the goodness in what we have done today.

Your earth, gracious Creator, has been here for eons; our world has been here for hours. How dare we humans, in our greed and selfishness, abuse your great gift! Ancient American Indian wisdom tells us to make every decision in light of its effect upon seven generations. Too often we, in our heedlessness, rush headlong into actions that threaten our children's very existence. Forgive us, O Merciful One. Open our eyes to eternal values, and help us to cherish our beautiful, fragile planet.

(Morning)
Starting right now, I resolve, through your grace,
to be a better steward of your creation.
(Prayers of Intercession)

(Evening)
You made the day for action, the night for rest. Thank you, God, for both. Help us to find a healthful balance.
(Prayers of Intercession)

The earth is God's and all that is in it.

(Morning)
Thank you that the earth brings forth its increase. Your wild abundance is beyond our comprehension. Amen.

(Evening)
More than the stars in the nighttime sky are your loving thoughts to us, O faithful God. Amen.

FRIDAY, MAY 15
(Read Revelation 21:10, 22; 22:5)

(Morning)
Spirit of God, help us to be with you as freely as was the writer of Revelation. It is only then that we can see the city of God.

(Evening)
Spirit of God, a city without temples is hard for us mortals to imagine. Yet you, at once almighty and vulnerable, are its temple.

Stars have always filled us with wonder. Visionaries have pointed to them. Van Gogh's *Starry Night* is a painted psalm of praise. A star led the royal trio to the manger at Bethlehem. How can we live without night? without stars? How can we live without Brother Sun and Sister Moon? And yet we know that the heavenly hosts are ornaments on your garment. In your presence is fullness of joy, where we shall find all we loved on earth plus more than we can imagine.

(Morning)
Loving God, you have surrounded us with signs of your beauty and love.
Help us to take the time to smell the roses.
(Prayers of Intercession)

(Evening)
Thank you for sunlight, moonlight, and starlight,
and for your light within our hearts.
(Prayers of Intercession)

The heavens are telling the glory of God.

(Morning)
Thank you for writers, painters, and musicians who speak of you in starry language. Amen.

(Evening)
Remind us, generous God, that eyes have not seen nor ears heard the things you have prepared for us. Amen.

SATURDAY, MAY 16
(Read John 14:23–29)

(Morning)
Thank you, Jesus, for calling us not servants but friends. Walk with us today.

(Evening)
Thank you, Jesus, for inviting us to come inside and rest for a while. Your love
is our refreshment.

What loving farewell words you spoke, Jesus, to your followers and, through
them, to us. You know that transitions are difficult and that it is not easy to
let go of those we love. Through the Holy Spirit you are still with us, teaching us and reminding us of all your wise and precious words. Give us open
hearts to feel your presence.

(Morning)
Transcendent One, thank you for coming to us in human form and
for making your home with us.
(Prayers of Intercession)

(Evening)
When anxiety strikes, help us to remember your words,
"Do not let your hearts be troubled, and do not let them be afraid."
(Prayers of Intercession)

If God is for us, who can be against us?

(Morning)
Help us, Gentle Guide, to see you in
all transitions and to trust you with
our pain and grief at parting with
loved ones. Amen.

(Evening)
Peace, dear Jesus, is your heart's gift—
an eternal one, not like the transient
things of this passing world. Help us to
share this peace with others. Amen.

SUNDAY, MAY 17
(Read John 5:1–9)

(Morning)
Loving God, help me to be aware, even in the midst of a festival,
that there are hurting people in need of love.

(Evening)
Loving God, at different times today, we have been both givers and receivers
of healing love. Bless us and those we have touched.

Sometimes, compassionate God, we have been critical of the disabled man
at the pool. We have tended to blame the victims—the impoverished, the
unemployed, the addicted—or their condition. Jesus did not do this. He
simply asked, "Do you want to be healed?" and empowered the man to
take up his bed and walk. Help us, too, to be empowering, not enabling,
knowing that we, too, are in need of your healing love.

(Morning)
Jesus was never self-righteous. Free us from the besetting sin of thinking of
ourselves as better than others. May we see all people as God's dear children.
(Prayers of Intercession)

(Evening)
Sometimes we feel as if we have taken one step forward and two steps back.
Comfort us when we fail.
(Prayers of Intercession)

There is none righteous. No, not one.

(Morning)
Thank you, God, for being in the
healing and forgiving business. Make
us always quick to forgive others and
to remember that only through forgiving are we forgiven. Amen.

(Evening)
As we attempt each day to take up
our beds and walk, be our strength
and our help. May we encourage our
companions. Amen.

MONDAY, MAY 18
(Read Revelation 22:12–14)

(Morning)
Dear God, as I brush the cobwebs of sleep from my mind, I give thanks to you.
As you are the beginning of this day I thank you for life.

(Evening)
Dear God, from the Alpha of life you have kept me in your care. Thank you.

Most precious and loving God, I come before you remembering that you were in the beginning, that you are in the present, and that you will be in the end. I thank you for being with me from my beginning, and I pray that you will continue to walk with me as I open my heart to your perfect will.

(Morning)
Holy God, as I start this day, keep me mindful of others
who do not know you and are in need of your love.
(Prayers of Intercession)

(Evening)
God, as the Omega of this day approaches, I thank you for your presence.
Be with me this day and every day until the Omega of my life comes.
(Prayers of Intercession)

As Jesus Christ taught, I pray.
(Pray the Prayer of Our Savior.)

(Morning)
Come, dear God, fill me with your
Spirit, that I may do your will
this day. Amen.

(Evening)
Thank you, gracious God, for your
presence with me this day. Amen.

TUESDAY, MAY 19
(Read Acts 16:16–34)

(Morning)
Dear God of freedom and liberation, free me from the prisons of selfishness as I greet those who have not been exposed to your love.

(Evening)
Dear God of freedom and liberation, help me to keep my covenant with you by sharing your forgiveness of sins with others as you have shared it with me.

God of love and life, who has been with us as we live in diaspora, struggle, and oppression, send another earthquake to free us from our prisons of hate and self-doubt. God, you would not have allowed us to remain if you did not have plans for our freedom. Have mercy on me this day, Savior God. Allow me to share your love and your freedom with someone who has lost hope in life.

(Morning)
Dear Jesus, free me from my apathy as I see the need to help others in their quest for liberation and freedom from sin.
(Prayers of Intercession)

(Evening)
Thank you, God, for giving me the courage to share your gospel with one who was in spiritual bondage, as you shared it with me in my bondage.
(Prayers of Intercession)

With hope I pray.
(Pray the Prayer of Our Savior.)

(Morning)
Dear saving God, keep me free from my addiction of selfishness. Amen.

(Evening)
Dear holy God, thank you for your power, which has been my strength this day. Amen.

WEDNESDAY, MAY 20
(Read Psalm 97)

(Morning)
Dear God, I awake today fresh in the knowledge that no matter what I am confronted with, you are in control of the situation.

(Evening)
Dear God, thank you for being the sunshine of my day and for making my enemies like wax in your light.

O God, I thank you for the knowledge that you are with me. As I engage with those who seek to hinder my service to you, I can take comfort that you are in control. As long as I keep steadfast and do your will, then all things will work out to your glory and honor.

(Morning)
Dear Jesus, thank you for your presence in my life. Holy God, as you control the flow of time, control me, and keep me from going against your will.
(Prayers of Intercession)

(Evening)
Thank you, God, for this day of freedom in Christ. Keep me in your way of freedom.
(Prayers of Intercession)

Ever-present God, I pray.
(Pray the Prayer of Our Savior.)

(Morning)
Dearest God, control my thoughts and actions this day and always. Amen.

(Evening)
Dear God, your mercy was evident in my life today. Thank you for loving me. Amen.

THURSDAY, MAY 21
(Read Revelation 22:16–17)

(Morning)
Good morning, loving God, who watched over me as I slept. Thank you for your touch this morning—a touch that allowed me to wake in the land of the living.

(Evening)
Good evening, loving God. As this day fades into night, my soul is buoyed by your light. You have smiled upon me and made me glad. Thank you.

Gracious and generous God, thank you for being the wellspring of love in my life. God, I acknowledge that I stand in need of your love as I go through this wilderness journey. In the middle of the desert of difficulty, you are there with a refreshing offering of "come and drink." Without you in my life I would dry up and burn out. But you are there, always ready to comfort and console me. I am coming to drink from the well that offers the water of life. Thank you, thank you, thank you.

(Morning)
Good morning, God, thank you for waking me with the cool running waters of life this morning. I pray that during the heat of this day
I will come to you to quench my thirst.
(Prayers of Intercession)

(Evening)
Thank you, Jesus, for your presence in my dealings today. I was truly in need of spiritual refreshment and you provided me with all that I needed. Thank you, Jesus. May I always have the good sense to call on you when I am thirsty.
(Prayers of Intercession)

Refreshed, I pray.
(Pray the Prayer of Our Savior.)

(Morning)
Good morning, Jesus. Truly this will be a blessed day because you are the bright and morning star. Amen.

(Evening)
Jesus, I end this day in the comfort of being blessed by your love. Amen.

FRIDAY, MAY 22
(Read John 17:20–26)

(Morning)
God, as I come to consciousness, I feel bathed in the light
of your revelation that Jesus is the Christ and that if we acknowledge Jesus
then we can be one with you.

(Evening)
God, today I saw the beauty in the diverse quilt of humankind and
not in the blanket of sameness.

Dearest God, you created us in your image of love and planted in our collective hearts the seeds of inclusiveness. Allow our love for one another to grow, so that we may be one in your sight. And may we be one in our sight as well. Not one in the sense of clones, but one in the spirit of Christ.

(Morning)
Sovereign God, who looks upon those called by your name, I pray that I will be
able to look beyond our differences to see the beauty of our diversity.
(Prayers of Intercession)

(Evening)
Loving God, you created us in your image, equal yet not same, like a tapestry as
beautifully woven as a field of wildflowers. Jesus, let us see the world through
different eyes today.
(Prayers of Intercession)

In awe of your mercy, I pray.
(Pray the Prayer of Our Savior.)

(Morning)
Dear God, let me see myself in the lives of those whom I normally pass by on the streets. Amen.

(Evening)
Thank you, God, for letting me see myself in the face of a hungry child, in the outstretched hand of a person asking for money, in a person who was challenged, and for letting me see you in each of them. Praise be to you, God. Amen.

SATURDAY, MAY 23
(Read Acts 16:16–34)

(Morning)
Dear God, I awaken this morning comforted by the knowledge
that I know in whom I believe. Thank you for caring enough about me
to allow me to be one of your children.

(Evening)
Dear God, thank you for keeping me out of harm's way.

Saving God, who threw me a rope of hope in a sea of despair, I come as
humbly as I know how to say thank you. If I had been left to my own
devices, I would have self-destructed. You entered my life in a mighty way.
You shook me like you shook that jail. You rocked the foundations of my
foolishness and brought me into a right relationship with you. You freed
me from a prison of self, and freed me to live in relationship with you.
God, I love you and I thank you for caring so much about me. Help me to
share the message of what it takes to be saved with others whom I encounter.

(Morning)
Good morning, Jesus, I take comfort in being rescued from sinfulness and
shame by your love.
(Prayers of Intercession)

(Evening)
God, you are the architect of the household of my life. Thank you for your
presence today.
(Prayers of Intercession)

Boldly I pray.
(Pray the Prayer of Our Savior.)

(Morning)
Dear God, may I feel your guiding
hand in every place that I venture
today. Amen.

(Evening)
Thank you, God. You protected me
from those who wanted to harm me,
and you helped me to help somebody
else today. Empower me to share a
message of love that comes from
Christ Jesus: Don't harm yourself;
instead choose life, choose Jesus.
Amen.

SUNDAY, MAY 24
(Read Revelation 22:20–21)

(Morning)
Good morning, God, I awaken with anxiety today knowing that you could come back at any moment or that I could leave this place at any moment. Regardless, help me to live this day in a manner that will be acceptable to you.

(Evening)
Good evening, God. Thank you for your mercy in my life.

Jesus, today is your day. Today I will try to live my life as completely as possible. Come into my life, Lamb of God, and you will see that the table has been set for your arrival. There is room in the inn of my soul for you to reside. Jesus, I pray that I will be able to help make this world as ready for your coming as I am ready for you to come back.

(Morning)
Help me, God, to make the world a better place in which all can live.
(Prayers of Intercession)

(Evening)
Well, Jesus, it is the end of another week, and I thank you
for having been with me. By your grace I have made it through,
and by your grace I look forward to the next week.
Your grace has sustained me through the narrow passageways
of difficulty and has guided me to the pastures of peace.
May your grace continue to be all that I need.
(Prayers of Intercession)

Confidently I pray.
(Pray the Prayer of Our Savior.)

(Morning)
God of life, I take great pleasure in waking in your arms this day. Amen.

(Evening)
Perfect and loving God, I am blessed because I am your child. Amen.

MONDAY, MAY 25

(Read Acts 2:1–12)
(Sing "Spirit of the Living God")

(Morning)
Holy Power, Love Divine, my eyes open to your wonder and my lips respond with praise. All night you have kept me and again this morning touched me with amazing grace.

(Evening)
Holy Power, Love Divine, thank you for a day of joyful surprises! I have seen you in many faces and felt you in many touches. Thank you for a day lived in wonder. Forgive my sin and make me one with you.

God, your touch is in every fabric of the world. As flowers begin to bloom, as trees continue to sprout buds and the refreshing rains water the earth, I see your hand. Your power is in every thread of my existence. It connects me in community, it grounds me in relationships, and it keeps me in harmony with you. The Pentecost fire continues to burn within my soul. I pray to be kept in the center of your will and used for your good and glory.

(Morning)
You have called me into community. Today I lift up my community before you.
(Prayers of Intercession)

(Evening)
All day long I have sensed your presence.
All day I have longed to bring others into your company through my prayers.
Now I leave them and myself in your care.
(Prayers of Intercession)

**Thank you for the gift of the Holy Spirit's power
yet being available to transform the world.**

(Morning)	(Evening)
Today I will live as one empowered by the Holy Spirit! Amen.	Now I lay me down to sleep. I pray you, God, my soul to keep! Amen.

TUESDAY, MAY 26
(Read Acts 2:13–21)

(Morning)
God of dreamers and visionaries, how good to awake with you!
Thank you for another opportunity to hear your voice.
My heart cries that your name be blessed!

(Evening)
God of dreamers and visionaries, you have fallen upon me again today.
I praise you for the outpouring of your grace and power
which have sustained me, encouraged me, and kept me this day.

Calling God, I have experienced love today from many whom you have called. My day has been greatly blessed by others. For every man, woman, boy, and girl you have used to make my life better, I offer humble thanks. You use whoever will call upon your name! Thank you for every respondent!

(Morning)
All-sufficient One, many need the outpouring of your Holy Spirit's power today.
(Prayers of Intercession)

(Evening)
Rush of Wind and Breath of Love, you have moved mightily in your world today. Thank you for all you have done. Forgive me for all I have left undone.
Bless these upon my heart, I pray.
(Prayers of Intercession)

The power and the glory of Pentecost is alive and well today in me!

(Morning)
Today I will be open to the dreams and visions which come to me from you, God. Amen.

(Evening)
Speak to me, Holy One, in the hours of quiet rest and solitude. Let me hear you clearly in the watches of the night. Amen.

WEDNESDAY, MAY 27
(Read Genesis 11:1–9)
(Sing "Halleluia, Halleluia")

(Morning)
Creation Builder, I hear you in the silence of this new day.
Let my words be few and seasoned with your grace as I walk
with humility before you in the world today.

(Evening)
Creation Builder, this day I have attempted to imitate you in my life.
I have sought understanding. Forgive my shortcomings and
the many walls I built instead.

God of unity, how awesome to know that you have given unto us the power
to re-create our world. Your living Word declares that when we are of one
accord we can accomplish anything! Yet I see the many broken places, lost
hopes, and wounded spirits among us. Give us understanding. Renew our
hope. Bring us into community again, we pray.

(Morning)
Amidst the noises of our world allow me to hear your voice and
to be your voice in the world.
(Prayers of Intercession)

(Evening)
I have sought to hear you and to follow your lead today.
Bless now these upon my heart who need to hear from you.
(Prayers of Intercession)

Noise does not mean unity. The presence of God is often in silence.

(Morning)
Today I will strive to understand the
language of the hearts of my sisters
and brothers. Amen.

(Evening)
Many times today, I have become
entangled in the many noises around
me. Help me in the stillness of the
night to know you better, I pray.
Amen.

THURSDAY, MAY 28
(Read Psalm 104:24–35)
(Sing "Morning Has Broken")

(Morning)
Wonder-working God, we enter your day with thanksgiving and
begin this day with praise. I honor and adore you.
I exalt you for your goodness and your mercy. I worship you!

(Evening)
Wonder-working God, I pause to offer my sacrifice of praise
for the experiences of this day. Many and great are your marvelous works,
and my soul magnifies you for another day of miracles.

I offer up the meditations of my heart as I ponder the spectacular creation
of which I am such a small part. I am amazed at how vast and full of splendor this world continues to be despite our pollution, mismanagement, and
waste of resources. From the tiny ant, to the fledgling bird, to the giant
redwood forest and enormous mountain ranges, your handiwork articulates
your care! And then you continue to care for me! With the psalmist I stand
in awe.

(Morning)
Again this morning, your new mercies I beseech.
(Prayers of Intercession)

(Evening)
For the matchless grace we have received, thank you. Now again hear the
petitions of my heart.
(Prayers of Intercession)

I will sing the praise of my God as long as I have breath!

(Morning)
God, today I will open my eyes and
see your glory in all I meet. Amen.

(Evening)
Sleep is a wonder! I commit myself
unto you in all its mystery. Amen.

FRIDAY, MAY 29
(Read Romans 8:14–17)
(Sing "We Shall Overcome")

(Morning)
Abba! What joy to awake to a new day of liberty in you! Thank you for the refreshment of the night. Help me to face the day with purpose and with confidence in your Holy Spirit's ever-freeing and ever-living power, I pray.

(Evening)
Abba! Thank you for the gift of being your child today.
I have felt your love. Forgive me for the times I allowed fear
to dictate my actions and did not show love in the world.

Thank you for purpose in my life. Thank you for the gifts of the Holy Spirit, which operate in me and keep me from being dominated by my fears. You are the God of power and love, and I have received your power by adoption into your family. Help me to always remember that I am an heir to greatness and not mediocrity! Give me clarity of focus and singleness of heart, I pray.

(Morning)
Many are enslaved today, God.
(Prayers of Intercession)

(Evening)
I have tried not to suffer today; forgive me for turning away from you.
Hear the pleas of my heart.
(Prayers of Intercession)

Get purpose! Keep it before you!

(Morning)
I will walk in love, courage, and power today. Amen.

(Evening)
The night has great restorative powers. Embrace me, I pray. Amen.

SATURDAY, MAY 30
(Read John 14:7–17)
(Sing "Amen!")

(Morning)
Great Amen, I awake with "Yes" upon my lips. Your claim upon my life calls me to exhibit your loving care in the world. Walk, talk, and live in me. My heart says "Amen" to your will!

(Evening)
Great Amen, today has been a gift. I pray that my life has been a gift to you.

It's difficult to believe that I am called to do "greater things" than Jesus. Yet I know that your Word does not lie. I look at the world around me, and my heart is filled with compassion for what I see. There are so many needs, so much hurt, such great sorrow, and such varied cares. And I'm to do greater things? Help me to know what to do. Help me to speak with your authority, to act with your boldness, and to be at one with you, I pray.

(Morning)
Greater things begin when I pray.
(Prayers of Intercession)

(Evening)
For the great things I have neglected today, I ask forgiveness. For the great needs upon my heart, I pray.
(Prayers of Intercession)

I will do greater things today because Jesus lives in me!

(Morning)
Greater things are my inheritance!
Amen.

(Evening)
For the greater things that can be accomplished in me while I rest, I now pray. Amen.

SUNDAY, MAY 31
(Read John 14:25–27)
(Sing "Jesus Loves Me, This I Know!")

(Morning)
Jesus, lover of my soul, unto you I lift my spirit.
For the night of rest and the mysteries before me, I give you thanks.

(Evening)
Jesus, lover of my soul, for enfolding my heart with love and
my day with grace, I lift my voice in exultations of praise.

In this world I have my share of troubles, but in the midst of every storm I find a place of refuge in you! Thank you for being my anchor. Thank you for the gift of the Holy Spirit, my comforter, my guide, and my powerful friend. Thank you for never leaving me alone. Thank you for the abiding peace which is not simply the absence of confusion and chaos in my life, but my blessed assurance!

(Morning)
Jesus, everybody ought to know who you are!
(Prayers of Intercession)

(Evening)
You have been the lifter of my head!
Lift now the heads and hearts of these, I pray.
(Prayers of Intercession)

There is no spot where God is not! I am never alone!

(Morning)
God, today I am filled with and
possessed by your shalom! Amen.

(Evening)
If I should die before I wake, I pray
you, God, my soul to take. Amen!

MONDAY, JUNE 1
(Read Romans 5:1–2)

(Morning)
Good morning, God. Thank you for letting me see another day. Give me the wisdom and insight that I need to remember that I am justified by faith.

(Evening)
Good evening, God. If I have wronged anyone this day, please allow me another day, so that I may seek reconciliation. Create in me a new heart, so that I may be more sensitive to the feelings of others.

Dear God, at times it is easy to forget that my good deeds, solemn prayers, and consistent tithing are not what characterize me as a follower of Christ. I would not do these things were it not for Jesus. Sometimes my faith feels strong; sometimes it seems quite weak. But, nonetheless, I do have faith. So I thank you, God, for your Child Jesus and for the faith and hope that have grown in me as a result of your faithfulness.

(Morning)
I pray now for those who feel they have no faith.
(Prayers of Intercession)

(Evening)
Here is my soul, O God. Please make it more faithful to you alone.
(Prayers of Intercession)

Jesus, lover of my soul, I now pray.
(Pray the Prayer of Our Savior.)

(Morning)	(Evening)
May my faith inspire faith in others this day. Amen.	Good night, God. May my rest and the rest of my family be peaceful. Amen.

TUESDAY, JUNE 2
(Read Romans 5:3–5)

(Morning)
God, in addition to hope, I can also boast in my suffering.
Help me to understand this truth more completely today.

(Evening)
God, thank you for pouring your love into my heart this day. May I use this
evening to reflect on your Word with even more precision: "Suffering produces
endurance, and endurance produces character, and character produces hope."

I believe that suffering produces character and character produces hope.
But sometimes, God, I really think I have enough character and hope. So if
it is your will, I don't mind missing any additional suffering. Yet, when I
look back on all the storms through which you have guided me, I can honestly thank you for them. Your Holy Spirit was there, making me a new
person, a stronger person, a wiser person, a more compassionate person.
Help me, O God, in difficult times as well as hopeful times, to know that
you are always pouring out your love.

(Morning)
I pray now for all Christians who suffer and feel they have no hope.
(Prayers of Intercession)

(Evening)
I pray now for those who do not have hope because they do not know you, God.
(Prayers of Intercession)

With hope I pray.
(Pray the Prayer of Our Savior.)

(Morning)
May the words of my mouth and the
meditation of my heart be full of hope
and inspire hope in all who meet
me today. Amen.

(Evening)
Whatever my lot, it is well with my
soul. Good night, God. Amen.

WEDNESDAY, JUNE 3
(Read Proverbs 8:1–4)

(Morning)
Creator God, when wisdom calls today, I pray that I am ready to listen.

(Evening)
Creator God, may I recognize the wisdom that you give to children
which adults often haughtily overlook.

Like Solomon, I too ask for wisdom and understanding. When I am confronted with a disgruntled coworker, make me wise. When my children or others seek my counsel but seem more content to ignore me than to take sound correction, make me wise. When my parents are no longer able to live independently and I must make arrangements for them, please, make me wise. O God, whatever the case, I do not want to be a fool who rushes into things and assumes that my years equal wisdom. I want wisdom that comes from being in touch with you. Whatever the circumstance may be, please grant me a portion of your wisdom.

(Morning)
Teach me to find wisdom's lessons wherever I go.
(Prayers of Intercession)

(Evening)
Thank you for granting me wisdom this day.
(Prayers of Intercession)

Humbly I pray.
(Pray the Prayer of Our Savior.).

(Morning)
May my life glorify you today. Amen.

(Evening)
Another work-filled day has ended. I lay my head to rest now. As I fall asleep, I think of your creation—the earth, the solar system, the universe. Amen.

THURSDAY, JUNE 4
(Read Proverbs 8:22–31)

(Morning)
Loving God, yesterday I prayed for wisdom, but today I marvel at the way in which your wisdom precedes all creation.

(Evening)
Loving God, I think of how you have put together all of creation with perfect understanding and wisdom. I think of the intricacies of the ecosystem and how you created us perfectly in your image.

In order to see your wisdom, God, we have to quiet our hearts by going to a quiet place. Perhaps now is a good time to look at the sun as it awakens, or just close our eyes and imagine a sun rising over the ocean. When all is quiet in our hearts, we may listen to Wisdom. What is she telling you about life, family, or creation?

(Morning)
Today I will reflect on the agelessness of wisdom.
Wisdom is as old as the universe.
(Prayers of Intercession)

(Evening)
Thank you, God, for letting me enjoy your creation.
Make me aware of my folly, so that I will not defeat the wisdom and understanding that you have given me.
(Prayers of Intercession)

To be wise is to humble oneself to the awesomeness of God.

(Morning)
It is time to spread my light. Amen.

(Evening)
It is time to let my light rest. Amen.

FRIDAY, JUNE 5
(Read John 16:12–15)

(Morning)
Inspiring God, thank you for waking me up this morning and allowing me to see a new day. I wait patiently for the revelation of your mysteries.

(Evening)
Inspiring God, thank you for the rest of this evening. I wait patiently for the revelation of tomorrow.

God, when Jesus announced his departure to the disciples, they appeared to be anxiety-ridden. They wanted to know what was next and they wanted to follow him. In John 14, Peter knew that Jesus was going somewhere, but Jesus was not clear about his destination. Jesus' words to his disciples may remind us that we, too, will know all that we need to know in due season. Christians need only to wait for the voice of the Holy Spirit. Help me, God, to understand that I do not have to know everything that is to come. It is just as well to trust in you.

(Morning)
I wait patiently for your revelation.
(Prayers of Intercession)

(Evening)
Teach me to wait patiently on the Holy Spirit.
(Prayers of Intercession)

Sing "Sweet, Sweet Spirit."

(Morning)
Reveal to me, Holy Spirit, the error in my ways. I know I am not always a loving person. I am not always quick to reconcile. I am not always eager to forgive. I throw myself at your mercy, and I lay before you my transgressions. Amen.

(Evening)
As I recline, I wait for the gift of sleep and restoration. Amen.

SATURDAY, JUNE 6
(Read Psalm 8:1–8)

(Morning)
God, I awaken to marvel at your love for me.

(Evening)
God, what am I that you are mindful of me?

When the mundane things that occupy our time threaten to dull our view of the universe, it is time to slow down. How many times have we not noticed the clouds in perfect formation? How often do we fail to notice the beauty of fruits and vegetables? And when was the last time that we were overwhelmed by the moonlit stars? If the universe is looking dull and ordinary, it is time for us to slow down and look once more at your work, Creator God.

(Morning)
May I recognize your glory in everything that you have created, especially other human beings, no matter what their state or circumstances.
(Prayers of Intercession)

(Evening)
Help me to remember that I am extraordinarily special to you. Help me to remember that I am a steward of creation. I must cherish it and protect it from careless pollution and destruction.
(Prayers of Intercession)

Tonight, spend a few moments enjoying the stars.

(Morning)
I thank you, God, for the birds of the air and the fish of the sea. Amen.

(Evening)
Nighttime is the work of your hands, O God. You tilted the earth perfectly and spun it on its axis at just the right speed, so that now another day has ended. I can finally rest from my labors. Amen.

SUNDAY, JUNE 7
(Read Psalm 8:9)

(Morning)
God, Creator of the heavens, I commit myself to your service.

(Evening)
God, may I always reflect on your name (Yahweh) with joy.

"O God our Sovereign, how majestic is your name in all the earth!" wrote the psalmist. The psalmist was glorifying you, Yahweh, and also distinguishing you from other gods. In short, the psalmist was identifying you as the God of the universe, a God whose magnificence and power surpassed all others. We, too, must remember this. The very reading or utterance of your holy name should move us to deep reverence and humility.

(Morning)
I reflect now on everything your name means to me.
(Prayers of Intercession)

(Evening)
I reflect now on your sovereignty.
(Prayers of Intercession)

In reverence I pray.
(Pray the Prayer of Our Savior.)

(Morning)
When I meet someone in need today, may the mere thought of your name lead me to greater service. Amen.

(Evening)
In all the earth tonight, you are majestic. Amen.

MONDAY, JUNE 8
(Read Luke 7:36)

(Morning)
Gracious God, let me seek the glory of this day. May its wonder rise in my eyes
as your dawn rises upon the world.

(Evening)
Gracious God, settle me from the hurry of the day. Let me listen with my heart
for the whispers of your Word.

Compassionate God, there are times when we are much like the Pharisee in
Luke: admonished by your living Word for choosing a path contrary to
your purposes. But in the same breath we see a glimpse of the resurrection
when that same Pharisee can invite your Child to come and share a meal at
his home. When Jesus accepts the invitation (even from one seen as "unworthy"), the living Word is revealed. The door is open for the confession
that we are people who can invite your presence into our lives.

(Morning)
Gracious God, through your guidance help me discover new ways to open my
life to the presence you offer; for in that presence is the true dawn which rises
upon my life.
(Prayers of Intercession)

(Evening)
Merciful One, I offer my thanks that, through your Holy Spirit, your Word has
been my companion in the course of this day. May its light guide the prayers I
offer on behalf of those who share this creation with me.
(Prayers of Intercession)

In the presence of God, I pray.
(Pray the Prayer of Our Savior.)

(Morning)
Set my feet on the path of the Risen
One this day. In Jesus' name. Amen.

(Evening)
May this night be one of peace, for
the joy that has been mine today, and
for the hope of the tomorrows you
hold in store. In Jesus' name. Amen.

TUESDAY, JUNE 9
(Read Luke 8:3)

(Morning)
Shepherd of Souls, I thank you for the peace of the night that is now past.
Waken my heart, as the dawn has opened my eyes, that I may rise
to the path of this breaking day.

(Evening)
Shepherd of Souls, for the wonder of knowing that in the heart of this day your
hands have encompassed my life, I raise my deepest prayers of thanksgiving.
Guide me to the blessings of your Word.

Caring God, your Gospel is one which stretches our picture of the kinds of
people surrounding the Christ, either as followers or as recipients of healing grace. The recognition of the ever-wider circles of Jesus' life opens us
to the rich blessings of the surprising ways you choose to move through
this creation. The marks of grace and faithful discipleship will show themselves in the lives of the least expected. We are called to watch for and
witness to you, living God.

(Morning)
Send me into this day, O God, with a discerning wisdom tempering my sight.
Help me look beyond the walls of convention, that I might see the variety of
those who have set their lives on the path of your Christ.
(Prayers of Intercession)

(Evening)
Help me this day to bring to mind the women, the men, and the children who
have offered their gifts to the ministry of Jesus Christ.
(Prayers of Intercession)

In reverence, I pray.
(Pray the Prayer of Our Savior.)

(Morning)
If your grace will suffice, O God,
allow my life to be counted in the
number of those who follow the
Christ. In Jesus' name. Amen.

(Evening)
For the blessings of such a cloud of
witnesses I offer my thanks. In Jesus'
name. Amen.

WEDNESDAY, JUNE 10
(Read 1 Kings 21:1–21a)

(Morning)
O God, stir me from the sleep of this night, that the energies of this day
will give rise to the song of Jesus Christ in my heart.

(Evening)
O God, the pace of the day may now change, but know that my devotion to your
Word will never wane. Mark me well, and make me yours.

God, the issues of power and stewardship come forth in King Ahab's desire for Naboth's vineyard. Although we may not speak of it, we too wield power: we effect change and we cause things to happen. The blessings of power, however, become evident when the intention and the result are seen through the prism of your shalom. Through stewardship, the people and resources around us are part of an interdependent creation where fullness is denied by exploitation. In seeing the vineyard merely as an object of desire, Ahab (and Jezebel) lost sight of the fact that in your eyes Naboth stood on equal ground with them.

(Morning)
God of pilgrimage, send me out into this world knowing how intimately I am a
part of it. Let me see your image in the people I meet.
(Prayers of Intercession)

(Evening)
For the legion of blessings this day has brought,
I raise my thanks to you, O God.
(Prayers of Intercession)

Humbly I pray.
(Pray the Prayer of Our Savior.)

(Morning)
Fill my steps with the blessings of your
Christ. In Jesus' name. Amen.

(Evening)
Bring me peace this night in knowing
that your graces will continue to
unfold. In Jesus' name. Amen.

THURSDAY, JUNE 11
(Read 2 Samuel 11:26; 12:10, 13–15)

(Morning)
Shepherd of All, I thank you for the blessings this day may bring. Make me
attentive to your Word.

(Evening)
Shepherd of All, companion through this day, let me breathe deeply of your
Spirit that this night may be one of peace and rest.

God, you ask us to be honest with ourselves about the direction of our
actions. It would have been easier for King David to declare that his sin
was against Uriah alone. But his words confess that his sin was "against
God." God, you are affected because you are intimately involved in this
world: the One who has set creation into motion; the One who has given
birth to the divine image in each of us; the One who continues revelation
through the living Word. Our actions are a confession of how seriously, or
lightly, we take our role in the covenant that you have established.

(Morning)
Light of All Light, allow me to remember and celebrate the eternal
companionship you have chosen to offer this world.
Through that presence, guide my actions as I make my way this day.
(Prayers of Intercession)

(Evening)
Forgive me, Holy One, if my words have denied your presence,
or if I have acted in abuse of your covenant.
Keep me mindful of the call you have placed in my heart.
(Prayers of Intercession)

I pray as our Savior Christ taught us.
(Pray the Prayer of Our Savior.)

(Morning)
Send me forth with eyes hungry to see
you and lips eager to confess you. In
Jesus' name. Amen.

(Evening)
Take into your hands that which I have
been unable to accomplish, that the
peace of this night might envelop me.
In Jesus' name. Amen.

FRIDAY, JUNE 12
(Read Psalm 5:1–8)

(Morning)
O God of steadfast love, as my body rises for the nourishment of the day, my soul hungers for the Living Bread of your Child, Jesus Christ.

(Evening)
O God of steadfast love, throughout this day I strove to follow your way. Hear my thanksgiving for the blessings revealed to my heart.

Gracious God, there is a strong conviction revealed by your psalmist which "gives light to all in the house." The faith of the writer is contrasted with the lack of faith seen in the writer's enemies. A strength of faith is seen through petitioning you, watching for your response, declaring your steadfast love, and yearning for your continued guidance. Such faith leads to a powerful proclamation: "But I . . . will enter your house, I will bow down . . . in awe of you." My house is flooded with your light! May our way in this world be marked by such devotion to your living presence.

(Morning)
Help me choose this day, O God, between the life found in service to you and the death which comes by turning from you. Allow your light to shine brightly in and through my life.
(Prayers of Intercession)

(Evening)
Give me your eyes, O God, to see where I have spoken strongly of your Spirit, and where I have missed such opportunities.
Forgive my sins, and strengthen my faith.
(Prayers of Intercession)

Faithfully I pray.
(Pray the Prayer of Our Savior.)

(Morning)
Be my guide and my companion in this world which hungers for your renewing presence. In Jesus' name. Amen.

(Evening)
May the rejoicing of this day serve only to strengthen this life in service to your Word. In Jesus' name. Amen.

SATURDAY, JUNE 13
(Read Psalm 32)

(Morning)
Wisdom of the ages, speak to me and I will listen.
Lead me and I will follow, Shepherd of my heart.

(Evening)
Wisdom of the ages, let me breathe deep of your gathering
Spirit that my scattered self may again be centered in you.

God, what are the weights that hang heavy upon our lives? From how many directions can threats to the fullness you intend come? They may be legion, but they do not have the ability to remove the blessings of your presence. In the midst of the personal siege the psalmist faces, the focus is on you, O God, and your preserving steadfast love. Precisely because of such a faith, the psalmist can declare safety from the threats that come as "the rush of mighty waters," and can find a hiding place, preservation, and deliverance. Through this example we learn again how to "shout for joy" to you, the living God.

(Morning)
May I journey into this day, led by the conviction of God's presence,
and waiting upon God's living Word.
(Prayers of Intercession)

(Evening)
You are a bulwark and a fortress, O God.
In you there is rest for my spirit and hope for my heart.
(Prayers of Intercession)

Humbly I pray.
(Pray the Prayer of Our Savior.)

(Morning)
Give me eyes to search for your steadfast presence and help my lips sing your praise. In Jesus' name. Amen.

(Evening)
Breathe your Spirit into my life, that I might find your peace this night. In Jesus' name. Amen.

SUNDAY, JUNE 14
(Read Galatians 2:15–21)

(Morning)
O God, the peace of your Sabbath washes about me,
and my heart sings your praise. Help me know that I am yours.

(Evening)
O God, as from a table set full, I push myself back from the banquet of this day.
Your Holy Spirit has served to fill me and I pray my thanks to you.

Our lives are filled with rules by which we are measured and hoops through which to jump—all in the name of fulfilling some expectation. What a gift to be reminded that our lives are justified in your eyes, O God, through our faith in your Child, our Savior Jesus, and not by how well we follow a set of laws. In faith, we step out into the world responding to the call we hear so deep within us. The faith is lived out as we seek to follow the path of the One who came to serve. May we discover how the obligations of the faith flow from the foundation we have in Jesus Christ.

(Morning)
Gracious Shepherd, teach me to live the faith which has washed over me
in the waters of my baptism.
(Prayers of Intercession)

(Evening)
Forgive me, O God, for those times when I have expected my achievements to
grant me greater standing in your eyes.
(Prayers of Intercession)

In the spirit of Christ, I pray.
(Pray the Prayer of Our Savior.)

(Morning)
On this Sabbath with the promise of your presence, may the light of Jesus Christ shine through my life. In Jesus' name. Amen.

(Evening)
O God, may the week which I will rise to greet know the graces of your Child Jesus Christ. In Jesus' name. Amen.

MONDAY, JUNE 15
(Read Galatians 3:23–29)

(Morning)
Gracious God, help me to remember I am baptized!
Strengthen my faith, that I might bear witness to this call.

(Evening)
Thank you, God, for the gift of baptism.
May I always be aware of this gift of your grace.

John Lennon wrote a song entitled "Imagine." The lyrics tell of a world where there are no divisions. The Scripture today speaks of a similar reality. Through baptism, we are part of a new creation through Christ. What would happen this day if we disregarded our differences? If gender, color, and background made no difference? Think about the universal Christian church which encompasses the world. Imagine this day that everyone you encounter is a part of the living Christ.

(Morning)
God of newness, today help me to remember
that I am clothed with the light of Christ.
(Prayers of Intercession)

(Evening)
God of hope and promise, let me see my brothers and sisters
with your eyes of grace.
(Prayers of Intercession)

By baptism, I am part of the new creation in Christ.

(Morning)
May the light of Christ be reflected in me today, so that I regard others in a new light. Amen.

(Evening)
I rest in the knowledge that I am an heir of your promise, O God. Amen.

TUESDAY, JUNE 16
(Read Psalm 42)

(Morning)
Keeper of our souls, you are the source of all hope. I long to hear your voice
this day among the cacophony of the world's noise.

(Evening)
Keeper of our souls, when I cannot perceive your presence, reassure me that you
are near. Let me not lose hope.

I feel surrounded by violence, oppression, and death. God, where are you
in all of this? Sometimes I cry. Sometimes I choose to ignore the pain.
Sometimes I just feel like giving up. I can easily be seduced into thinking
that you are not present. But I read the Scriptures and find hope and assurance. I am able to perceive your presence anew in my life and in the world.

(Morning)
Hear the stirrings of my soul this day.
Hear the stirrings of all your people, God of mercy.
(Prayers of Intercession)

(Evening)
Remind me of the songs of praise I have sung to you, O God.
Remind me of your gracious help, given to those who love and serve you.
(Prayers of Intercession)

Even when I cannot perceive it, God's steadfast love is present in my life.

(Morning)
Ever-present God, may I go about this
day proclaiming your steadfast love in
all I do. Amen.

(Evening)
God of steadfast love, grant me
assurance of your presence this night.
May I awaken to sing your praises
once again. Amen.

WEDNESDAY, JUNE 17
(Read 1 Kings 19:1–15a)

(Morning)
God of earthquake, wind, and fire, it is often in quiet,
still moments that you are heard. May I have such moments this day.

(Evening)
God of earthquake, wind, and fire, night closes in around me like a cave.
May I find rest from the struggles of this day.

God, at times I feel that the work I do on your behalf makes no difference.
I become fearful, disheartened, and self-pitying. The rigors of being one of
your people are difficult. I get exhausted physically, emotionally, and spiritually. I want to run away, hide, and be left alone. God, I am ready to give
up on you. Yet you are never ready to give up on me.

(Morning)
May I hear your gentle yet firm call, O God.
Feed my heart and soul with your Word.
(Prayers of Intercession)

(Evening)
Holy One, you rescue me from the terrors of life.
You calm my fears and give me renewed hope.
(Prayers of Intercession)

Let me be attentive to the quiet voice of your Spirit in my life.

(Morning)
Send me out into the morning with
renewed hope and faith. May I not
retreat from doing your will. Amen.

(Evening)
Waken me to a new day, refreshed and
ready to hear your Word. In the name
of the One who came and
embodied your way in this world,
Jesus the Christ. Amen.

THURSDAY, JUNE 18
(Read Psalm 43)

(Morning)
Gracious God, may the light and truth of your Word guide me this day.

(Evening)
Gracious God, fountain of all light and hope, I thank you for your guiding
presence this day.

There are times when I feel like I am in a courtroom: I am on trial for my
faith. God, the values and attitudes of the society and culture I live in are
often in direct opposition to your intentions. When I attempt to witness on
behalf of Christ to the injustices and inequities around me, my testimony is
mocked. But I do not have to defend the faith; I only need to live it. God,
you are my defense. You will vindicate those who seek to live their lives
faithfully.

(Morning)
God of truth and justice, may I follow your way faithfully. Let my life proclaim
the joy I find in serving you.
(Prayers of Intercession)

(Evening)
I thank you for your companionship this day. My hope is renewed and my faith
is strengthened by your defense.
(Prayers of Intercession)

God is my defender, my truth, and my light.

(Morning)
Let me enter this new day with praises
on my lips to you, saving God. Amen.

(Evening)
Holy Defender, my refuge and my
strength, in you I place my hope
this night. Amen.

FRIDAY, JUNE 19
(Read Isaiah 65:1–9)

(Morning)
God of righteousness, to your divine call may I respond,
"Here I am," and serve only you.

(Evening)
God of righteousness, forgive me for inattentiveness to your call, for rebellious-
ness against your will, for provoking your anger.

It is easy to point fingers at others in this world. We can see their sinfulness
and transgressions. It is easy to condemn others for lack of fidelity to your
will. I can be caught up in self-righteousness. But if I hold up the mirror of
faithfulness, I see a reflection of myself in this reading. Forgive me, God,
when I do not embrace your call to be one of your chosen!

(Morning)
Guide me this day, that I might follow only your way, O God.
(Prayers of Intercession)

(Evening)
Forgiving God, by your gracious mercy restore me to your servanthood, that I
might bring you joy.
(Prayers of Intercession)

**Forgive me for provoking your anger and
help me to live out your righteous Word.**

(Morning)
I am called to be one of your chosen
servants. May I live out that
servanthood to you, Holy One. Amen.

(Evening)
God of grace, forgive me for turning
away from you. May your words of
rebuke be changed into words of
forgiveness. In the name of our Savior,
Jesus the Christ. Amen.

SATURDAY, JUNE 20
(Read Psalm 22:19–28 and Luke 8:26–30)

(Morning)
Divine Helper, may I feel your presence close to me as this day unfolds.
May I praise you in word and deed today.

(Evening)
Divine Helper, I give you thanks for your protection and guiding hand.
I praise your steadfast and compassionate love.

God, at times I feel overtaken. My life is not my own. I am anxious and fearful. Others share with me these same concerns. Nights are filled with brief and restless sleep. We cry for help. We do not know how to save ourselves. Our faith reminds us it is you who rescues us from adversity. The first step is to seek you, O God. You are the one who hears our anguish and pain.

(Morning)
When I am consumed by the pressures of this day, may I seek your help,
O merciful and compassionate God.
(Prayers of Intercession)

(Evening)
Holy One, help me to heal my soul and spirit from those things that seek to
possess it from you.
(Prayers of Intercession)

God will hear our cries of anguish and deliver us from oppression.

(Morning)
Send me out knowing that you alone,
O God, have sovereignty over my life.
Amen.

(Evening)
My heart is alive with praise for you,
my Savior God. I give you thanks for
guiding me through this day. Amen.

SUNDAY, JUNE 21
(Read Luke 8:32–39 and Psalm 22:19–28)

(Morning)
Holy Deliverer, you have saved me.
Through Jesus the Christ, I proclaim your power!

(Evening)
Holy Deliverer, from the insanity of this hectic world
you have restored peace to my soul. You are my redeemer and my strength.

I need to be reminded that only from you can I receive the gift of peace and wholeness to my soul. Today we are called to rest from work and responsibilities. We gather with our community of faith to remember who we are as your people. The demons of this world which seek to control our lives are destroyed by the saving presence of Christ. Wholeness of soul and spirit come only from you.

(Morning)
God of all power and might, may I proclaim today
all that you have done for me through Christ.
(Prayers of Intercession)

(Evening)
Gracious God, deliver me from the demons of this world
which seek to own my heart and soul.
(Prayers of Intercession)

Only in the saving power of Jesus Christ are we made whole.

(Morning)
Grant me a respite this day from all that make demands upon my life. Let me know your saving presence. Amen.

(Evening)
Holy Redeemer, may I rest quietly by your feet this night and awaken tomorrow refreshed and renewed to proclaim to all the saving power of Jesus Christ. Amen.

MONDAY, JUNE 22
(Read Galatians 5:13–18)

(Morning)
My Creator, as I open my eyes to a new day, I am filled with the freedom that comes from your mercy and constant love. Thank you for another day and another opportunity to serve you.

(Evening)
My Creator, thank you for your guiding presence in my life today.

When desires of the flesh become more powerful than our love for our neighbor, we become enslaved and lose sight of your glory, dear God. If I truly love my neighbor as myself, I will not give way to fear, lust, or greed. If I live to serve you, God, your love will set me free. Your mercy will heal the weaknesses that bind me.

(Morning)
God, may I be a channel of your love for those who are enslaved by their own fears and desires and for those who are oppressed by the greed of others.
(Prayers of Intercession)

(Evening)
God, please forgive me if I have failed you in any way today.
(Prayers of Intercession)

I pray as Christ taught the disciples.
(Pray the Prayer of Our Savior.)

(Morning)	(Evening)
As I go about my duties today, I have nothing to fear, for you set me free. Amen.	As I lie down to rest, my heart is filled with gratitude for the many blessings that fill my life. Amen.

TUESDAY, JUNE 23
(Read 1 Kings 19:15–16)

(Morning)
God, thank you for the many who serve you.

(Evening)
God, thank you for those who spread your message of love and justice.

God, I realize that to bring justice and peace to this earth and to do your will, there must be many of us. We must help one another to be strong and we must strengthen and support those leaders who will be role models and teachers. As Elijah anointed new kings, so must we anoint others to carry out your work for love and justice. Grant me wisdom, patience, and perseverance to share your love and encourage others to do the same. Let my words be yours, and let your light shine through me.

(Morning)
God, help me to be an example to others—to support other people to be strong, so that they in turn can strengthen others.
(Prayers of Intercession)

(Evening)
Help me to see the strengths of my brothers and sisters and to help them recognize the power they have within themselves.
(Prayers of Intercession)

Anointed by your power, I pray.
(Pray the Prayer of Our Savior.)

(Morning)	(Evening)
I commit myself to your service. Let me be an instrument of your love. Amen.	God, please grant me peace and rest tonight, so that I can be strong to do your work tomorrow. Amen.

WEDNESDAY, JUNE 24
(Read Psalm 77:11–20)

(Morning)
God, thank you for the many blessings you have bestowed upon me—for the love which surrounds me, all made of your hands.

(Evening)
God, thank you for the many wonderful things which you have created and which I take for granted every day.

Dear God, Creator, your power is so immense. I see your work in the smallest of living things and in the grandest sights of mountains, skies, canyons, and seas. In this vast universe, we are so small. How could we ever think that we could come close to your power to create and destroy? Today negligence, greed, and arrogance threaten to destroy your work. Nature responds and warns us to be respectful of creation. Strengthen us and guide us to be your humble servants, to live in a just and peaceful world.

(Morning)
God, teach us respect for your creation.
Teach us how to nurture it and to understand that to respect your creation means also to respect one another as human beings.
(Prayers of Intercession)

(Evening)
God, grant us the strength to overcome the greed and fear which poison our mind and spirit and the toxins which poison our bodies and environment.
(Prayers of Intercession)

In the love of Jesus, I pray.
(Pray the Prayer of Our Savior.)

(Morning)
I praise you, God, for your immense power and glory. Amen.

(Evening)
Praise to you, God, for the beauty of all your creation. Amen.

THURSDAY, JUNE 25
(Read Luke 9:51–62)

(Morning)
God, thank you for your unselfish commitment to me. Thank you for never looking back from your plow and for giving me hope and strength.

(Evening)
God, I thank you for watching over me this day and for showing me your unselfish commitment through the many gifts and love which surround me.

It is so difficult to walk a path of righteousness. With all the fears, pressures, and anger of the world today, it is so hard to keep one's hand to the plow and not look back; to let the dead bury the dead; to follow your path without taking leave of our loved ones. We struggle to hold on to those people and things that nurture us and give us love in this world. Yet I know that all I know and love of this world ultimately belongs to you.

(Morning)
God, grant me guidance and strength today to do your will.
(Prayers of Intercession)

(Evening)
Please bless my family, friends, coworkers, and all those who are struggling on this day. Grant us guidance and strength to do your will and the humor and spirit to celebrate the life you give us.
(Prayers of Intercession)

In awe of God's mercy, I pray.
(Pray the Prayer of Our Savior.)

(Morning)
I commit myself to do your will here on earth. Amen.

(Evening)
May my eyes always be open and looking forward. Amen.

FRIDAY, JUNE 26
(Read Psalm 77:1–2)

(Morning)
God, thank you for the beauty of your creation,
which gives me comfort and hope in times of distress.

(Evening)
God, thank you for hearing me, for knowing my thoughts and fears.

You have always been there for me, God. Whenever I am lost, when I am stressed from the pressures of this world, when I am afraid, my prayers to you give me comfort and hope. At times when I have neglected you; when I am naive, negligent, or too arrogant to know how important your relationship is to me; when I look for you, you are always there. I thank you for never refusing to listen to me.

(Morning)
Walk with me this day, please, God.
Be my friend and guide me in troubled times.
(Prayers of Intercession)

(Evening)
Grant me strength and guidance, O God. Bless me and hear my prayers.
(Prayers of Intercession)

Knowing that you are my comforter, I pray.
(Pray the Prayer of Our Savior.)

(Morning)
Please bless all those who cry out to you today, God. Hear the prayers of all those who are sick and in need. Amen.

(Evening)
Grant me the patience and wisdom to hear others, to be a companion to them in their time of need, as you have always been for me. Amen.

SATURDAY, JUNE 27
(Read 1 Kings 19:19–21)

(Morning)
God, thank you for another day and another opportunity to serve you in faith and love.

(Evening)
God, thank you for the direction and guidance you have provided me throughout this glorious day.

We live in a world full of distinctions. We are constantly encouraged to strive for wealth, power, and fame. I pray for the strength to detach myself from worldly objectives, for I am called to your service, God. I desire to do your will today and every day. For it is only in communion with you, my Creator, that I will find true wealth.

(Morning)
My God, allow me to be of service to those who cross my path today. Teach me to love.
(Prayers of Intercession)

(Evening)
My Creator, if I have failed in any way today to be a channel for your goodness and love, please forgive me. Keep me in your loving care and renew my spirit.
(Prayers of Intercession)

Caring Creator, I pray.
(Pray the Prayer of Our Savior.)

(Morning)
God, I turn my will and my life over to you. Use me and direct me to be your instrument today. Let your love flow through me and to all who surround me. Amen.

(Evening)
I rest with assurance that my Creator watches over me. May I be strengthened, so that I might better do your will. Amen.

SUNDAY, JUNE 28
(Read Galatians 5:1)

(Morning)
Dear God, thank you for this day, for the warmth that summer brings, and for those who struggle for freedom.

(Evening)
Dear God, thank you for watching over me on this day and for allowing me to feel the light of freedom. Thank you for those who have struggled for us to know the warmth of this day.

God, how can we truly glorify you if we are enslaved? Through the struggle for freedom and justice, I seek to glorify you. I pray for strength and guidance to know what is just, to free my mind and spirit, and to avoid being poisoned by fear or greed.

(Morning)
Allow me to be a medium for your love, to know what is just, and to be an instrument of salvation not oppression.
(Prayers of Intercession)

(Evening)
Dear God, please bless those who sleep tonight captive in mind and spirit, whose energy, voice, and creativity are denied to the world.
(Prayers of Intercession)

I pray as my Savior taught.
(Pray the Prayer of Our Savior.)

(Morning)
Dear God, I praise you for this beautiful day, for the warmth of summer and the life that it brings. Amen.

(Evening)
Tonight I lie down to sleep knowing that there is much to be done. I praise you, God, for the prophets, through whom you have spoken, calling for freedom. Amen.

MONDAY, JUNE 29
(Read Isaiah 66:10–14)

(Morning)
Creator God, we rejoice and give thanks for the wonder of your creation.
Awakened afresh to your world and its wonders, we praise your name. For the
gift of life, we thank you and ask your steadfast presence throughout the day.

(Evening)
Creator God, as evening enfolds me, quiet me and make me attentive to the
lessons you offered this day.

In the midst of life's joys and sorrows, God, you are ever present with us
and for us. You offer comfort by day and by night. Within the goodness of
creation, you have given us all that we need to sustain life. In your presence, our hearts shall rejoice, certain of the abiding presence and presents
of One who comforts us as a mother comforts her child.

(Morning)
For all those this day who seek your comforting presence,
Creator God, we are mindful.
(Prayers of Intercession)

(Evening)
We lift up in prayer those who in this day are bereft and alone. May they know
your comfort.
(Prayers of Intercession)

God's creation is beloved. God will not forsake Jerusalem or us.

(Morning)	(Evening)
To a day of faithful service and discipleship I commit myself. Amen.	By your comforting hand give me rest and refreshment to serve you tomorrow. Amen.

TUESDAY, JUNE 30
(Read 2 Kings 5:1–14)

(Morning)
O God, as I greet the morning sky, I greet you with thanks for the rest and safety of the night and seek you and your will in this day, which you created.

(Evening)
O God, as shadows lengthen, I turn again to you and seek in your Word the peace and truth you offer your people.

Why is it we modern women and men seek a complex and unfathomable God? Like Naaman we do not receive your good gifts with joy and thanksgiving but often puzzle over your love, O God. In our desire to create you in our own image, we often seek to thwart your generosity by finding complex approaches to you or even in seeking false gods. Just for today, I will seek your good gifts where I find them. And without question or doubt, I will receive them with thanksgiving.

(Morning)
God, I lift up to you all those who know brokenness today and ask your healing touch upon them.
(Prayers of Intercession)

(Evening)
Forgive, O God, our reluctance of heart and instill in us the spirit of gratitude and confidence.
(Prayers of Intercession)

I will forsake all false gods and seek the God of creation.

(Morning)
Give me this day an eye for seeing your wonders, an ear for hearing your call to faith, and a heart for believing! Amen.

(Evening)
For the blessing of this day and its activities, perfect them by your grace and grant me peace. Amen.

WEDNESDAY, JULY 1
(Read Psalm 30:1–5)

(Morning)
Strong and Present One, "our help in ages past, our hope for years to come,"
we awaken when day is new and draw near to you for strength and guidance.

(Evening)
Strong and Present One, as this day runs its course, I look once again to you,
grateful for your promise to be near at hand in waking or in sleeping.

So often life offers up challenges to our minds, our spirits, even our very lives. God, were it not for your reassuring presence, how would we find the courage to live? The church in all ages has been sustained in every land and tongue by your graciousness. Today, may I face the troubles I confront with the confidence that there will truly be "joy in the morning," for you, O God, are with me.

(Morning)
In this day, there will be those whose concerns and troubles lead them to
despair. I lift all who are struggling for justice, mercy,
and peace to your strong embrace.
(Prayers of Intercession)

(Evening)
As the world turns to sleep, I give thanks for this day with its challenges and
your sure promise. Keep this night those who know loneliness, fear, and anxiety.
(Prayers of Intercession)

In life's sorrows and trials I will call upon you alone, O God.

(Morning)
I will find new ways today to sing praises to your name and witness to the salvation you offer. Amen.

(Evening)
As I grow still and calm in the day's closing, I take comfort in your promise that weeping will not linger but that joy awaits me. Amen.

THURSDAY, JULY 2
(Read Psalm 30:6–12)

(Morning)
Precious God, I wake today calling, "God be my helper," and praising your wondrous deeds.

(Evening)
Precious God, throughout the day, I have cried out to you and you have been there for me in the large ways and the small.

The psalmist sings of crying out to you, precious God, for help. Do you have the capacity to hear all the cries from those who seek help? in every tongue and language? with concerns great and small? The psalmist has no concern for such matters, being certain that you will hear every word of praise or prayer whether whispered alone in a desperate situation or proclaimed from the grandest cathedral. We should be as confident that you will hear us and be gracious.

(Morning)
Ever-present God, hear the cries of all your people.
When they cry out, be their helper.
(Prayers of Intercession)

(Evening)
As I turn in prayer, I recall others who plead for help and reassurance.
(Prayers of Intercession)

**We give thanks for the gift of prayer and
for the assurance of prayers heard.**

(Morning)
As I go about my day, I will pray in thanksgiving and in times of need, always sure that you hear. Amen.

(Evening)
At the end of a day filled with prayers both spoken and unspoken, I turn toward slumber with a final prayer of thanksgiving and of praise. Amen.

FRIDAY, JULY 3
(Read Galatians 6:1–6)

(Morning)
God, this *is* the day that you have made for your children to rejoice and be glad
in it. Let me live today conscious of this gift of life.

(Evening)
God, with the close of day, I return to you and wonder if you brood as
I do over the events and missed opportunities of the day.
Attend me as I seek your guidance in reflection and prayer.

Our lives of work, family, neighbors, and strangers bring us often to some
conflict or misunderstanding. The letter to the Galatians reminds us of the
freedom to be gained not in faulting others but in a spirit of *gentleness,*
restoring those who err. How much we long for that gentle correction but
fail to offer it. How quick we are to spot the flaw in another but slow to
recognize it in ourselves. How much more fully we would live if truly we
recalled this kindly word of love to one another.

(Morning)
Forgive me, O God, for my too-quick and sharp correction of others and my
slowness to see those ways in which I contribute to the world's woes.
(Prayers of Intercession)

(Evening)
Uphold, loving God, those whom I was quick to fault and
grant me a gentleness of spirit.
(Prayers of Intercession)

I will study the ways of gentle restoration and the art of forgiveness.

(Morning)
Grant me in this day a ready forgiveness and kindly spirit. Amen.

(Evening)
I have sought this day to "carry my
own load" in reliance on you.
Strengthen me this night to assist
others with burdens too heavy to carry.
Amen.

SATURDAY, JULY 4
(Read Galatians 6:7–16)

(Morning)
God in three persons, you attend us each through the presence of the Spirit
among us. We give thanks for this companion on life's journey.

(Evening)
God in three persons, weary in good-doing and not-so-good-doing at day's end,
I turn to your Word looking for guidance and meaning.
By your Spirit grant me a listening heart.

How it frightens us to recognize that we may indeed reap what we sow. Yet
your promise of mercy sustains us and your invitation to "sow in the Spirit"
beckons us to another way. In life's busy tumult we are often tempted to
ignore our spiritual formation and spiritual disciplines in favor of activity
and entertainment. God, you still call us to the work of the Spirit, prayer,
and working beyond weariness for the good of all.

(Morning)
In company with the Spirit I continue my faith journey,
rededicating myself to work for the common good.
(Prayers of Intercession)

(Evening)
Commending the day's efforts to you, God, through the Spirit,
I now reflect on the good I have left undone this day.
(Prayers of Intercession)

God's will for the good of all is served by women and men of faith.

(Morning)	(Evening)
Empowered by the Spirit of the living God I approach today in hope and confidence. Amen.	Lifting today's work to you, O God, with thanksgiving for the calling of all Christians, I seek now peace and renewal and a night's rest to serve all of your children tomorrow. Amen.

SUNDAY, JULY 5
(Read Luke 10:1–11, 16–20)

(Morning)
Creator God, as morning comes afresh, we give thanks that in every age you still call people to serve you in love. I give thanks for my own baptism today.

(Evening)
Creator God, the demands of the day weigh heavy, but amid them I still hear you calling us to the faithful Christian life, and I give thanks.

The Gospel of Luke records so clearly the message for our day. God, you still call us in the name of the Christ, not to be a people apart but to go out into the very midst of life with the message of peace. The great calling for the church and for all Christians is to find ways to proclaim your peace in a world too busy and self-absorbed to listen. As people of faith, we need always to remain together in a bond of unity, pronouncing that word of peace even in the least peaceful settings.

(Morning)
This broken world longs for peace among countries and peoples, in families and communities. Hear my prayers for peace.
(Prayers of Intercession)

(Evening)
Wars and rumors of war abound today and in all days.
Hear my prayers for peace.
(Prayers of Intercession)

Bringer of Peace, make me an instrument of your peace.

(Morning)
Answering Christ's call, I will seek to serve peace this day and in all my days. Amen.

(Evening)
O God, I have worked for your peace and sometimes fallen short. Join my efforts with others, that all may know the blessing of your peace. Amen.

MONDAY, JULY 6
(Read Colossians 1:1–14)

(Morning)
O living God, I rise to meet your Spirit and thank you for your gift of sleep.

(Evening)
O living God, I give thanks for your grace and appreciate those who labor in the summer heat to prepare the bounty that graced my table tonight. Remember them as evening comes.

Our gracious God, I am reminded how dependent I am on you for my daily existence. Your love provides all that I need, making this life of privilege possible. I am also thankful for the challenges you bring to my life each day. Help me fulfill them.

(Morning)
Eternal Creator, I have often failed to bear fruits of justice, equality, and hope. Lead me in paths that build and do not destroy human dignity within our communities.
(Prayers of Intercession)

(Evening)
O God, just as grass cannot survive without water, I cannot live without your Spirit which created me from the clay of the earth. Remind me to be thankful for this gift today.
(Prayers of Intercession)

"May you be made strong with all the strength that comes from God's glorious power."

(Morning)
Thank you, O God, for rescuing me from evil and bringing me into the community of Jesus' forgiveness and grace. Help me live a life that reflects this reality and love. Amen.

(Evening)
Today has been another joyful gift of life. Help me be thankful and appreciative when I awaken to tomorrow's new promise of life. Amen.

TUESDAY, JULY 7
(Read Amos 7:7–9)

(Morning)
O God, by your grace I was spared.
Open my heart to understand all that this means.

(Evening)
O God, truly my heart is glad for the moments of joy I experienced today.
Continue to make me a believer of your truth through love.

By all measures of what I should be doing with my life, I fall short of your glory and requirements, O God. Spare me and judge me not for those things I have left undone, but move me to be a true witness of your grace, peace, and truth wherever I go today. Only your truth, O living God, is the final measure of faithfulness; let me not be satisfied with anything less in my life.

(Morning)
Loving God, I need your Spirit to help me distinguish the untruths of this world from your truth, and I pray you will give me the courage to act appropriately.
(Prayers of Intercession)

(Evening)
O God, I thank you that you have not judged my life harshly for what I have left undone this day. Forgive my shortcomings with your Spirit of love.
(Prayers of Intercession)

"See, I am setting a plumb line in the midst of my people Israel."

(Morning)
It is easy to be a judge if I see things only from my point of view. It is more difficult when I consider our world through your eyes and your judgment, which is infallible. Amen.

(Evening)
I am thankful after this long day. Thank you, God, for sparing me your judgment. Amen.

WEDNESDAY, JULY 8
(Read Amos 7:10–17)

(Morning)
O God, thank you for this amazing morning. May your goodness be with me all the day long.

(Evening)
O God, it is a joy to be part of the human community which supports our life, and we give you thanks. We remember it was Jesus who said, "I am the way, the truth, and the life."

O God, you are the maker of heaven and earth, yet you allow us freedom and choice. We cannot fathom the trust you have in us, but we can appreciate it when we realize how quickly we grab power for ourselves. Never forsake us, God, for we are an unfaithful generation.

(Morning)
Restore a right spirit within me, O God, that my life might be saved.
Restore a right relationship between my heart and your heart,
that I might be wise.
(Prayers of Intercession)

(Evening)
It is within your power to take everything I own and
strip me of my possessions, yet you have given me so much.
Make me responsive to your generous Spirit of acceptance this night.
(Prayers of Intercession)

"Therefore thus says God: 'You yourself will die in an unclean land.' "

(Morning)	(Evening)
To accept our life of ease without concern can be our downfall. Our God wants a clean and contrite heart. God, may you be merciful unto us this day. Amen.	Today the world moved closer to being more humane because I took a moment to hear another person's troubles. Thank you, Jesus, for giving me the patience to listen. Amen.

THURSDAY, JULY 9
(Read Psalm 25:1–10)

(Morning)
Merciful God, what a joy it is to awaken to a world you have given us today.
It is, indeed, an Easter morning again.

(Evening)
Merciful God, it is good to come home to a clean home and running water,
yet I remember many places where these basic needs are not being met.
Be mindful of them this night.

When I see the stars in the sky, I am reminded of your promise to Abraham.
Renew that sense of hope within me, for in the vastness of space my life
seems so small. Thank you, God, for the promise of your presence to even
the least of those in your creation.

(Morning)
Lift my spirits to a level of compassion for others this day, O God.
Do not let me be put to shame, nor let my enemies exult over me.
Then, lead me in paths of your light and truth.
(Prayers of Intercession)

(Evening)
Forgive me for those I have ignored today. In my rush
to accomplish my tasks, I did not hear your cries for understanding.
"Whoever welcomes me, welcomes the one who sent me."
(Prayers of Intercession)

**"Lead me in your truth, and teach me,
for you are the God of my salvation."**

(Morning)
O God, I am committed to making
this day have meaning for me. Teach
me the pathways that lead to your
righteousness and joy, as I seek
your face. Amen.

(Evening)
The news on television sounds bleak
tonight. It is good to know there are
also many acts of kindness done in
your name, O God, renewing my faith
in humankind. Amen.

FRIDAY, JULY 10
(Read Deuteronomy 30:9–14)

(Morning)
O God, "Choose life" is a powerful commandment for me today.
May I choose to bring down barriers so I can learn
to live by this commandment and enjoy its many benefits.

(Evening)
O God, the promised land for Moses was never realized in his lifetime.
If it pleases you, allow me to enjoy this life of promise and
hope for many more years.

I understand little of how I became the person I am. I am learning that I am more than just a mind with a body. I also have a spirit where your compassion and feelings abide. Teach me to coordinate my life though mind, body, and spirit as I follow Jesus who teaches me.

(Morning)
Moses was right: Your commandments are not beyond
our understanding or beyond our doing. It is our spirit that is weak.
Let us turn our hearts toward you, God, today.
(Prayers of Intercession)

(Evening)
O God, our God, when I am blinded by anger and hate, calm my spirit and bring
your focus to my life again. In the name of Jesus, our redeemer.
(Prayers of Intercession)

"I have set before you life and death, blessing and curses. Choose life."

(Morning)
The admonitions of Moses are clear,
yet I so often choose evil over good.
May the spirit of the Christ be my
guide for making ethical decisions that
are best for all concerned. Amen.

(Evening)
For Asians, harmony is the highest
community value. May the American
spirit soon begin to appreciate Jesus'
call to peace which comes from this
ancient Eastern teaching. Amen.

SATURDAY, JULY 11
(Read Luke 10:25–28)

(Morning)
Our gracious God, remind me to work toward eternal life by loving you with all
my heart, and soul, and strength, and mind.

(Evening)
Our gracious God, it is hard to consider Jesus' question:
"Who is your neighbor?" I pray for honest answers.

In a busy life, it is hard to take time to consider the costs of that lifestyle. O
God, your Child Jesus is asking all of us to consider a larger question about
eternal life. Is that a priority for me, or do I choose to ignore it and miss an
excellent opportunity for growth? Help me choose wisely.

(Morning)
It is a hard thing to consider Jesus' call to "Love your neighbor as yourself."
It is easier to isolate myself and not take time to know others.
Open my heart and make me generous.
(Prayers of Intercession)

(Evening)
How have I injured another? Forgive my short-sightedness which made me act
in haste. I am sorry. Give me your peace that will empower me.
(Prayers of Intercession)

"What must I do to inherit eternal life?"
He said to him, "What is written in the law?"

(Morning)
It is becoming more evident that I
need to deal with my isolationism.
What can I do to change this today?
God, you call me to be in community,
but I find myself too weak. Why?
Amen.

(Evening)
Do not let this night fall before I deal
with my anger. Perhaps some of my
anger is justified; let it become an
avenue for needed changes. Help me
be honest about this. Amen.

SUNDAY, JULY 12
(Read Luke 10:29–37)

(Morning)
God, as I go about my daily routines today, how will this story of the good
Samaritan make me think differently? Let it sink in and challenge me anew.

(Evening)
God, I did not find time enough to stop; but I wish I had,
because my life is not getting better. I need to reach out more
to those who are suffering with me on the roadside of life.

"Too busy!" "Too much to do." These are excuses I have used to keep from
getting involved in the lives of other persons who have needed my help.
Renew your Spirit of love within me, O God, and put a right spirit within
me.

(Morning)
God, I did not mean for it to end that way today,
but it was almost beyond my control.
(Prayers of Intercession)

(Evening)
God, tonight we both ended up being upset. It is important that we take time to
bind up each other's wounds and heal our broken spirits,
so the spirit of cooperation can live again.
(Prayers of Intercession)

**"Which one of these three do you think was a neighbor
to the man who fell among robbers? Go and do likewise."**

(Morning)
It is dangerous to get involved in other
people's lives on the side of the road.
Is there an easier way? Perhaps Jesus
was right. The gate is narrow and not
many will pass through it. Amen.

(Evening)
It felt good to be a neighbor. Perhaps
those who have been helped will
remember it and not be so hesitant to
help someone if the opportunity
arises in their lives. I live in that hope
this night. Amen.

MONDAY, JULY 13
(Read Colossians 1:15–28)

(Morning)
Empowering God, I am on a quest, continually seeking answers to innumerable questions about life and living. How fruitless this quest often seems.

(Evening)
Empowering God, I have so many unanswered questions about life and ask your patience with me.

Life has a purpose. And in the living of it, I often question. Searching for its purpose has brought me to the realization that answers to my questions are not what is most important. What is infinitely more important to my well-being is my experience of a centeredness in Christ. A Christ-centeredness frees me from pursuing fruitless questioning and frees me to accept what I have decided is inexplicable. This enables me to embrace love, joy, and a passion for living, despite suffering pain and all manifestations of evil.

(Morning)
Holy God, when I experience Christ risen, God among us who walked on earth and knows the pain of human suffering, I am able to embrace life in the midst of setbacks and difficulties.
(Prayers of Intercession)

(Evening)
Invisible God, revealed in Christ Jesus, when I am centered in you, resting in your presence, you infuse me with a serenity that quiets my feverish search.
(Prayers of Intercession)

What joy to discover that in Christ all the fullness of God is made available to us!

(Morning)
I seek the comfort, serenity, and reassurance that only your presence can provide. Amen.

(Evening)
There is no meaning to my life apart from you, Divine One. Amen.

TUESDAY, JULY 14
(Read Luke 10:38–42)

(Morning)
Gracious, living God, I greet this day, fresh with new possibilities.
It offers me an opportunity for renewing my commitment to being your disciple.

(Evening)
Gracious, living God, thank you for the gift of this day and
its opportunities for discipleship.

The world in which I live rewards noise and activity. The phone rings, others need my assistance, and job responsibilities demand my presence. You have given me this day, O Holy One, with its many demands competing for my attention. You call for my undivided attention, but your call is not the loudest. In the midst of the noise of these competing demands, I must make a choice. Only the stillness which comes from centering on you will quiet this frenetic pace, so that I may discern your voice and hear your guidance.

(Morning)
Listening God, I turn to you for guidance and discernment as to what is
"the better part" for me today.
(Prayers of Intercession)

(Evening)
Holy One, I give you thanks and praise for the opportunities
to be your disciple during the day that has passed.
Forgive me for the times when I failed to discern your call.
(Prayers of Intercession)

**Today I will reevaluate my priorities and
the influences on my thoughts and time.**

(Morning)
Open my heart to hear and receive
these words of Scripture with the
freshness and curiosity of a child and
the eagerness of an earnest seeker of
the Word. Amen.

(Evening)
Bless me as I, your disciple, now turn
to renewing rest and sleep. Amen.

WEDNESDAY, JULY 15
(Read Amos 8:1–12)

(Morning)
God, you are hard on me. I fear your silence and judgment.

(Evening)
God, I hunger for your presence to guide and encourage me.

The ringing of bells may herald an occasion for rejoicing or one of doom. So it is when I turn to your message, O God. I want it to be pealing the good news that you are a God of love who forgives my sins, not a God of judgment. When the message being tolled is that of frightful judgment, I recognize that it is deserved—deserved because of my complicity in accepting unjust and oppressive conditions and in neglecting to speak out against injustices. This warning of judgment is dreadful.

(Morning)
God who cannot be fully comprehended, you always expect justice and righteousness from your people.
(Prayers of Intercession)

(Evening)
God of total and complete judgment, you stand in solidarity with those who are treated with contempt and malice, with the poor and the oppressed. Where am I?
(Prayers of Intercession)

Yes, I want to participate in your divine plan of justice for all.

(Morning)
My complacency is disturbed by the clanging warning that I must confront an awful and awe-full hour of judgment. Amen.

(Evening)
I have committed my life to following you, but I must renew that commitment daily. Amen.

THURSDAY, JULY 16
(Read Psalm 15)

(Morning)
God of wisdom, I pause to discern your way among competing claims
for my allegiance and my time. Only you are true.
Only you are deserving of my devotion.

(Evening)
God of wisdom, guide me in my quest to be your follower.
I thirst for your righteousness in my life.

I am seeking guidance to follow your ways, O God. The directions seem murky, unclear. You say to love you and to love my neighbor as myself. But sometimes, often, I fail and find the mote in someone else's eye when there is a log in mine. I forget your commandments in the cacophony of the demands and distractions of everyday life. In the comfort of my life, it is easy to lose sight of my neighbors, persons who live in continual want and distress. Faithful God, have mercy on me. I ask your forgiveness.

(Morning)
You show me, O God, what it means to be a righteous person, a follower of your ways. Guide my steps, that I may speak and live according to your truth.
(Prayers of Intercession)

(Evening)
Gracious, loving, caring God, guide my steps,
that I may speak and live according to your truth.
(Prayers of Intercession)

It is difficult to live according to God's ways in an un-God-ly world.

(Morning)
Guide my steps in seeking the well-being of all other persons, my neighbors near and far, in this world of diversity. Amen.

(Evening)
May your righteousness and your righteous people infiltrate our global city, bringing to all love and goodwill. Amen.

FRIDAY, JULY 17

(Read Genesis 18:1–10a)

(Morning)
God who calls us, the status quo seems so comfortable. Then you burst in, startling me with new creative prospects. My preconceived notions of self are called into question. You instruct me to shake up my life. Is that good news?

(Evening)
God who calls us, infuse me with courage if I am to confront the startling news that fruitfulness can replace the barrenness with which I had grown content.

I have become comfortable with a certain nonproductivity, which I have accepted as normal and to which I am accustomed. Now a promise of creativity challenges and startles me. I hear your challenge that I am capable of giving birth in a totally new way. The prospect is both scary and exciting. Can I, will I allow myself to relinquish the familiar in order to embrace the promise of a new possibility?

(Morning)
You, surprising God, have disclosed the potential for new life.
This revelation leaves me feeling very vulnerable.
What does this mean for my future?
(Prayers of Intercession)

(Evening)
Ingenious God, my preconceptions are shaken, shattered.
You dare me to change.
(Prayers of Intercession)

Is anything too hard for me with God?

(Morning)
The newness and challenge of this day bring the delight that you, God, and I are collaborating in a new adventure. Amen.

(Evening)
Praise be to you, O Christ, for revealing the possibility of fruitfulness and the likelihood of new beginnings. Amen.

SATURDAY, JULY 18

(Read Genesis 18:1–10a; Amos 8:1–12; Luke 10:38:42)

(Morning)
Timeless God, praise to you for Scripture which disturbs and challenges,
sustains and nurtures me. It connects me with people of faith from earlier times.

(Evening)
Timeless God, praise to you for your Word which disturbs and challenges,
sustains and nurtures me.

Scripture serves as an icon through which I experience you, Creator God,
Jesus Christ and the Holy Spirit. Amazingly, I recognize people I know or
know about in the lives of Mary, Martha, Abraham, Sarah, and the prophet
Amos. They come alive when they confront the challenge to welcome you
and your incredible message. They come alive when they respond to injustice in a world where the powerless and the oppressed suffer, and when
they are faced with determining what is "the better part." This, too, is our
dilemma.

(Morning)
God who calls us into relationship, praise to you. The Word lived out in the
lives of our spiritual ancestors is alive in people today.
(Prayers of Intercession)

(Evening)
Holy Deliverer, I praise you for the wonderful stories in Scripture.
(Prayers of Intercession)

**Scripture is a vehicle for developing a right relationship
with God and God's people.**

(Morning)
May my mind be open to your Word.
Amen.

(Evening)
Praise to you, O Holy One, for the
inspiration and challenge of
Scripture. Amen.

SUNDAY, JULY 19
(Read Genesis 18:1–10a)

(Morning)
Welcoming God, what persons with new ideas and insights
may come my way if I am receptive? I struggle with being surprised
by you and those who come in your name.

(Evening)
Welcoming God, help me to show hospitality to your surprises.

God, you challenge me to openness by treating each person sent by you with hospitality and respect. To toss aside my plans to be hospitable to others—to stop and share words of welcome and a listening ear, to offer a cold drink and a comfortable chair to everyone—can be really upsetting. Then, in addition, when I am confronted with questioning my ideas and insights, I'm not sure that I wish to receive your message.

(Morning)
God, how bewildering it is to be hospitable. Open my closed mind to be what
you want me to be, and open my arms to be welcoming to all persons.
(Prayers of Intercession)

(Evening)
Holy God, I thank you for all the ways I have been offered hospitality. I am
astonished to have found myself the welcomed and honored guest.
(Prayers of Intercession)

Have you come my way before and I have not known?
Have you spoken when I was not ready to hear?

(Morning)
I will be open to being surprised and
amazed. Amen.

(Evening)
It is with a sense of contentment and
joy that I approach the coming night of
rest. You, hospitable God, make me
feel welcomed and secure. Amen.

MONDAY, JULY 20
(Read Genesis 18:20–32)

(Morning)
God, let us take our time and appreciate the surprise that comes
with this new day.

(Evening)
God, order in the universe reminds us of the reason we are alive.

O God, as the sun rises in the east, your love warms our hearts. Today, remind us of grandparents who could not read or write but who knew they were created in your image. Help us to see their dreams and know their desires. Thank you for their lives, although often stymied by oppression and disappointment. Thank you for their unfaltering faith, which sustained them and drew them closer to you. Thank you for their smiles, which carried them through painful years and provided confidence which they instilled in us. Help us to be obedient to your Word and pass their legacies on to our grandchildren.

(Morning)
O God, as our breath inhales, fill us with your Spirit. As our breath exhales,
receive our thanks and spread new life throughout your world.
(Prayers of Intercession)

(Evening)
O God, listen to the laughter of your people,
and dry the tears that drip from their hearts.
(Prayers of Intercession)

Let our courage lead us into the lives of unknown friends.

(Morning)
Christ, help us to know your face and voice today when you greet us in the streets. Amen.

(Evening)
How can we say thank you when we fail to obey your Word? Thank you for your mercy. Amen.

TUESDAY, JULY 21
(Read Psalm 138)

(Morning)
Creator God, today let us practice gratitude and joy, no matter what happens.

(Evening)
Creator God, praise to you tonight comes from the lowly creatures
creeping through the grass to the sparkling,
celestial symphony light-years above our heads.

Great Creator, dance gently to your glorious music and hum sweetly as your Spirit gracefully sweeps across your universes. Touch our ears softly and fill us with your beautiful truth. Turn our hearts into cotton cushions absorbing your love and reflecting your majestic presence. Sing through our voices and bless your people. And, O God, make us sensitive enough to hear our brothers and sisters whose voices are silent and whose ears are impaired.

(Morning)
My feet cannot dance. My hands cannot clap. My body cannot stand. My eyes cannot see. My ears cannot hear. My voice cannot sing. Thank you, O God, for the life you have given me.
(Prayers of Intercession)

(Evening)
After all you gave us today, O God, why didn't we do more for you?
(Prayers of Intercession)

**It is impossible to be grateful and resentful at the same time.
So let's celebrate LIFE!**

(Morning)	(Evening)
O God, you have awakened us to sounds of fresh life. Teach us a new song today. Amen.	What a wonderful gift of new memories. Help us to tell your story. Amen.

WEDNESDAY, JULY 22
(Read Luke 11:1–13)

(Morning)
Merciful God, love sounds so nice, but it requires unusual discipline.

(Evening)
Merciful God, forgive us for turning our backs on people today
who reached out for love.

O God, thank you for opening the door when we knocked at midnight. You did not turn us away when we needed an answer. Sometimes, it seems easier to sleep through the night and ignore the stranger or even the friend at the door. But you, O God, heard our cries and pitied our needs. Through Jesus, you taught us how we are to love one another just as you have loved us. Jesus told us also to love our enemies. What did you have in mind, God, when you sent Jesus to teach us how to live on your earth? When he said, "Love your enemies," did he also mean nations with their armies? Or was he just talking to people like us?

(Morning)
Teach us, O God, to say sincerely to others, "We are going to love you in word,
thought, and deed, no matter who you are."
(Prayers of Intercession)

(Evening)
Help us, O God, to know with confidence that your love
shines through us and touches everyone we meet.
(Prayers of Intercession)

Love breaks into every encounter. Don't dismiss it.

(Morning)
Jesus prepared breakfast at daybreak
for his disciples because he loved
them. Thank you for loving us. Amen.

(Evening)
The garden of Gethsemane at night-
fall was changed into a sacred space
of blood, sweat, and tears. Have
mercy. Amen.

THURSDAY, JULY 23
(Read Psalm 85)

(Morning)
Loving God, may the desires of our hearts be consumed by your Spirit.

(Evening)
Loving God, did we do one thing today that pleased you and brightened
someone's face or lightened a stranger's burden?

You gave us life, O God, and we did not always say, "Thank you." You
watched us poison the water, and we did not say, "Sorry." You heard us
curse our children, and we were not ashamed. You wept over your cities,
and we did not comfort you. And now, O God, we want you to restore our
lives and fill our hearts with joy. Forsake us not. Forgive us and teach us.

(Morning)
Speak your Word of peace and righteousness into the ears of your faithful
people, and restore us again, O God.
(Prayers of Intercession)

(Evening)
You did it, O God! You made your Word flesh and walked with us. Have mercy.
(Prayers of Intercession)

When there is nothing we can do, thank God for Jesus.

(Morning)
We can be peaceful today and give
smiles to those who pass our way.
Maybe Jesus will laugh with us.
Amen.

(Evening)
You did not let us down as you lifted
our spirits. Did you smile today, O
God? Can we try again tomorrow?
Amen.

FRIDAY, JULY 24
(Read Hosea 1:2–10)

(Morning)
Sustaining God, from whose bed did we arise this day?
Into whose arms will we return?
Can faithfulness be measured as anything less than whole?

(Evening)
Sustaining God, cleanse our hearts and make us completely faithful to you.

You know, O God, no matter how hard we try to do what is right, we must confess, like Paul, that we too easily do what is wrong. In searching for partnership, sometimes one meets a "soul mate" who is one's co-walker in life. But one does not always have a choice about who one falls in love with. Emotions can overcome the rational self and lead a person into the life of someone who becomes a lover. Sometimes we are not always faithful. Sometimes our partners in life may not honor our covenants. Disappointments may discourage us. Heartaches may afflict us. But, you, O God, have loved us despite our infidelity. Have mercy.

(Morning)
Teach us this day, O God, the true meaning of faithfulness.
Let our lives demonstrate fidelity and honor.
(Prayers of Intercession)

(Evening)
Did we honor your name today, O God?
Did we act like the "children of the living God"?
(Prayers of Intercession)

The chaste and the unchaste are God's children.

(Morning)	(Evening)
As the children of God, what shall we do that will please the Creator? How can we be as you intended? Amen.	Jesus showed us how the child of God is to be faithful, obedient, and loving. Teach us, Jesus. Amen.

SATURDAY, JULY 25
(Read Colossians 2:6–15)

(Morning)
O God, in the busyness of this day, help us to focus on you.

(Evening)
O God, there are so many distractions that lead to empty spaces.
Help us to discern your way through faith.

Voices are raised and lowered to attract our ears. We seek to know the truth, so that we can be free to serve you, O God, and live according to the Word. Yet we are tempted to lean toward the most persuasive and authoritative voices that come near us. We must listen carefully and faithfully to the tiny sounds that enter our hearts and long for our souls. Through prayer and meditation we are able to hear and know you. The foundation of our understanding is built on our love for you. Grant to us wisdom to know you, and give us the desire to obey you and you alone.

(Morning)
O God, how can we know your way?
Abide in us and whisper your Word all day long.
(Prayers of Intercession)

(Evening)
Thank you, O God, for giving us new life in Jesus Christ.
You forgave us even when we were dead in spirit. Have mercy.
(Prayers of Intercession)

Breathing alone does not mean we are alive. We must live.

(Morning)
Don't let us be fooled by sweet words that leave us hungry. Give us your truth, that we may be fully alive in you. Amen.

(Evening)
Dwell in us and let your Spirit fill our lives with courage. Allow us to know victory over sin. Amen.

SUNDAY, JULY 26
(Read Colossians 2:16–19)

(Morning)
Merciful God, how wonderful it is to know you are renewing our connection.

(Evening)
Merciful God, attempts are made to separate us from you. It is our choice to strengthen the tie that binds us to you, our Creator.

It seems so foolish to worry about offending you, loving God, by the food we eat or what we drink. You want us to enjoy the full bounty of life. How we treat one another is of far greater concern to you than what we consume. How we respect the whole of your creation is more important than our holidays and festivals. Knowing with reverence that we are created by intention in your image gives us appreciation of who we are in truth. Jesus joins us in our exploration to know your greatness. Each discovery renews our souls and makes our hearts rejoice. Hallelujah.

(Morning)
Surprise us today, O God, with a visit by the Spirit.
(Prayers of Intercession)

(Evening)
Liberation has come through Jesus Christ.
Thank you, O God, because you knew we could not free ourselves.
(Prayers of Intercession)

God bless the ties that bind.

(Morning)
What shall we select to honor you today? How can we show how much we love you by caring deeply for all people? Give us the opportunity today to share your wealth. Amen.

(Evening)
Thank you, loving God, for giving to us your gifts of food, drink, and compassion. Help us to receive with gratitude what you give us. Amen.

MONDAY, JULY 27
(Read Hosea 11:1–11)

(Morning)
Merciful God, who cares for me and holds me like a parent even when I turn
away, watch over me today in all my thoughts and actions.

(Evening)
Merciful God, I give you thanks for not turning away from me throughout this
day, for keeping me in your tender care, and for hearing me when I call to you.

We see in the prophecy of Hosea that the disobedience of Israel was transformed into obedience by your mercy. God, you "bent down to them and
fed them" even as you taught them to walk. To experience such love is life-
transforming. Once we have known it, nothing is ever the same again. Once
we have known the grace of forgiveness of undeserved love, the gratitude,
wonder, and love we show to others are the marks of daily life.

(Morning)
God of mercy, grant us grace to return to you and
keep all of your children in your tender care.
(Prayers of Intercession)

(Evening)
God of compassion, for all your mercies I give you thanks and ask you to
continue to forgive our wandering ways.
(Prayers of Intercession)

God said: "I led them with words of human kindness, with bands of love."

(Morning)
O God, let me not turn away from you
this day. Show me your kindness in
temptation and your constancy in
trouble, as I have known them fully in
Jesus Christ. Amen.

(Evening)
Holy God, I am filled this night with
wonder and gratitude for your goodness and mercy. I rest in your mercy
and rejoice in knowing its fullness in
Jesus Christ my Sovereign. Amen.

TUESDAY, JULY 28
(Read Ecclesiastes 1:2, 12–14; 2:18–23)

(Morning)
Holy God, Creator of all things, giver of life and source of meaning and purpose, teach me to look to you this day and to seek your will.

(Evening)
Holy God, grant me the grace to find my rest tonight, not in the vanity of false choices and hollow endeavors, but only in your purpose and presence in my life.

In a culture geared to goals and objectives, to climbing ladders and celebrating human accomplishments, the writer of Ecclesiastes reminds us of the vanity of it all. All that striving with its attendant pride is, ultimately, just huffing and puffing before you, O God. It does not bring happiness or rest or fulfillment. Only life lived in your presence is true life. O for the vision and courage to live such a life and not ask for any reward save that of being in your presence!

(Morning)
Holy God, help me and all your children to see the hollowness of vain striving, to recognize cheap rewards for what they are, and to seek only your will.
(Prayers of Intercession)

(Evening)
Creator God, who alone gives meaning to our lives, may our hearts this day be grounded in you. Forgive whatever has been vain and hollow.
In your mercy, teach us all to rest in you.
(Prayers of Intercession)

**I saw all the deeds that are done under the sun; and see,
all is vanity and a chasing after wind.**

(Morning)
Holy God, cut through the trappings and falseness of living and show me how to trust in your will, revealed in Jesus Christ. Amen.

(Evening)
Merciful God, I give thanks this night for the love and hope I have known today from your hand. Amen.

WEDNESDAY, JULY 29
(Read Psalm 107:1–9, 43)

(Morning)
Gracious God, grant me the grace today to recognize your abiding love in creation, in your leading and forgiveness, and in your deliverance from shadows within and without.

(Evening)
Gracious God, I give thanks for your steadfast love
throughout this day, for your light where I could not see the way,
for your healing presence, and for hope itself.

Our culture is geared to goods and objectives, to the rewarding of human accomplishments, to thinking in terms of what humankind does or fails to do. The wonder of creation and the mystery and power of love teach us how great you are, merciful God, and how infinite yet vulnerable. We have seen delicate flowers emerge from rocks and the hands of a little child bring healing to grief and remorse. Time after time, your steadfast love is known in fragile, tender ways.

(Morning)
Merciful God, come to me this day, in its ordinary moments,
with your light and truth.
(Prayers of Intercession)

(Evening)
Holy God, as the shadows lengthen and the evening falls, watch over this wondrous world and forgive the sin of your children.
(Prayers of Intercession)

Let the redeemed of God say so.

(Morning)
Teach me, O God, your ways and your laws. I have no light for my path save with you. My ways with you are bright and ordained. Amen.

(Evening)
For this day and its grace, I give thanks. For its signs of your love and mercy, I am humbled. For my life and its wonder, I praise you. Amen.

THURSDAY, JULY 30
(Read Colossians 3:1–11)

(Morning)
Creator God, source of every good and perfect gift, turn my soul to you so that I
may seek only the new life Christ gives.

(Evening)
Creator God, ruler of the world and of all things visible and invisible, show me
how to abide in you in Jesus Christ.

God, the writer of Colossians tells us to seek the things that are above
where Christ is seated at your right hand. The behavioral implications of
that are: to set our mind on things that are above is to live the marks of
baptism; and to die to old ways is to live out of the new life that has been
made possible though Christ. The implications of the phrase "raised with
Christ" are concrete and specific. They bring theology and discipleship
together in a rich tapestry of image and practice.

(Morning)
Heavenly God, farther off than the stars, yet nearer than a breath of wind, speak
to your people through Jesus Christ.
(Prayers of Intercession)

(Evening)
Merciful God, help all who seek you to find themselves in the brilliant light of
the risen Christ beside you.
(Prayers of Intercession)

**"When Christ who is your life is revealed,
then you also will be revealed with Christ in glory."**

(Morning)
Holy God, let me not be far removed
from you. Give me the vision of your
glory. Come to me in Jesus Christ.
Amen.

(Evening)
Merciful God, take my life this night
into your loving care. Give me the
benediction only you can give, so that
I may rest in your peace. Amen.

FRIDAY, JULY 31
(Read Colossians 3:1–11)

(Morning)
God of my life, I trust in you. Come to me today with the light
I have known in Jesus Christ.

(Evening)
God of my life, bless this day. I long to have lived it in
the brilliant light of the risen Christ.

God, the life that is lived in the risen Christ is described in Colossians. These are not demands of the Christian life. They are, rather, pictures of life without divisions. Everyone in Christ is a new being, and that new being is evident in the quality of daily life, in the absence of anger, slander, and abusive language. To be raised with Christ is to live Christ's love for all.

(Morning)
Everlasting God, Sovereign of heaven and earth,
come to us in the risen Christ to bring love, kindness, truthfulness,
and healing love to all people in their need.
(Prayers of Intercession)

(Evening)
God of all mercy, may the fragrance of the risen Christ spread over
the brokenness of the world with healing and hope.
(Prayers of Intercession)

**"If you have been raised with Christ, seek the things that are above
where Christ is seated at the right hand of God."**

(Morning)
Holy God, take my life and ground it in Christ. Make me a new being in the One who is the way, the truth, and the life. Amen.

(Evening)
Holy God, as evening falls, grant me the peace of knowing that I rest in you and in your beloved Child, Jesus Christ. Amen.

SATURDAY, AUGUST 1
(Read Luke 12:13–21)

(Morning)
Gracious God, grant me a sense of my need. Teach me to look away from what is empty and passing toward what is fulfilling and eternal.

(Evening)
Gracious God, I give you thanks for watching over me today and for reminding me of the one hope that abides. Keep me in your tender care this night.

God, Luke the evangelist tells the truth of the human inclination to seek security in goods and wealth. He tells of a man who looked to Jesus, of all people, to intervene in an inheritance arrangement. Life, real life, is not possessions. We are, in this Gospel reading, brought up short by Jesus' refusal to enter such negotiations and his clear view that real life is to be rich toward you, our God.

(Morning)
God of mercy, deliver your people from the temptation to turn away from you and to seek security in wealth and possessions.
(Prayers of Intercession)

(Evening)
God of compassion, deliver me and all your people from false choices and hollow lives. Bring us somehow to see in your presence the only place of grace and security we have.
(Prayers of Intercession)

"Take care! Be on guard against all kinds of greed; for one's life does not consist in the abundance of possessions."

(Morning)
Holy God, come to me throughout this day. Teach me your will and show me your way, that I may not be tempted to seek what will not satisfy but rather to seek rest in you. Amen.

(Evening)
Merciful God, I give thanks for your forgiveness and direction today. I rest tonight in your presence and care. You alone are my peace in Jesus Christ. Amen.

SUNDAY, AUGUST 2
(Read Luke 12:13–21)

(Morning)
Holy God, you have come in Jesus Christ to teach us in parables
the truth of life itself. Open my heart to your will.

(Evening)
Holy God, I give thanks tonight for your grace, which has kept me
close to you today, which filled me with joy and trust in your promises.
I rest in that confidence.

Jesus tells a parable of a man who amassed wealth in order to ensure his security and yet died unexpectedly without ever using that wealth. The future is not ours to know. God, whatever you have in store for us is in your hands. We live in confidence that your promises are good and gracious, that you will watch over us and give us life now and forever. This parable brings us right up against a future that is unknown and a promise that is eternal.

(Morning)
Holy God, forgive our nation for its worship of material possessions.
And forgive me my complicity in that false choice.
(Prayers of Intercession)

(Evening)
Holy God, I pray this night for all who restlessly pursue empty lives.
Fill us with abiding joy and teach us to wait with confidence
for the future you will bring.
(Prayers of Intercession)

"But God said to him, 'You fool! This very night your life is being demanded of you. And the things you have prepared, whose will they be?' "

(Morning)
Open my life today to the wonder and beauty of your world and to the promises only you can fulfill. Let my peace be your will. Amen.

(Evening)
Merciful God, I give thanks that you have brought me safely to the end of this day in the sure and certain hope of the resurrection to eternal life. Amen.

MONDAY, AUGUST 3
(Read Isaiah 1:1, 10–20)

(Morning)
O Holy One, with some trepidation I bow before you this morning. I come before you to pray and to worship. Prod me today to honor you in all I do.

(Evening)
O Holy One, as I scan the day's horizon, I confess my failure to do good and seek justice. And I celebrate the ways you have worked through me to rescue, defend, and befriend those who have depended on me.

You have spoken, O God, and so often I have refused to listen. I want to be safe. I ache for comfort and reassurance. Time and again, with all my sisters and brothers, I have betrayed you by seeking security and safety and forgetting that I am responsible for my neighbor. Each day I encounter someone in need—recently widowed, perhaps, or without a home, or grieved or abandoned—someone who could use my presence, my word, my resources, my love. Grant me the wisdom and the fortitude to be a gift to others.

(Morning)
God, help me to begin this day by remembering someone in my circle or beyond who struggles or aches. May I be a blessing to that person today.
(Prayers of Intercession)

(Evening)
Because I am a frail earthen vessel, I have not accomplished all that I would have liked today. Forgive me for the ways in which I have failed to do good and seek justice. Hold in your arms those whom I have not reached.
(Prayers of Intercession)

**Help me to conquer my various idolatries and
to put your work at the center.**

(Morning)
Today I give myself to you to be a person for justice and righteousness and peace. Amen.

(Evening)
Forgive me my shortcomings, O God, and inspire me this night, that your great work of justice might begin again in me tomorrow. Amen.

TUESDAY, AUGUST 4
(Read Psalm 50:1–8, 22–23)

(Morning)
O Most High, you have given me this day. I could not have created it myself.
Both its joys and its sorrows will find your hand in them.
You shine forth in it all. Thank you.

(Evening)
O Most High, from the rising of the sun to its setting, this entire day has come
to be at your behest. Heaven and earth declare your righteousness.
I thank you for your dominion and presence.

How hard it sometimes is, O God, to confess that my faith has missed the mark. I am often convinced that I need little correction. Where I have neglected you and put my own needs and desires at the forefront, gently correct me. Where I have been too sure of what is right, set me straight. Plant within me this day a seed of gratitude that will flower into a constancy of praise. Show me again that I am utterly dependent on you.

(Morning)
This morning I thank you for the abundance of the gifts that have come from
you, and I name them now.
(Prayers of Intercession)

(Evening)
As day recedes, I give thanks for the many wonders this day has brought me.
Hear now my recital of them.
(Prayers of Intercession)

**Though life may not be everything that I had hoped it would be,
thank you for the many marvels you have given to me.**

(Morning)
Today, O God, keep me from taking
for granted the marvelous world that
surrounds me and the extraordinary
life you have given me. Amen.

(Evening)
You have shone forth in countless
ways today, O God. As I give thanks,
show me your salvation. Amen.

WEDNESDAY, AUGUST 5
(Read Isaiah 1:1, 10–20 and Psalm 50:1–8, 22–23)

(Morning)
O God, teach me and let me attend to you. Sometimes I am proud,
sometimes haughty. Sometimes I just pay no attention. But all too often,
for whatever reason, I dismiss you. Envelop me. Let me not escape you.
Speak, and I will hear. Command, and I will obey.

(Evening)
O God, it is tempting as I pray to think that it is in this alone that I do my duty
to you. Hear my prayers, I ask, but remind me, as well, that my faithfulness is
lived out in my love. O God of goodness, justice, and righteousness,
let me care for someone who needs me.

Too often I have taught, O God, that faith is a matter of intellect and feelings, of proper prayers and suitable sacrifices. I may say the right words
and do the appropriate ritual, but if I "do not have love, I am a noisy gong
or a clanging cymbal." Lead me today and tomorrow to do something for
someone else's sake, to stand by the side of someone for whom sorrow or
injustice or loneliness is crushing. May I devote myself to you.

(Morning)
As I begin this day, instill in me a sense of justice, O God.
(Prayers of Intercession)

(Evening)
Take me back over this day, O Holy One. Where I have been just, I offer my
gratitude. Where I have failed to be just, I confess. Forgive me and strengthen
me for tomorrow.
(Prayers of Intercession)

**I know that you require mercy and not sacrifice,
O Most High. Make me more merciful.**

(Morning)
Awaken me from slumbers of self-
centeredness, O God. Make me alive
and responsive to aches and pains all
around me. Amen.

(Evening)
As I rest from my labors, strengthen
me to be ever more faithful
tomorrow. Amen.

THURSDAY, AUGUST 6
(Read Hebrews 11:1–3, 8–16)

(Morning)
O God, where will you lead me today? Will I dare to follow?
May I trust you in all your ways.

(Evening)
O God, guide and protector, you have led me on a journey today and
will lead me again tomorrow. You have promised much.
Give me the wisdom and persistence to follow.

Throughout all of history, you have led your children. Some have dared to
follow, and many have not. It is not always easy to follow you, O God. The
territory into which you call us is scary and unknown. In this moment, may
I trust you. Make me wise enough to live toward what you promise, even
when I cannot see the end. Give me a sense of adventure that is unbowed
by fear. Make me perceptive about your ways. And let me not be dependent
on having to reach the goal, but rather let me be satisfied with the pilgrimage itself.

(Morning)
In all that I do today, may I trust and obey, O Holy One. If you lead me on new
paths, let me not resist, but give me the wisdom to respond and follow.
(Prayers of Intercession)

(Evening)
Today in some ways I followed you, O God. I give thanks for your leading, and
I rejoice in my following. In other ways, I said no to your leading.
In my sleep, build my trust.
(Prayers of Intercession)

O God, make me bold in faith, a servant of trust and not of fear.

(Morning)
Lead me today, O God. I promise to
try to follow. Reassure me in my fear.
Bring me to the true home you
promise. Amen.

(Evening)
Lead me in my sleeping as in my
waking, O Holy One. Bring me ever
closer to you. Make me a persistent,
dogged follower of you. Amen.

FRIDAY, AUGUST 7
(Read Luke 12:32–40)

(Morning)
O God, how startling it can sometimes be to hear your reassurance: "Do not be afraid." I have known my share of fears, and I rejoice in the comfort of those embracing words. Let me live fearlessly today.

(Evening)
O God, may my whole life be a gift to you. You have given me life and energy. Without my having to earn anything, you have received me as I am. Let me live boldly, gratefully rejoicing in your unfailing presence.

As much as I wish it weren't so, I sometimes live as though "whoever has the most toys at the end wins." I hoard or crave this or that, and I value worldly possessions. Meister Eckhart once said, "Do what you would do if you felt most secure." Let me celebrate my security today, O God. Give me grace to remember that I live not by bread alone but by every word that comes from you. Let me bury my treasure in your heart alone.

(Morning)
Release me from my clinging ways. At every opportunity, guide me to give rather than to get. Let me be your gift to those whom I meet today.
(Prayers of Intercession)

(Evening)
Where I cling tightly to lesser things, free my grip. Let me live in the light of your promises rather than in the prison of my fears.
(Prayers of Intercession)

May I live generously today, confident in your promises.

(Morning)
Turn me back toward you today with your never-failing promises. Amen.

(Evening)
As day closes and light fades, remind me that my treasure and my heart belong to you. Amen.

SATURDAY, AUGUST 8
(Read Luke 12:32–40)

(Morning)
O Holy One, as I embark on this day, remind me that everything I do or say makes a difference. Let me live not casually but passionately and intensely.

(Evening)
O Holy One, guide me in my living to an alertness that expects to encounter you at every moment. Keep me from being bored and uninvolved. Make me ready.

How easily I fall into ruts, O God. I forget that my life is brief, that you have made each moment holy, and that you have charged me to pay attention. Let me not pretend that what I do has no meaning or that my ethical shortcuts will be greeted with impunity. Remind me that my slightest action is charged with meaning. Make me ready to convey your love in all I do today.

(Morning)
As I live through this day, O God, make me attentive to you
in everything that happens.
(Prayers of Intercession)

(Evening)
Let me be as alert for you, O God, as I would be for a thief
prowling outside my door.
(Prayers of Intercession)

May everything I do be attentive to you, O Holy One.

(Morning)
I promise today to look for you, and to find you, again and again and again. Amen.

(Evening)
Make me vigilant in my faith, O God, that I might not miss you when you come. Amen.

SUNDAY, AUGUST 9

(Read Hebrews 11:1–3, 8–16; Isaiah 1:1, 10–20; Psalm 50:1–8, 22–23; Luke 12:32–40)

(Morning)
O God, how awesome you are. How great the faith you offer me.
I cannot help but be intimidated yet enthralled and
nourished by the challenge you put before me.

(Evening)
O God, I have not lived up to your hopes for me today. But I trust that you
forgive me and that you will start me again fresh tomorrow.

You ask much of me, O Holy One, that I live justly and righteously, that I hold my neighbor's welfare as dear as my own, and that I stop worrying about my own security. You ask that I give with abandon. It is hard, O God. I find myself coming up short. So remind me again of your promises: that you bless and keep me and shine forth in my life, and make me thankful.

(Morning)
I give thanks this day for all that is special in my life, and I remember that all of
it comes from you.
(Prayers of Intercession)

(Evening)
Let me live this day not by sight but by trusting in you. Let me relinquish my
hold on false treasures and cling tightly to you.
(Prayers of Intercession)

Let me live this day, and always, by the light of your promise.

(Morning)	(Evening)
Though aware of my failings today, O God, let me not be weighed down by them. Let me rejoice in all that you have given me. Amen.	Hear me as I recite my blessings. Reassure me again of the certainty of your grace. Amen.

MONDAY, AUGUST 10
(Read Luke 12:49–56)

(Morning)
All-wise God, discerner of my thoughts, help me to remain calm and
trust you to guide me through life's difficult lessons today.
I want to follow your instructions.

(Evening)
All-wise God and patient Friend, my heart is filled with praise to you as this day
draws to a close. Without a doubt, I experienced your hand holding mine as I
faced some difficult situations. Thank you for taking me through each new
learning experience.

God, sometimes there are obvious divisions and difficulties among families and friends which feel like the way of the cross. I do not always accept
the fact that you are refining my life at these times. Following you today
has shown me the need for constant cleansing in many areas of my life.
Keep your consuming fire alive in me, so that I will accept your discipline
for my life.

(Morning)
Patient Teacher, let my agenda and work be filled with your priorities in both
word and deed.
(Prayers of Intercession)

(Evening)
Thank you for your presence in every trying situation today. As the evening
shadows fall, be with others who walk this path of difficult lessons.
(Prayers of Intercession)

**I will look for good in all of life's experiences
instead of complaining about the things that seem wrong.**

(Morning)
I choose to accept every challenge as
a new learning experience. Amen.

(Evening)
Holy One, into your hands I commit all
my problems, and into your arms I
climb for a night of sweet rest. Amen.

TUESDAY, AUGUST 11
(Read Jeremiah 23:23–29)

(Morning)
Creator of dreams, Revealer of thoughts, whatever today brings,
my desire is to hear and accept the truth of your Word. Help me not to seek an
easy way out of responsibilities but to face each task with courage.

(Evening)
Creator of dreams and Purifier of even my secret thoughts, thank you for
helping me face the truth about myself and the sources on which I rely.
Forgive my foolishness for not accepting your full counsel in all I did today.

God, sometimes it seems difficult to separate the real truth from the
well-constructed lies that we constantly face. Grace me with the ears of a
true prophet who will always faithfully speak your Word without fear of
the consequences. There is no comparison of your Word to the empty lies
of the arrogant.

(Morning)
Voice of Truth, your insistent whispers have awakened me to a new dawn.
Make me ready to look for you as I abandon empty promises.
Be with all of us today in our pursuit of your truth.
(Prayers of Intercession)

(Evening)
Dear Friend, it was you who helped me make the right decisions
in life today. Thank you for staying with me all day long,
even when I struggled against your truth.
(Prayers of Intercession)

**Let the power and truth of your Word be revealed
to all people who trust you.**

(Morning)
This day I endeavor to seek for truth in
all people and all things. Amen.

(Evening)
Comforter, let my rest be sweet and
my dreams pure. Amen.

WEDNESDAY, AUGUST 12
(Read Isaiah 5:1–7)

(Morning)
Beloved Companion, the thought of sharing this new day with you creates ideas
of celebrations. My heart is open to receive and share the gifts and graces you
will give, the ones I have not yet imagined.

(Evening)
Beloved Companion, what a day of unexpected surprises in the smiles and
support of others, as well as those who chose to complain and cause problems.
Your provisions were more than adequate for me today. Thank you for opening
my eyes to see beyond my limited imagination.

Generous One, you provide balance in beauty and judgment. We are so
accustomed to receiving without being accountable for sharing our gifts
with others. Teach us to celebrate the periods of plenty in our lives and also
to give thanks during the unproductive seasons.

(Morning)
Today open my eyes to see your love in the things of beauty
as well as the unpleasant events.
(Prayers of Intercession)

(Evening)
It has been a wonderful day with you, Jesus. Keep reminding me that life
consists of fruitful seasons as well as times of pruning.
(Prayers of Intercession)

God, teach me to celebrate your gifts in all the seasons of life.

(Morning)	(Evening)
Gardener of my soul, now I am open to your planting and pruning. Amen.	Beloved, as the sun closes another day, continue your pruning even in my sleep. Amen.

THURSDAY, AUGUST 13
(Read Hebrews 11:29–12:2)

(Morning)
O Faithful Friend, as my eyes open to greet a new day, I am determined to continue working toward those goals that appear to be beyond my grasp. My confidence is in your promises to me and not only in what I see at this moment.

(Evening)
O Faithful Friend, looking back on what you have helped me to accomplish, my heart swells into a song of thanksgiving. Pardon my lack of faith in thinking that you would abandon me during the difficult moments.

My God, I join the writer of Hebrews in recalling the names and fine examples of ancestors who have preceded me in life's race. They persevered to the end, so I will not stop. With my confidence in Jesus, I must harness my strength and stay focused on the distant finish line. Those things that have held me back are released—yes, thrown away. I must continue with patience toward my goal.

(Morning)
Good morning, God. Ah, it's a new day! I am ready to return to life's race.
Others before me completed the course. I can do it, too.
(Prayers of Intercession)

(Evening)
Awesome God! Thank you for your everlasting arms,
which supported me and kept me steady as I forged ahead in the race.
Forgive my pride in thinking I could do it by myself.
(Prayers of Intercession)

Faithful Companion, keep my feet on the path and my eyes on the goal.

(Morning)
Give me faith that is equal to the race.
Amen.

(Evening)
Evening time has brought renewal and restoration. Spirit of quietness, bring rest. Amen.

FRIDAY, AUGUST 14
(Read Psalms 80:1–2)

(Morning)
Gentle Shepherd, my first waking thoughts are toward you.
Through the light of your Word, let me really see you for who you are,
as you sit on the throne of my heart.

(Evening)
Gentle Shepherd, you are still high and lifted up above all life's circumstances.
Forgive the many times I focused on problems and not your presence.

O beautiful Spirit, elevate my thoughts high above the present confusion and noise. Show me your mighty hand working for my deliverance. Lead me, restore me, help me see your way. Save your very own. I am the creation of your hands.

(Morning)
My soul longs for your protection, Eternal Helper.
Hide me in your secret place.
(Prayers of Intercession)

(Evening)
My eyes are raised toward your throne,
the place where I always have found help.
(Prayers of Intercession)

**Thank you for the answers that come today
and at unexpected times in days gone by.**

(Morning)
Grace me with your compassion and
love in the midst of life's struggles.
Amen.

(Evening)
Your eyes are on the sparrows. Surely
you are watching me under the canopy
of night. Amen.

SATURDAY, AUGUST 15
(Read Psalm 80:8–19)

(Morning)
Strong Deliverer, as dawn scatters the shadows of night,
my cry for help is to you alone.
How long must I try to explain to others what they cannot see or feel?

(Evening)
Strong Deliverer, like a loving parent you heard my cry and came to rescue me.
I repent from the sins of unbelief and impatience.

In times like these, I confess that my faith is weak. Increase my confidence as you transform my worries into your plans for my life. Guide me, Jehovah, like the shepherds of old did their sheep. Take me to a place of safety from these present threatening dangers.

(Morning)
God, lead us to a place of safety, a refuge from harm's way.
(Prayers of Intercession)

(Evening)
You have been our strong tower and anchor in these turbulent times. Calm our fears and wipe our weeping eyes.
(Prayers of Intercession)

**Grant peace and comfort to all your children facing difficulties
in their lives today.**

(Morning)
I know you will be with us in places of danger and uncertainties. Let your presence shine upon us today. Amen.

(Evening)
In your presence we are always safe, even when night falls. Amen.

SUNDAY, AUGUST 16
(Read Psalm 82)

(Morning)
Righteous Judge, I stand up with the rest of the world as you open heaven's
court. Let your counsel and power be known to the wicked.
You alone rule the whole earth.

(Evening)
Righteous Judge, you cleared away the shadows and let in the light, and what
was wrong you set right. Your righteous judgment has satisfied my quest for
justice. Save us from the evil of our arrogant ways.

Wonderful Counselor, you were not silent when my enemies spoke against
me. I was weary of unnecessary argument, then you stood up and spoke in
my defense. Your Word is forever settled in heaven, and nothing more can
be added to your righteous judgment. All wisdom belongs to you!

(Morning)
Bring to shame the evil counsel that has been planned against
the innocent this day.
(Prayers of Intercession)

(Evening)
It has been a good day; you have judged righteously and rescued the helpless
from their oppressors. Forgive my lack of courage for not standing up and
speaking on behalf of the poor and oppressed when there was opportunity.
(Prayers of Intercession)

Hear the cry of the oppressed, Loving Protector. Grant their petitions.

(Morning)
Eternal One, everything begins and
ends with you; even power and glory
are yours. Amen.

(Evening)
In quietness I lie down to sleep. I am
safe because the whole world is in
your hands. Amen.

MONDAY, AUGUST 17
(Read Psalm 103:1–12)

(Morning)
Creator God, I know that storms come in life and that the rain of trial and temptation will fall, even on me. But as I meet the new day, I do so with great faith that you will walk with me, not letting me drown in the midst of the storm.

(Evening)
Creator God, thank you for being with me today. No matter where I went, you were there and I felt strong.

Creator God, sometimes I feel as though I am in the midst of a quiet storm. Nevertheless, I know that I must hold on because help is on the way. God, when you forgive my iniquities, I am forgiven. When you heal me from all my diseases and transgressions, I am healed. When you redeem me from the pit of problems, I am crowned with love and mercy. No matter what storm is raging in my life, you forgive me. Your anger will cease and you will be merciful to me. Thank you for calming the quiet storms.

(Morning)
O God, help me to start this new and wonderful day, assured that if I hold my peace and let you fight the battle, you will say to my storms, "Peace, be still!"
(Prayers of Intercession)

(Evening)
Loving God, thank you for being with me today. Forgive me if I, at any time today, doubted your ability to protect me from the storm. Let me sleep the sleep of renewal in you.
(Prayers of Intercession)

Thank you for your work of vindication and justice for all.

(Morning)
I pledge to develop a great faith in you and in your mighty power. Amen.

(Evening)
O God, let me awaken tomorrow with a strong conviction to meet whatever and whomever knowing that you are with me and in me. Amen.

TUESDAY, AUGUST 18
(Read Psalm 103:13–22)

(Morning)
O God, I need you today more than I ever have needed you. I come to you because there are situations in my life that are raging. I need strength for this day, and I know that you are the only one who can make me strong. Thank you, God, for being God all by yourself.

(Evening)
O God, thank you for always reminding me that you are in charge of everyone and everything and that you are in complete control. I rest easier because your throne is everlasting.

God, as a child I would exclaim, "Just wait until I become an adult, then I will be in charge!" However, one of the most interesting things about being an adult is that when storms rage I often wish I could run to my parents for protection and comfort. But while I cannot run to my parents, you are the Great Parent who always has compassion for me. You know me and love me. God, help me always to remember that I can run to you for shelter from the storm.

(Morning)
O God, may I start this new day with the blessed assurance of knowing that if I need to run to you for comfort, you will be there.
(Prayers of Intercession)

(Evening)
Thank you, God, for continuing to prove yourself to me. Every time I get weak, you are there to comfort me. Every time I doubt your love, your love lifts me. Let me sleep assured that you will never leave me or forsake me.
(Prayers of Intercession)

Thank you for your angels who watch over me. Bless God, O my soul.

(Morning)
I pledge to witness to the world your love for me, as a parent loves a child. Amen.

(Evening)
O God, let me awaken tomorrow assured that while I am frail like the flowers and the grass, you make me strong. Amen.

WEDNESDAY, AUGUST 19
(Read Jeremiah 1:4–10)

(Morning)
O God, you have richly blessed me. You have seen me through many storms, but today I face a problem that I am not sure I'm strong enough or seasoned enough to handle. Be my guide today.

(Evening)
O God, thank you for calming my fears of inadequacy. I did not believe that I would be able to meet the challenge, but you are the one who promoted me and set me in such a high place. I should have known that you would not lift me up just to let me down.

God, I can remember the first time I was in charge of something, and while at first all was going well, problems developed. I felt that I was not good enough to meet the challenge. But then I remembered that I was chosen by you for such a time as this. What you did for me yesterday, you will do again for me today. God, thank you for reminding me that you are with me to deliver me.

(Morning)
O God, touch my mouth with your hand of guidance and wisdom, so that your words and will might be spoken through me.
(Prayers of Intercession)

(Evening)
Thank you, God, for speaking to me and through me today. I know that I must constantly submit my will to yours so that you might be glorified through me. Grant me a rest that will not only refresh me but encourage me to serve you even more.
(Prayers of Intercession)

**Thank you for choosing me to build and to plant.
Thank you for your divine guidance.**

(Morning)
I pledge today to do the very best I can for others and to use wisely the gifts that you have given me. Amen.

(Evening)
O God, let me awaken tomorrow determined to make a difference where I live, so that your light will shine from me. Amen.

THURSDAY, AUGUST 20
(Read Isaiah 58:9b–14)

(Morning)
O God, I continue holding on in the midst of this storm in my life.
Help me to move away from my problems,
so that I might minister to someone else who is in greater need.
Help me to minister to others even in the midst of my pain.

(Evening)
O God, thank you for helping me to move away from my problem and help
another find joy and meaning in life. I am encouraged that, despite my state of
affairs, I am still worthy to be used by you to help others repair what the storms
in their lives have wrecked.

God, there have been times when I have felt totally immobilized. All was
very bleak. But during those times, a knock on the door or a call on the
telephone broke through my despair. It was a cry for help from someone
else. I disregarded my troubles and went to assist another. God, you remind
me that if I make myself available to others, you will guide me and make
me strong. You will enable me to endure and overcome.

(Morning)
God, help me to be determined to get the most out of my worship experience
this week at church.
(Prayers of Intercession)

(Evening)
Thank you, God, for helping me take my mind off of my troubles by giving me
the opportunity to serve others in their hour of need. As I go to sleep tonight,
anoint me so I am able to discern when another is in need.
(Prayers of Intercession)

**Thank you, God, for your gift of worship. I will strive ever to delight in you
and your glory. O God, repair the breaches in my life.**

(Morning)	(Evening)
Today, I pledge to be open to your Spirit, so that if you send someone to me to serve, I will do so with gladness. Amen.	O God, should I awaken tomorrow, give me the yearning to worship you more and more. Help me to give you the honor and glory tomorrow. Amen.

FRIDAY, AUGUST 21
(Read Psalm 71:1–6)

(Morning)
O God, I'm stepping out on your promise of deliverance. Today I leave my
home trusting in you, because I know that if I run into trouble,
you will be there to protect me.

(Evening)
O God, thank you for looking out for me today. When I had to take time out and
regroup, you made it possible for me to take shelter in you. I regained my
balance, despite the storm winds blowing upon me. You became for me a rock
of refuge. I survived the day and was victorious.

Storms in life come, and storms in life go. But you, O God, remain constant during the time of trauma and trial. Even from our birth, we have depended upon you. God, you delivered us at birth, and you will continue to deliver us from the storms in our lives.

(Morning)
O God, as I face a new day, deliver me from anyone or anything
desiring to do me harm. Be my fortress and my rescue from the storm.
Give me the strength to meet this day.
(Prayers of Intercession)

(Evening)
Thank you, God. I was not sure how the day would turn out, but you let me lean
upon you. In you I placed my trust, and because of this I was delivered.
As I leaned upon you today, let me sleep in you tonight and
rest assured that you are with me.
(Prayers of Intercession)

Thank you, God, for protecting me today. My praise is continually of you.

(Morning)	(Evening)
I pledge today to put my trust in you. Be my strength and my guide; let me ever lean on you. Amen.	O God, as I prepare to retire for the night, thank you for protecting me. Keep me as I sleep and encourage me to do better tomorrow. Amen.

SATURDAY, AUGUST 22
(Read Hebrews 12:18–29)

(Morning)
O God, I realize that without you I would be lost. Thank you for your Child, Jesus Christ. In Jesus I find my direction and am coming to know my purpose in life. In Jesus I am steady and focused.

(Evening)
O God, thank you for your precious grace. Without your grace I could not have accomplished all that I did today. I embrace you and look forward to one day being with you in your heavenly realm.

God, sometimes in this life I am called upon to sacrifice something of great importance to me. Your Child Jesus, through the shedding of his blood, brought into being a new covenant between you and humankind. Because of Jesus' sacrifice, I have the opportunity for eternal life. Jesus experienced a storm that cost his life. But because Jesus sacrificed his life, I gained mine. When I sacrifice myself, I actually gain more than I have lost.

(Morning)
Dear God, if I am faced with the opportunity to make a sacrifice for someone else, help me to do so cheerfully so that my gift will be from my heart.
(Prayers of Intercession)

(Evening)
O God, today you called upon me to make a sacrifice. Thank you for helping me work through my difficulty in making it. Help me to rest in you and learn from you, so that I might better serve and love you.
(Prayers of Intercession)

God, you are worthy, and your realm is forever. Let me be worthy of it. In you I stand strong and firm, no matter what is asked of me.

(Morning)
Jesus, I thank you for your sacrifice. Let me hear your voice today. Amen.

(Evening)
Now God, as I lie down to sleep, help me to be worthy of your promise. I will trust in you to face tomorrow. Amen.

SUNDAY, AUGUST 23
(Read Luke 13:10–17)

(Morning)
O God, I was in the midst of a terrible storm last week. My life was in trouble,
and I sought you. You heard my cry. I trusted in you, and you healed me. I
awaken to stand tall and strong again because of you.

(Evening)
O God, thank you for your concern. I rest tonight assured that because I claim
Jesus as my Sovereign Savior, no matter what might happen, you will deliver
me.

God, your work cannot be confined to one specific time or place. My mission in life is to daily serve you. There will be times when I must stop what I am doing because there is a greater demand placed on me. I cannot be worried when what I am called to do appears to some to be strange or different. I cannot let ceremony get in the way of healing. However, I must be Spirit-led. When I operate under your power, my service becomes anointed and healing occurs.

(Morning)
Dear God, give me the ability today to discern when you need me to
do something for another. Help me to place in proper perspective
what I should do and when I should do it.
(Prayers of Intercession)

(Evening)
Thank you, God, when you made an opportunity for me to assist someone today
in their healing. As I go to sleep, be with me. Should I awake to see the morning
sun, help me to be a blessing to someone else.
(Prayers of Intercession)

**God, you are my healer, my sustainer, and my life. I submit my dreams to
you. Never cease from calming the storms in my life.**

(Morning)
Jesus, you have been my salvation
from the beginning of my life. Help me
to do good. Amen.

(Evening)
O God, as another day ends, thank
you for being with me. Even when I
fell short, you were still there. Amen.

MONDAY, AUGUST 24
(Read Psalm 112)

(Morning)
Spirit of Water, Spirit of Life, the powerful steadfastness of your streams,
mighty rivers, and great oceans, cut through rock and land, cleanse me, refresh
me, and quench my thirst for justice. Awaken me.

(Evening)
Spirit of Water, Spirit of Life, Spirit in motion, of waves, ripples,
swirls, and seasons, always changing. May I learn to appreciate
the constancy of your change.

God, when we are called to live the life of the righteous, we are called into
living a life that may be risky, dangerous, challenging, and contrary to the
norms of society. Facing strong winds and rushing currents, we are promised courage and steadfastness that will not falter. You may not promise us
an easy or momentary victory, but instead, the fearlessness and firmness to
be true to our heart's belief.

(Morning)
Forgive me, God, for when I have not stood up for justice,
for when I have doubted that you would give me the boldness and
strength of heart to proclaim a new vision.
(Prayers of Intercession)

(Evening)
May I remember that my strength does not come from my will, but yours,
O God, and from the courage of those who stood for justice before me.
May I take a moment to remember those whose legacy,
spirit, and tradition of righteousness and justice I carry.
(Prayers of Intercession)

Grant me a firm heart to hear your call.

(Morning)
As I go out into the world today, give
me the steadfastness of the mighty
rivers, the fearlessness of the great
oceans, and the power of all the
earth's waters behind me. Amen.

(Evening)
Thank you for this day, blessed with
water that is life—that embraces me
and reminds me of your faithfulness.
Amen.

TUESDAY, AUGUST 25
(Read Jeremiah 2:4–13)

(Morning)
Spirit of truth, awaken me to truth, so I am not blinded by the distractions of daily life. Help me to notice the richness and flavor of each moment, the strains, stretches, pulls, tensions, emotions. The roundness of truth.

(Evening)
Spirit of truth, open me to your presence, your ever-presence in the multitude of the rainbow, the sea of faces, and the grassy field.

My two-year stay in Brazil taught me to appreciate your presence, God, in the everyday language of the *favelados,* or poor people. "Thank God for this . . ." "God willing that . . ." Not only were you present in their language, but they had a keen awareness that without you, very little, including their own survival, would be possible. Upon returning to the United States, I missed hearing your name in a heartfelt way in everyday language. It is as if people here do not have to count so hard on you. It is as if we forget about you, or rather hide you in the church, removed from everyday life, and go on digging for living water in "cracked cisterns."

(Morning)
Forgive me, O God, for my false idols, my false sources of power, image, and security. I know where living water lies. I know the true sources of peace. Keep me committed to what truly matters.
(Prayers of Intercession)

(Evening)
Forgive me where I have failed and become distracted from my path. Keep me committed to what truly matters.
(Prayers of Intercession)

Because you are the living water, I pray.
(Pray the Prayer of Our Savior.)

(Morning)
Grant me this day open eyes, a mindful heart, an acute spirit, and faithfulness to remain authentic to our call to wisdom and love. Amen.

(Evening)
Thank you for your presence this day. Keep me looking in the "right" places for authentic sources of truth and connection. Amen.

WEDNESDAY, AUGUST 26
(Read Hebrews 13:1–6)

(Morning)
God of understanding, wide expanse, and that which encompasses
all truth and beauty, open my mind and my heart to listen.
Open my soul to the gifts of the universe.

(Evening)
God of understanding, who has walked by my side, comfort any hurts and
wounds that lead my soul to close, to distrust and fear. Remind me of the gifts
of the universe, the gift of life, and the miracle of being.

We are called to have mutual love, true solidarity, true compassion, Creator God. Perhaps we have felt this close to someone, maybe a child, parent, or loved one. But what about someone in prison? Or someone dying of AIDS? The call to "feel with others," particularly those who are in pain, imprisoned, and tortured, is a radically frightening challenge. Why would we want to seek feeling with those in pain? We are called to solidarity because our own salvation lies in seeing the truth, exposing the invisible, recognizing the pain, and "feeling with" those who are suffering. Solidarity and compassion expand our understanding of truth, and your truth will set us free.

(Morning)
Forgive me when fear closes my heart and when fear turns me toward separation
and hate. Give me the courage to feel vulnerable, and open me to new growth.
(Prayers of Intercession)

(Evening)
Forgive us for the callousness of the world which divides and separates us.
(Prayers of Intercession)

In truth and understanding, I pray.
(Pray the Prayer of Our Savior.)

(Morning)
I honor the oneness of all beings, the
hope in solidarity, and the power of
change and song. Amen.

(Evening)
May I have understanding and compassion which knows no end. Amen.

THURSDAY, AUGUST 27
(Read Luke 14:1, 7–11)

(Morning)
Creator Spirit, I awaken, touched by light, greeted by sound and movement and color of all creatures and creation. Open me this day to the wonder into which I was born. Center me into the fullness of being.

(Evening)
Creator Spirit, may I enter into awareness of your presence and of grace in my life and in this world today.

Creator God, what is a spirit of true humility—not the false humility that seeks praise, but the humility that truly honors and is awed at the wisdom and unique gifts of others? What does it mean to be humble in means and humble in truth? Where does the spirit of humility reside within me? What gets in the way of a humble spirit?

(Morning)
O God, grant me the openness to truth—all truth,
that is indeed bigger than all of us. Grant me humility to hear your wisdom and seek you in varied faces and places. May I gain the fruits of all of your creation and not stumble on my own ego.
(Prayers of Intercession)

(Evening)
God, forgive me when my heart is not humble. Remind me of the unexpected moments of truth. Keep me open to the wisdom and beauty around me.
(Prayers of Intercession)

With an open spirit, I pray.
(Pray the Prayer of Our Savior.)

(Morning)
May I go with an open heart throughout this day, with the emptiness of grace, a spirit of humility and equity, honoring all life, wisdom, and truth.
Amen.

(Evening)
Grant me rest, blessed by your presence, surrounded by all in which you are manifest. Amen.

FRIDAY, AUGUST 28
(Read Luke 14:12–14)

(Morning)
O Great Spirit, who connects me with *all* things and weaves all life into an intricate web of wholeness, be with me today as I seek to do your will.

(Evening)
O Great Spirit, weaver and shaper of color and fiber, line and pattern, remind me of your beauty and power, so I may better know you and myself.

A banquet gives an image of abundance and festivity: the finest foods and drink, warmth and hospitality; the very best for a special occasion and special guests. In the northeastern part of Brazil, there was a campaign called *"portas abertas"* ("open doors") which sought to address problems of hunger and bridge human relationships. Families posted *"portas abertas"* signs on their houses, which meant their doors were open to anyone to join their family for a meal. God, this is how the teachings say we are to treat the stranger, the newcomer, the migrant, the shunned, the outcast of society. The banquet allows us to see our sameness in your eyes, dear God.

(Morning)
God, forgive me for the places in my life where there is separation and disconnectedness from you and all that you have created. May I be conscious of the walls that keep me apart from others and seek ways for our connectedness.
(Prayers of Intercession)

(Evening)
God, who is weaver, potter, gardener, painter of the fields, skies, and waters, thank you for your beauty. Forgive me when I did not notice. Thank you for your ever-present faithfulness.
(Prayers of Intercession)

Humbly I pray.
(Pray the Prayer of Our Savior.)

(Morning)
Gather me as I reflect the profound ways my life is connected to all life. Give me the courage to cross boundaries and open doors. Amen.

(Evening)
Rest me. Grant me peace and dreams that go beyond all boundaries. Amen.

SATURDAY, AUGUST 29
(Read Psalm 81)

(Morning)
Giver of breath, breathe life and Spirit into me, fill me with love, so that in song
and motion, I may embody joy.

(Evening)
Giver of breath, I gather here collecting every moment of the passing day,
of stress, worry, tension, disappointment, joy, and elation.
Gather me in mindful reflection.

How hard it is sometimes to choose the way of life, your way, Creator God,
the way of love. How much easier it is sometimes to fall into patterns of
fear, doubt, suspicion, blame, separation, and hopelessness. How easy it is
to forget and disregard the divine beauty and light within ourselves and in
the "other." Fill us with divine wonder. May I turn away from fear, so that
I may taste the abundant life.

(Morning)
Forgive me my moments of separation, hopelessness, and cynicism.
Free me, O God, from the burden of distrust and fear. Fill me with your light.
(Prayers of Intercession)

(Evening)
God of grace, life, and abundance, forgive me when I have failed myself and my
sisters and brothers around me.
(Prayers of Intercession)

Filled with your Spirit, I pray.
(Pray the Prayer of Our Savior.)

(Morning)
This day, as I walk on this earth, whose
beauty surrounds me, may your love
move through me. Amen.

(Evening)
Thank you, God, for today's blessing
and grace. May I enter into tomorrow
remembering all that has been given
to me. Amen.

SUNDAY, AUGUST 30
(Read Hebrews 13:15–16)

(Morning)
Creator God, remind me of the morning water, the fresh ocean,
the placid lake, the quiet spring, the morning dew, the drops of rain.
Rain upon me, river of living water.

(Evening)
Creator God, take me to the place of ever-flowing waters, the fountain and
source within me, the bubbling brook, the steady stream, the constant sea where
body and soul embrace.

"Do not neglect to share what you have." Simple words and teachings, yet
words that we easily stumble over. God, how do we share what we have? I
best learned the meaning of these teachings from a neighbor in the poorest
of communities in the northeast of Brazil. Dona Nené woke up every morning not knowing how she was going to feed her seven children. She shared
even the tiniest bit of food when neighbors asked for help. It was hard for
me to believe that the tiniest piece of salty pork would again get divided.
How do we challenge ourselves to share what we have—freely?

(Morning)
Forgive me, Mother Earth, when I have taken and not given back; when I have
accumulated and not shared; when I have not recognized that all is yours.
(Prayers of Intercession)

(Evening)
Forgive me for the moments today when I have failed to remember the gifts of
the earth and the bounty that is only ours to share. Forgive me when I have
drawn human lines of division and separation.
(Prayers of Intercession)

Blessed by your grace and mercy, I pray.
(Pray the Prayer of Our Savior.)

(Morning)
Bless us throughout this day. Touch us
with the abundance of creation. Let
fountains come forth. Amen.

(Evening)
Nourish me this night with the wonders of the making of the rain, the
feeding of the earth, and the peace of
all peoples. Amen.

MONDAY, AUGUST 31
(Read Deuteronomy 30:15–20)

(Morning)
God, enable me to make the right choice. Guide me in your ways
so that I may choose life over death. If I stumble and fall,
pick me up and hold me in your loving embrace.

(Evening)
God, thank you for giving me the power of choice, so that I may choose life, not
death; choose love, not hate. Keep me as I keep you, close to my heart.

Every day I am faced with an abundance of choices. These choices affect
my life, as well as the lives of others. Continue to create in me a clean
heart, O God, so that the choices I make lead to life.

(Morning)
As I step out into the world today, I will make good use
of the gift of choice you have given me.
(Prayers of Intercession)

(Evening)
Everlasting and omnipotent God, I have felt your presence today. You enabled
me to choose life. For this, I am so thankful. Guide me through the dream
world, so that I may return to you anew.
(Prayers of Intercession)

I truly do possess the power of choice. Thank you, God.

(Morning)
I am responsible for the choices I make
in life. Therefore, I will make choices
that support and enable life. Amen.

(Evening)
I will search for you in my dreams, O
God. I know that your omnipotence
will enable me to choose life, even
while I sleep. Amen.

TUESDAY, SEPTEMBER 1
(Read Psalm 139:1–6)

(Morning)
O God, as I watch the little pearl drops of dew in the morning sun, myriad little rainbows appear. I am reminded of your covenant with humankind.

(Evening)
O God, your name should be "Awesome." For when I think of you I stand in awe. Thank you for bringing me to this place.

I have no desire to walk on hot coals; neither do I have a desire to stretch my body upon a bed of nails. Just knowing that you love me, O God, is good enough for me. What a wonderful thing your love is! I sifted through the many layers of self to experience the joy of finding you there. You are the essence of my being.

(Morning)
I am in awe of your magnificence, Great Spirit!
(Prayers of Intercession)

(Evening)
Wonderful One! Everlasting and ever-present God, whose great Spirit is all-knowing, thank you for granting me another day to experience your creation.
(Prayers of Intercession)

Thank you for instilling in me the willpower to attain higher heights.

(Morning)
I will continue to be amazed and awestruck by your perfect knowledge.
Amen.

(Evening)
I will try to attain higher heights, knowing that such knowledge and heights are not easily attained. But it is comforting to know that you know me.
Amen.

WEDNESDAY, SEPTEMBER 2
(Read Jeremiah 18:1–11)

(Morning)
God of all creation, whose power is fathomless,
you are indeed the most skillful potter! Keep bringing me to the place
where I hear your words. Your creation is a marvelous work of art.

(Evening)
God of all creation, thank you for reminding me I am but a piece of clay
on your potter's wheel. Shape me to your liking.

It has been said that in art there are no mistakes. As I look around me at
your work of art, I can attest to this truth. Not only are you the potter who
takes me to your potter's wheel, you are also the painter who paints the
sunshine in my sky. Enable us, O God, to be potters and painters. Help us
to shape our lives in a way that is pleasing to you.

(Morning)
As I journey into this day, I will be open to the many places and spaces
where I may hear your Word.
(Prayers of Intercession)

(Evening)
O God, thank you for this day. Your Word came to me as I watched the children
play. So much joy, hope, and laughter. Thank you for allowing me to be an
apprentice potter in their lives, for you are their most skillful potter.
(Prayers of Intercession)

You are the changer, O God, and I am the changed.

(Morning)
I commit myself to your potter's wheel,
O God. Amen.

(Evening)
When tomorrow comes, continue to
work on me, O God, so that I may be
a vessel for your goodness. Amen.

THURSDAY, SEPTEMBER 3
(Read Psalm 139:13–18)

(Morning)
Great Spirit, whose breath I first breathed as an infant,
your works are indeed wonderful! And your thoughts are deeper than still
waters. Enable me to be more present to my body, mind, spirit,
so that I may become more balanced and whole.

(Evening)
Great Spirit, lead me to the still waters,
so I may drink of your life-sustaining thoughts.

Modern science enables us to see, in living color, just what our inner parts look like. While the psalmist would surely be mesmerized by the microcameras that can gain access to our inward parts, the wisdom the psalmist brings to us remains timeless: "I praise you, for I am fearfully and wonderfully made." Thank you, Great Spirit, for the breath of life.

(Morning)
I want to begin this day by acknowledging the intricate details of my body,
mind, and spirit, which you have formed into one body, mind, spirit.
(Prayers of Intercession)

(Evening)
You have brought me through one more day, O God.
Walk with me through the dream world.
(Prayers of Intercession)

**Thank you for creating the human family with such intricate details,
so well planned. I sing with the psalmist,
"How weighty to me are your thoughts, O God!"**

(Morning)
I will respect my body, which you
have made wonderful. Amen.

(Evening)
May I awake with a new readiness to
be all that you have created me to be.
Amen.

FRIDAY, SEPTEMBER 4
(Read Philemon 1–21)

(Morning)
Most compassionate and loving God, teach me the "ways of the heart."
Enable me to use the tools of love, not force.
You have shown me that through the eyes of love, all things are possible.
Thank you, O God, for another day to practice love.

(Evening)
Most compassionate and loving God, you are my everything. Fill me with
compassion for the world until my cup runs over. Enable me to quench the thirst
of the thirsty, with your ever-flowing love.

God, the letter Paul wrote to Philemon should be of keen interest to all
Christians. It reminds us of how Christians ought to be. Jesus teaches us in
Mark 10:42–44, "You know that among the Gentiles, those whom they recognize as their rulers lord it over them, and their great ones are tyrants over
them. But it is not so among you; but whoever wishes to be great among
you must be your servant, and whoever wishes to be first among you must
be slave of all." As Dr. Martin Luther King Jr. said, "We all can be great,
because we all can serve." Help me, O God, to keep my self-importance in
balance.

(Morning)
O loving God, help me to become a better servant to your people.
Allow me to sow seeds of love in your garden of creation.
(Prayers of Intercession)

(Evening)
O God of my salvation, strengthen me, so that I may be impeccable in the
struggle for a more just world order.
(Prayers of Intercession)

Enable me to forgive those who have wronged me, O God.

(Morning)
I will commit myself to being a faithful
servant. Your will be done, not mine.
Amen.

(Evening)
As I surrender to sleep, O God,
continue to instruct me in your ways.
Enable me to break down the barriers
that keep me from being a loving and
forgiving human being. Thank you,
God. Amen.

SATURDAY, SEPTEMBER 5
(Read Psalm 1)

(Morning)
Everlasting and loving God, I can feel you this morning.
Enable me to face this day with a new determination,
a determination to do what is pleasing in your sight.

(Evening)
Everlasting and loving God, everything about you is good.
There is no injustice in your law. Let me not stand with the wicked,
for there is no justice in the ways of the wicked.

Thank you, God, for being my shepherd. When the wicked come to devour me, you will protect me. The wicked cannot claim me. I belong to you, O God. I will profess my faith in you, God Almighty, and send the wicked running for cover. I will delight in the way of the righteous, so that I may choose life. You are the life.

(Morning)
Loving God, lead me to your will, so that I may quench my thirst
with your living water. Grant me clarity,
so that I may recognize the wicked in all their disguises.
(Prayers of Intercession)

(Evening)
"And do not bring us to the time of trial, but rescue us from the evil one."
(Prayers of Intercession)

For the sake of righteousness, use me as you will, God.

(Morning)	(Evening)
Enable me to be discerning, for the ways of the wicked are devious and misleading. I will rejoice in your justice. Amen.	As sleep beckons me, O God, I am thankful for your guidance. Guide me through the dream world to that place by the streams of water where the righteous are planted. Amen.

SUNDAY, SEPTEMBER 6
(Read Luke 14:25–33)

(Morning)
God of all creation, you are the Alpha and the Omega. Strip me of all that is superficial in my life. And when my ears become dull from the noises of this world, whisper into them, so that I may listen and await your instruction.

(Evening)
God of all creation, help me as I seek ways to rid my life of the superfluous. Take my life, for only you can restore the saltiness.

Asleep or awake, the body rests, but not the mind. And God, why does the mind not rest? It is our unwillingness to let go. Seek the power of silence, and the mind will rest. By letting go, we begin to trust in the natural order of your creation. We begin to trust our own natural order. When the ways of the world attempt to interrupt my loving you, Creator God, shore up my shoulders so that I may carry my cross.

(Morning)
Eternal and loving God, when the burdens of this world rest heavy on my shoulders, lift my burdens as only you can do.
(Prayers of Intercession)

(Evening)
God of all creation, show me the middle way. Your children are living in a world full of avarice. Guide me so that I may be greedy for spiritual wealth and not material wealth.
(Prayers of Intercession)

"Have salt in yourselves, and be at peace with one another."

(Morning)
Grant me the wisdom, O God, to think before I act, so that the consequences of my actions build upon your foundation. Amen.

(Evening)
As I come to the close of a most wonderful week basking in your world, it is comforting to know that in "your house there are many dwelling places." Thank you for Jesus, who prepared a place for me. Amen.

MONDAY, SEPTEMBER 7
(Read Luke 15:1–10)

(Morning)
Most compassionate God, stir in me the sensitivity to see people not as the
world sees them but as those who are precious in your sight.

(Evening)
Most compassionate God, help me to see and feel the expansiveness of your
love for those who seem least important in ordinary life.

God, your love is inclusive and seeks out especially those who are least
able to do for themselves. The woman in the parable must be someone with
limited means, or else she would not have searched so carefully. A rich
woman could have decided easily that the lost coin was not worth bother-
ing about.

(Morning)
Loving God, grant me wisdom, so that I may see the faces of my brothers and
sisters in all people and not just those who are like me.
(Prayers of Intercession)

(Evening)
Ever-present God, let me not forget that when I am lost, you are present.
Help me to be in touch with you.
(Prayers of Intercession)

**"Jesus is easily seen as the Good Shepherd
but seldom seen as the Good Housewife." —John Dominic Crossan**

(Morning)	(Evening)
Guide my steps, O God, that I may walk in the steps of those who are considered expendable in this world. Amen.	God, in whom there is rest, calm my spirit, so that I may go to sleep and awake refreshed in the morning. Amen.

TUESDAY, SEPTEMBER 8
(Read Jeremiah 4:11–12)

(Morning)
O God of righteousness, I feel the heat of your anger when people stray from
your ways, and I want to shield myself from your judgment.

(Evening)
O God of righteousness, you are angry because your people do not listen to you.

When the war in Kuwait was ending and the Iraqis were fleeing to their
own country, they set fire to all the oil wells. The scene looked as though a
hell had been created on earth. God of creation, when human beings resort
to wanton destruction of other human beings and the earth's resources, how
deep your anguish must be.

(Morning)
Anger is very often a cover-up for hurt and disappointment. Help me, caring
God, to understand my anger and teach me to listen to the anger of others.
(Prayers of Intercession)

(Evening)
O God, I confess that I am sometimes angry at you
for what seems to be unfair in this world.
Help me to work through my anger so I may feel your compassion.
(Prayers of Intercession)

"For I have redeemed you; I have called you by name, you are mine."

(Morning)	(Evening)
Let not the anger of others blind me to the possibility of understanding and compassion for what lies beneath the anger. Amen.	When the heat of my anger has spent itself, help me, O God, to look within and view my relationship to you. Grant me rest for the night, that I may awaken to a new day. Amen.

WEDNESDAY, SEPTEMBER 9
(Read Jeremiah 4:22–28)

(Morning)
Creator God, the signs of your presence in this world are everywhere. Open my eyes and tune my ears so I may see and hear more keenly.

(Evening)
Creator God, you gave us a good creation and placed your people as stewards. Guide me in my ways so that I might be a worthy steward.

Creator God, your presence is everywhere, in Scripture and in your land. Like your Word, all things become new when your spirit abounds. In the midst of your destroyed creation, the signs of your presence are coming forth in places like Kaho'olawe. Restoration returns.

(Morning)
I pray that restoration and conservation of the earth's resources will prevail. May I do my part to make it so.
(Prayers of Intercession)

(Evening)
O God, pour your healing into the devastated places of the earth and let your people correct their destructive ways.
(Prayers of Intercession)

**"Have regard for your covenant,
for the shadowy places of the land are full of the haunts of violence."**

(Morning)
O God, signs of your presence in this world are everywhere. Amen.

(Evening)
O God, you know that all things need rest. May the stars and the moon keep watch while the earth sleeps in your care. Amen.

THURSDAY, SEPTEMBER 10
(Read Psalm 14)

(Morning)
O God, who is the refuge of the poor, keep me alert to see the signs of your presence, even as the world tries to convince me that you are absent.

(Evening)
O God, bless all those who call on your name.

God, when cynics say you do not exist, they do not know what they are saying. All forces of evil, sloth, pride, and destruction could be unleashed and no one made accountable if your realm did not exist. The hearts and minds of human beings would be cold and calculating, and no one would care for their neighbor. Save us, O God, from such a fate.

(Morning)
O God who gave human beings the freedom to choose either good or evil, guide my thoughts and actions, so that I may seek that which is right in your sight.
(Prayers of Intercession)

(Evening)
God of mercy, may the poor seek refuge in you tonight. Grant them the Spirit that will kindle hope.
(Prayers of Intercession)

"Where God is, everything is possible." —Walter Brueggemann

(Morning)	(Evening)
God who is with the righteous and the poor, do not count me among the cynics who say there is no God. Amen.	Grant me rest, O God, as I go to sleep, knowing that you are with me. Amen.

FRIDAY, SEPTEMBER 11
(Read Exodus 32:7–14)

(Morning)
O God, whose compassion is greater than your wrath, I am thankful that you can change your mind—even with people who may have offended you.

(Evening)
O God, grant me the humility to know when I have been too harsh and unyielding with others.
Help me to be supportive of those who have had a change of heart.

God, when a Canaanite woman asked Jesus to heal her daughter who was tormented by demons, he, at first, refused. He said he was sent "only to the lost sheep of the house of Israel." Later, however, he changed his mind and healed the daughter because of the woman's great faith. Great is your faithfulness!

(Morning)
O God, whose realm overcomes distinctions of race, color, or creed,
keep me open to receive and respond to different expressions of faith.
(Prayers of Intercession)

(Evening)
O God, help me to know that your love never fails those
whose hearts are repentant.
(Prayers of Intercession)

**"As often as I speak against him, I still remember him.
Therefore I am deeply moved for him; I will surely have mercy on him."**

(Morning)
Most compassionate God, your people are easily led astray by the attractions of false gods. Let not your wrath consume them. Grant them wisdom and courage to change their ways. Amen.

(Evening)
Most compassionate God, it has been a demanding and perplexing day. Grant me rest for the night and fresh energy when I awake. Amen.

SATURDAY, SEPTEMBER 12
(Read Psalm 51:1–10)

(Morning)
Most merciful God, you know me better than I know myself.
Help me to begin the day with the gift of a clean spirit within me.

(Evening)
Most merciful God, you have known me since I was in my mother's womb.
What evil I have committed, knowingly or not, was my doing and mine alone.
Forgive me, that I might start anew.

God, forgiveness is a gift from you. It is seen in your Scripture and in times of pain. When families fight and tragedy strikes, you are an intermediary. Your love can rise above all evil and unrest. You are always transforming lives.

(Morning)
Help me, O God, to understand that when I mistreat my neighbor or consider my neighbor to be less important than myself, I am sinning against you. Forgive me and help me to correct my ways.
(Prayers of Intercession)

(Evening)
O God who forgives and makes new, enfold me in your Spirit like a wind that blows through and around me, so that I may be clean and fresh again.
(Prayers of Intercession)

"The sacrifice acceptable to God is a broken spirit; a broken and contrite heart, O God, you will not despise."

(Morning)
I thank you, God, for being ever watchful over me and demanding that I be true to you. Amen.

(Evening)
You have called forth in me, O God, my deepest loyalty, which is to you. And now I go to rest with thankfulness and peace. Amen.

SUNDAY, SEPTEMBER 13
(Read 1 Timothy 1:12–17)

(Morning)
Most merciful God, immortal and invisible yet most patient and forgiving,
I thank you for giving me life and turning me around
when I have not heeded your ways.

(Evening)
Most merciful God, immortal and invisible, you call us into your service even if
we have done evil things. If we repent and turn to you, you are gracious and
eager to receive us. Thank you.

God, your grace and mercy sustain me. When we run away from our faults,
you are there; when we steal, you are there; when we are imprisoned, you
are there. Your Child, Jesus, came into the world to save us from sin. Thank
you for your mercy and for those who are merciful.

(Morning)
It is easy for me, O God, to condemn those who break human laws and hurt
their families. Teach me wisdom in my heart, that I may know your mercy.
(Prayers of Intercession)

(Evening)
O God, teach me not to judge others' failings. I, too, am a failure when I turn
away from you. Temper my pride so I can ask for your forgiveness.
(Prayers of Intercession)

"So if anyone is in Christ, there is a new creation."

(Morning)
O God, often I do not understand the
motives of people I know, but you do.
And for those who truly repent, your
mercy is abundant. Thank you, God.
Amen.

(Evening)
Most merciful God, I lay before you
all that I have thought and done this
day. Grant me rest for the night and a
fresh start when I wake in the morning.
In the name of Christ Jesus, I pray.
Amen.

MONDAY, SEPTEMBER 14
(Read Jeremiah 8:18–9:1)

(Morning)
Source of comfort, grant me peace of mind in the midst
of difficulty and turmoil. May I always sense your nearness,
and may your presence lighten my burdens.

(Evening)
Source of comfort, thank you for watching over me. I give to you the stresses
and trials of this day, and I rest secure in your love.

From time to time, the challenges of life threaten to overwhelm me. Alone I am inadequate to meet the seemingly insurmountable obstacles. God, sometimes it even begins to feel as if you have ceased to watch over me. It is during these times that I question your presence. Help me always to remember that your hand is guiding me through the difficult passages. Thank you for the security of your presence and strength, and thank you for the opportunity to use these challenges to grow stronger in you.

(Morning)
Make me aware of your presence throughout this day.
(Prayers of Intercession)

(Evening)
I commit to you, all-knowing God, the tensions and worries of this day. Grant
me rest and peace of mind.
(Prayers of Intercession)

Strengthen me as I pray.
(Pray the Prayer of Our Savior.)

(Morning)
May I meet today's challenges with renewed confidence, knowing that you, loving God, are my strength and comfort. In Christ's name I pray. Amen.

(Evening)
Eternal and everlasting God, who is without beginning or end, thank you for your guidance and protection throughout this day. Amen.

TUESDAY, SEPTEMBER 15
(Read Jeremiah 8:18–9:1)

(Morning)
Compassionate God, let my mind be turned from my own troubles
to the distress of my neighbors.
Keep my worries from blinding me to the needs of others.

(Evening)
Compassionate God, thank you for Christ's example of compassion and
selflessness. Make me, like him, sensitive to the needs of others.

Merciful God, you care even for the tiny sparrow, and you alone know
what every man, woman, and child is going through. It is easy to insulate
myself and to become immune from the sorrow and suffering in the world.
You created us to care for one another. Grant me the strength to seek out
the hurting and the helpless, and grant me the courage to minister to them
as Christ would—selflessly and tirelessly.

(Morning)
May I be mindful throughout this day of the needs of others. Grant me patience
and humility, that I may serve others without thought of reward.
(Prayers of Intercession)

(Evening)
Loving God, whose gentle Spirit encompasses all people, grant me a night of
peaceful rest, that tomorrow I may be refreshed and renewed to serve you.
(Prayers of Intercession)

In your Spirit, I pray.
(Pray the Prayer of Our Savior.)

(Morning)
It is so easy to become immune or insensitive to the pain of my neighbors. Help me, O God, to be compassionate. In Christ's name. Amen.

(Evening)
Compassionate God, thank you for loving us enough to send Christ Jesus to be an example of your pure and selfless love. With your guidance, I will strive to be Christlike in my dealings with my neighbors. Amen.

WEDNESDAY, SEPTEMBER 16
(Read Psalm 79:1–9)

(Morning)
Merciful God, I pray this morning for the nations of the earth. Deliver us from
our willfulness and hard-heartedness, and grant us your peace.

(Evening)
Merciful God, whose loving Spirit enfolds the earth,
tonight I lay at your feet all the troubles and conflicts in this world.
Have mercy on us, and grant us peace.

It is impossible to watch the news or pick up a newspaper without seeing
the destruction that people all over the world are wreaking on one another.
King David cried out to you as my heart cries out now: How can you allow
such things to happen to innocent people? Where are you in all of this? As
you revealed to Elijah, you are not in the fire, in the wind, or in the earthquake; you are in the absolute silence. You are sorrowful at the injustice
and cruelty, but you know and understand the pain.

(Morning)
O God, to the leaders of nations grant wisdom and
the ability to reconcile differences. To the casualties of conflicts
too numerous for any except you to know, grant eternal rest.
(Prayers of Intercession)

(Evening)
Hear my prayer this night for peace. Quiet the rage of those
who are angry, reconcile those who are in conflict,
and comfort the innocent victims of violence.
(Prayers of Intercession)

Peacefully I pray.
(Pray the Prayer of Our Savior.)

(Morning)
You alone, O God, comprehend the
extent of the suffering in the world.
Forgive us for our pettiness, stubborn-
ness, and selfishness. Amen.

(Evening)
God, have mercy upon the people of
this world. Amen.

THURSDAY, SEPTEMBER 17
(Read Amos 8:4–7)

(Morning)
Righteous God, I am accountable to you for all of my actions.
Help me to glorify you in everything I do today.

(Evening)
Righteous God, you are the final authority and the supreme justice.
I tremble before so righteous a judge. Have mercy on me,
and forgive me my many, many sins.

God of Creation, you endowed humans with the will to choose right from wrong. When Adam and Eve disobeyed you, they bequeathed to all humanity the predisposition to sin. There are a great many people who deliberately defy you. There are also many people who strive to do your will and never seem to get ahead in the world. You, righteous God, will not forget what any of us have done, and at the judgment, you will require us to answer for our actions.

(Morning)
As much as I want to do your will, my flesh is weak. I have sinned against you
time and time again, and you have forgiven me time and time again!
Thank you for being patient with me.
(Prayers of Intercession)

(Evening)
Help me to recognize in myself my disobedience to you.
Make me aware of my unworthy thoughts and actions.
(Prayers of Intercession)

Obediently I pray.
(Pray the Prayer of Our Savior.)

(Morning)
I come before you this morning, knowing that no matter how much I strive to be a good person, my attempts are inadequate. Today guide my thoughts, words, and deeds so that I am all you want me to be. Amen.

(Evening)
Merciful God, forgive me for my sinful deeds, both those I know and those of which I am not aware. Thank you for your promise of eternal love and eternal life. In your name I pray. Amen.

FRIDAY, SEPTEMBER 18
(Read Psalm 113)

(Morning)
Glorious God, I give thanks this morning for your love, mercy, and graciousness. I will praise you with my whole heart and soul, from the rising to the
setting of the sun. Praise be to you, Sovereign God!

(Evening)
Glorious God, I rest secure in your power and majesty, knowing that you are the
Alpha and Omega, eternal and everlasting, and that I am your child.

You, O God, are the Creator of all; without you, nothing was made. Your
glory is over all of heaven and earth—in the song of the birds, the smell of
mown grass, the warmth of a fire, the expanse of the starry sky. It is in the
company of family and friends and in the touch of a loved one. Everywhere I turn, I find a new reason to praise you. I will trust you to raise my
thoughts above the tasks of everyday life, and I will seek to glorify you in
everything I do.

(Morning)
Today, God, I will look around me with new eyes. In everything, I will see your
presence and your glory, and for everything I will give thanks.
(Prayers of Intercession)

(Evening)
Eternal God, thank you for making me aware of your presence
in everything and everyone I saw today.
(Prayers of Intercession)

With praise I pray.
(Pray the Prayer of Our Savior.)

(Morning)
This day, everlasting God, help me to
see and feel you all around. Make me
aware of those times when I lose sight
of you; forgive me, and grant me the
ability to see you more clearly. In your
name I pray. Amen.

(Evening)
Everlasting God, you are so much a
part of everything around me. May I
fall asleep tonight feeling the presence of your Spirit, and may my first
thought upon waking be of your
glory, power, and love. In your name
I pray. Amen.

SATURDAY, SEPTEMBER 19
(Read 1 Timothy 2:1–7)

(Morning)
Heavenly God, I pray this morning for all humankind.
Grant wisdom to those who lead, peace to those at war,
comfort to those who suffer,and healing to those who are broken.

(Evening)
Heavenly God, Creator of everyone and everything,
hear my prayer for the people of this world.

O God, you sacrificed your Child, Christ Jesus, to redeem us all and to give us a living example of your goodness and love. I choose this day to live as Christ lived—with selflessness, kindness, patience, and generosity. Today, with your help, I will be a Christlike example of your love for all humankind. Enable me to see people as you see them, and grant me courtesy, kindness, and patience in my dealings with others. Today, I will pray for everyone as the apostle Paul instructed Timothy.

(Morning)
Loving God, let your love shine through all my words, thoughts, and deeds.
Grant me courage and patience in the face of confrontations.
(Prayers of Intercession)

(Evening)
Loving God, may tonight's rest renew and refresh me for the new day.
Forgive me if my actions or words today did not honor you.
(Prayers of Intercession)

In your honor I pray.
(Pray the Prayer of Our Savior.)

(Morning)
Creator of all humankind, both good and evil, help me today to be more like Christ: selfless, kind, patient, and generous. May everyone who meets me recognize your love, and may all of my actions glorify you. In Christ's name. Amen.

(Evening)
May tomorrow and every day bring new opportunities to glorify you and to share your love with others. Let your light shine through me, so that I may be an example of willing obedience to you. For Jesus' sake. Amen.

SUNDAY, SEPTEMBER 20
(Read Luke 16:1–13)

(Morning)
Giving and forgiving God, you have entrusted me with both time and material goods. Help me manage them in such a way that you are pleased and honored.

(Evening)
Giving and forgiving God, thank you for your guidance today. Forgive me if my actions had any impure or selfish motives, and grant me a night of peaceful rest.

God, you have generously blessed me, and I am thankful not only for what you have given me but for the opportunity to use these resources to serve you. Again today I commit myself to be a good steward of the things you have bestowed on me: I will manage my time and my material wealth so that you are honored and glorified. I will seek ways, both big and small, to be of service to others. Help me to manage all my resources so that you are pleased, and never let me forget that without you, my belongings are hollow and unimportant.

(Morning)
Grant me, O God, the clarity of insight to manage my affairs so that you are glorified. With your help, I will strive this day to turn over to you my greed, selfishness, and unkindness. Enable me to serve you humbly and completely.
(Prayers of Intercession)

(Evening)
Heavenly God, you have been generous and gracious to me.
Thank you for the opportunity to serve you by wisely managing your gifts.
(Prayers of Intercession)

Unselfishly I pray.
(Pray the Prayer of Our Savior.)

(Morning)
Giving and forgiving God, you have entrusted me with material possessions. With your help today, I will use these possessions and resources to serve and glorify you. Amen.

(Evening)
Gracious God, you have entrusted me with material possessions. Make me a worthy steward of these worldly goods, tomorrow and for the rest of my life. In Christ's name I pray. Amen.

MONDAY, SEPTEMBER 21
(Read Psalm 146)

(Morning)
Loving God who made the heaven, the earth, the sea, and all that is in them,
thank you for keeping faith with me as I begin another busy week.

(Evening)
Loving God, your faithfulness throughout this day has been astonishing.
Thank you!

Faithfulness is one theme that is interwoven in many of the readings for
the coming week. Monday is an appropriate time to reflect on your faithfulness as I begin to see the week unfolding. God, please be faithful to me,
no matter what happens.

(Morning)
Beginning this week, I look forward to knowing and experiencing your faithfulness. Help me to be lovingly faithful to the people and concerns
for which I now pray.
(Prayers of Intercession)

(Evening)
It has been difficult being your incarnate loving faithfulness today. I ask you to
help me reflect and learn from the occasions where I have fallen short. Help me
to be faithful in my prayers and in my intercessions as I pray for . . .
(Prayers of Intercession)

Happy are those whose hope is in God.

(Morning)
I go forward knowing that you, O
God, are faithful to me. Amen.

(Evening)
Your loving faithfulness enfolds me
even as I sleep. Amen.

TUESDAY, SEPTEMBER 22
(Read Jeremiah 32:1–3a, 6–15)

(Morning)
Dear God, today I am given the opportunity to be a loving, faithful person. Help me to experience these opportunities as real chances to demonstrate to those I meet how loving and faithful you are to me.

(Evening)
Dear God, at times today I have felt besieged with my worries and the concerns of others. Remind me again of your loving faithfulness as this day comes to a close.

The days are getting shorter now that we have passed the fall equinox. The gloom of winter is slowly creeping towards us, but creation is preparing in myriad ways. The promise of spring is packed away in seeds, roots, cocoons, and the mud of ponds. The earthenware jar of Jeremiah was a similar promise of new life to a defeated nation. God, you are loving and faithful and have filled many jars with promise and hope. They only wait to be opened.

(Morning)
God of all faithfulness, help me by my example to assist those for whom I now pray to find hope and promise in their lives.
(Prayers of Intercession)

(Evening)
Thank you being faithful, even in the littlest things.
Be with those for whom I now pray.
(Prayers of Intercession)

I am an earthenware jar that has been filled with God's promise of new life.

(Morning)
I set off today wanting to walk with you in faithfulness and love. Amen.

(Evening)
Help me relax and rest in your love all night long. Amen.

WEDNESDAY, SEPTEMBER 23
(Read Amos 6:1a, 4–7)

(Morning)
Loving God, I rest myself today in you as I set aside time
for Scripture reading and prayer. Thank you for the circumstances of my life
that permit me to have this leisure.

(Evening)
Loving God, rest and nourishment are what I seek this evening. Enfold me once
again into the firmness of your loving arms. Refresh me, so that I may be loving
and caring to those with whom I spend the closing hours of this day.

God, you are lovingly faithful to all and require us to be the same. Prophets
like Amos remind us that we are part of your way to love and care for
others. We are your mind, heart, and hands present in the world. This theme
now becomes interwoven with that of faithfulness.

(Morning)
This quiet time has been good for me. I now pray that those for whom I pray
will also find time to be enfolded in your loving arms. Enfold especially . . .
(Prayers of Intercession)

(Evening)
The day is coming to a close, and I am prayerfully fortunate to be in your
presence. I look forward to the leisure and rest of sleep, and remember those
who will be restless this night, especially . . .
(Prayers of Intercession)

**I am the mind, heart, and hands of God
working for justice in the world today.**

(Morning)	(Evening)
Send me forth today to respect the dignity of every human being. Amen.	A new day will soon dawn. Let me rest in your loving arms this night, so that I may rise tomorrow renewed and strengthened to work for justice and peace. Amen.

THURSDAY, SEPTEMBER 24
(Read Psalm 91:1–6)

(Morning)
God, every time I walk through a shadow today, remind me
that I live in your shelter and that you shield me with your wings
as parent birds protect their young.

(Evening)
God, as a parent bird gathers its young under its wings, I return to you at the close
of this day. I am tired, but this time the shadow of your wings refreshes me.

The psalmist provides us with a wonderful image of you as a loving, faithful God who wishes us no harm. We live, move, and have our being under the shadow of your protecting wings. The wings that shelter us also carry us ultimately to safety, which is why pestilence and destruction may cause us pain but no fear. It is without fear that we face our troubles, knowing that you are a loving, caring, and faithful God.

(Morning)
Thank you for sheltering me under your wings. Call those for whom I pray also
under the cover of your pinions.
(Prayers of Intercession)

(Evening)
At times today, I wandered away from the protective shadow of your wings, but
I scurry back to your loving faithfulness. I bring with me others who need to
experience your love. I bring . . .
(Prayers of Intercession)

God, I delight in being your fledgling.

(Morning)
As I explore the world away from this quiet time under your wings, remind me of your ever-present loving faithfulness. Amen.

(Evening)
Loving God, once again I return to you in sleep. Watch over me, so that tomorrow I may go out into the world refreshed and ready to love. Amen.

FRIDAY, SEPTEMBER 25
(Read Psalm 91:14–16)

(Morning)
Creator God, I bless you because of your loving faithfulness. I take delight in
your promise to hear my prayer, as it makes the morning even more beautiful to
be assured of your love for me. I want to walk with you in beauty today.

(Evening)
Creator God, the daily walk is almost over, and I am glad
to be able to come into your restful beauty this evening.
Today you have filled my senses with so much beauty.

God, you honor and bless us at all times; however, it is often difficult to
sense your loving faithfulness in terrible times. It is in these times that we
can turn to the psalms and read of your loving faithfulness in the beautiful
words of poems and songs. We must make the words of the psalms your
own. When we pray the psalms, we will know of your love for us.

(Morning)
Because of your loving faithfulness, you surround me in beauty—the beauty of
creation and the beauty reflected in the faces of those I meet.
I pray for inner beauty and wholeness for . . .
(Prayers of Intercession)

(Evening)
It was beautiful today! Thank you, Creator. During this time of reflection,
help me recall and remember the beauty that I witnessed today.
(Prayers of Intercession)

Creator God, your beauty is seen in all your creation.

(Morning)
Challenge me, loving God, to see the
beauty around me today and to
consciously give praise to you. Amen.

(Evening)
Today I know the meaning of beauty
rest. It is knowingly safe rest in the
beauty of your presence. Amen.

SATURDAY, SEPTEMBER 26
(Read 1 Timothy 6:6–15)

(Morning)
Caring God, I awake to a new day that will be filled with many temptations.
Kindly turn my mind and help me remember to seek to be righteous,
godly, gentle, and lovingly faithful.

(Evening)
Caring God, thank you for the gift of Holy Scripture.
This morning I was inspired. This evening, once again,
Scripture brings me into your special presence.

Loving God, being a caring, loving, faithful person is difficult in a world that encourages self-indulgent consumerism. Words of advice from one Christian to another, when given from the heart, can be inspiring and healing while helping us live more simply. We need one another as we journey together, walking the way of Christ.

(Morning)
Wonderful God, who has given us the gift of Scripture to remind us of your
loving faithfulness, help me to be faithful to those who have asked
for my prayers. I hold in my heart today . . .
(Prayers of Intercession)

(Evening)
As the day comes to a close, I still need your loving presence in my life, as do
these people for whom I pray . . .
(Prayers of Intercession)

Pursue righteousness, godliness, faith, love, endurance, and gentleness.

(Morning)	(Evening)
Once again, God, together we immerse ourselves in life. Amen.	The day is done, and I seek rest in your loving faithfulness. Amen.

SUNDAY, SEPTEMBER 27
(Read Luke 16:19–28)

(Morning)
God, it is Sunday. Cultivate in our hearts the ability to hear and respond to the
call of the poor who lie outside the gates of our comfort.

(Evening)
God, I have lived a comfortable life today. My comfort has probably dulled
my sensitivity to the needs of many around me
who I assume can be comfortable with less.
Help me live more simply, so that others may simply live.

The media are a two-edged sword. On the one hand, advertisements tempt
us to indulge and overconsume. On the other hand, the media connect us
with the poor, sick, hungry, and dying around the world and around the
corner. God, how do we respond to your people? How can we be lovingly
faithful to you without working to aid the poor?

(Morning)
Loving God, open my eyes, that I may see the pain and suffering of people.
Help me work to bring comfort and aid. I begin my work by praying for . . .
(Prayers of Intercession)

(Evening)
God, this is the day which you have made, and I rejoice and am glad in it, even
though I could have done more to aid those who lie outside my gates of comfortable living. God, comfort those who need rest this night, especially.
(Prayers of Intercession)

I rejoice that God's loving faithfulness reaches even into death.

(Morning)
God of resurrection, reach into the
dead and insensitive places in my
spirit and bring new life. Amen.

(Evening)
God of resurrection, reach into my
sleep and renew my body and spirit, so
that I may arise as a more loving,
caring, compassionate person. Amen.

MONDAY, SEPTEMBER 28
(Read 2 Timothy 1:1–7)

(Morning)
Good morning, God! I awaken this day with the promise of life
that is in Christ Jesus!

(Evening)
Good evening, God! The day is spent. I am tired and weary. Rest cannot come
soon enough. My prayer is that I lived this day in its entirety in your will. If not,
please forgive me.

God, I am grateful this day for those who saw something in me years ago
that I did not see in myself. Those persons believed in me and taught me
how to believe. They encouraged me and never stopped praying for me. I
am grateful for their continued prayers. There are days when I forget who I
am and whose I am. When faced with the challenges of life and ministry, it
is easy to become timid or fearful. Thank you, God, for reminding me at
those times that you did not give me a spirit of timidity or fear, but a spirit
of power, love, and self-discipline.

(Morning)
Giver of every good and perfect gift, help me to fan into flame the gift that you
have placed in me.
(Prayers of Intercession)

(Evening)
As I prepare to retire for the evening, I do so remembering those with whom I
share the joy of loving relationship.
(Prayers of Intercession)

In faith, I pray to you, O God.

(Morning)
As I enter the day, may I do so with a
sincere faith—the faith of one who
accomplished great things for you,
O God. Amen.

(Evening)
May the promise of life be renewed in
me as I sleep, O God. Amen.

TUESDAY, SEPTEMBER 29
(Read 2 Timothy 1:8–14)
(Sing "Evening Prayer")

(Morning)
O God, renew in me this morning a sense of your purpose for my life and for this day. I don't want to waste a minute of the life you have given me.

(Evening)
O God, it was a tough day. Fulfilling your purpose for my life and living up to your holy calling is not easy.

I'm really not ashamed of you, God. I just don't like conflict. Being in places every day with persons who question whether or not you are real is a challenge for me. I want to defend you, but at times I'm not sure what to say. I suppose I should just tell them my story. It is only by your grace that I am who and what I am. The grace that was revealed to me in Christ Jesus has made me who I am. You have called me with a holy calling to share with others the good news of grace found in your Child Jesus. I am not ashamed. I will tell everyone I have an opportunity to tell who Jesus is, even if they shun me.

(Morning)
Give me the words to say this day that will bring honor and glory to you!
(Prayers of Intercession)

(Evening)
What a wonderful day this was! I claimed your power to speak boldly for you and to take a stand on some pretty tough issues. I pray for those who may have seen my witness so that they, too, will claim the power of a new life in Christ and boldly witness.
(Prayers of Intercession)

I am praying today with renewed confidence in the power of prayer!

(Morning)
I know I believe in you, O God, and I know you will guard what I entrust to you this day. Amen.

(Evening)
If I have wounded any soul today, if I have walked in my own willful way, if I have caused one foot to go astray, dear God, forgive me. Amen.

WEDNESDAY, SEPTEMBER 30
(Read Lamentations 3:19–26)

(Morning)
God, what a joy to wake up this morning with the assurance
of your love and mercy.

(Evening)
God, thank you for keeping me safe this day!

I was tempted to give up today, God. I had lost all hope. I thought about all that I have already been through, and at times it looks like things are getting worse and not better. I didn't know how much more I could take. I wasn't sure I wanted to take any more until I remembered how loving and compassionate you are. You know what I am going through. You have been faithful to keep me thus far, and I know that you will continue to be faithful. My hope has been restored. I will be delivered. All I have to do is wait for you.

(Morning)
You are so good to me, God! Your Word says that you are good to those whose
hope is in you. I will live this day in anticipation of your goodness
and your love.
(Prayers of Intercession)

(Evening)
I am still waiting for you, Compassionate One.
I know that you know what I need.
(Prayers of Intercession)

Waiting for you, my strength is renewed.

(Morning)	(Evening)
Every morning, your love for me is renewed. I feel brand-new in the fullness of your love for me. Amen.	I can lie down and rest secure in knowing that I am loved by you. Amen.

THURSDAY, OCTOBER 1
(Read Habakkuk 1:1–4, 2:1–4)

(Morning)
Creator God, this is the day that you have made. I will rejoice and be glad in it.

(Evening)
Creator God, rejoicing in you this day gave me the courage to see it through.

God, I know that it seems like I am always complaining, but I have some concerns about the way things are going in the world. Violence has never been so prevalent. Young people make plans for their funerals rather than their graduations. It is not safe for children to walk the streets. Some of them are not even safe at home. How long must I cry to you about the injustices in the land? Isn't it time that we dealt with racism, sexism, classism, and ageism? Why are you tolerating these wrongs? Say something, God!

(Morning)
I lift up to you this day all those who work for and practice peace with justice.
I pray for myself, that I may be a part of the solution and not the problem.
(Prayers of Intercession)

(Evening)
I bring to you all those who have been the perpetrators and victims of violence.
(Prayers of Intercession)

I am waiting patiently for an answer from you.

(Morning)
Your Word makes clear to me that the righteous shall live by faith. I have faith this day that those things that concern me are of concern to you as well. Amen.

(Evening)
I don't always understand your timetable, but I know that you are always on time and in time. Your timing is always perfect. I trust that! Amen.

FRIDAY, OCTOBER 2
(Read Psalms 37:1–9)

(Morning)
Sustaining God, trusting in you I am safe. Delighting in you I have the desires
of my heart. What can anyone do to me?

(Evening)
Sustaining God, I had another day of rest in you and your love for me.
I am so blessed!

Today, I am clear that I am not to fret, even when evil persons succeed in
their plans or when they carry out their wicked schemes. Their plans and
schemes soon come to nothing, just like them. But the righteous flourish,
and your just cause will overcome the wickedness of those who are unjust.
You see to that, God, in your own time and in your own way.

(Morning)
One day the wicked will cease from troubling and the weary will be at rest.
Thank you, O Giver of Rest, for this blessed promise.
(Prayers of Intercession)

(Evening)
God, give me the strength not to want to seek revenge or to get even when folks
mess with me.
(Prayers of Intercession)

I will live each day in peace with my neighbor.

(Morning)	(Evening)
As I begin this new day, I commit everything to you, God: all my hopes, dreams, and desires. Amen.	As I end this day, I commit to you, God, all my hurts, disappointments, fears, and frustrations. I will lie down in peace. Amen.

SATURDAY, OCTOBER 3
(Read Luke 17:5–6)

(Morning)
God, I have only one request of you this morning: Increase my faith!

(Evening)
God, I believe you. It is by faith that I find myself in relationship with you.
Help my unbelief.

God, you keep challenging me to trust you more, to take you at your word, and step out on your promises. I keep asking myself, "What have I got to lose?" It's not like you are asking a lot of me. If I had faith the size of a mustard seed . . . A mustard seed isn't very large; it is quite small, actually. It doesn't take a whole lot of faith to do great things for you. You can take nothing and make something of it. If I can conceive it, I can achieve it. Help my unbelief.

(Morning)
I have faith in you to help me accomplish the following tasks or
to help me achieve victory in the following areas of my life.
(Prayers of Intercession)

(Evening)
I have faith in you to do great and small things
in the lives of the following persons.
(Prayers of Intercession)

With faith, nothing is impossible to me!

(Morning)
Faith sees the invisible, claims the unreachable, and does the impossible. Faith can conquer anything! Amen.

(Evening)
Without faith it is impossible to please you, God. I want to please you. Amen.

SUNDAY, OCTOBER 4
(Read Luke 17:5–10)

(Morning)
God, I ask so much of you, what is it that you would have me do for you today?

(Evening)
God, I am not worthy of all that you do for me. I give you the best of my
service. I owe it to you.

God, I am so fortunate that you would even let me serve you. I know that I
am not worthy. Whatever I give is my duty. I need to remember this, because sometimes I want to act like I am doing you a favor. I really don't
mean to be so arrogant. Forgive me when at times I tend to think of myself
and my gifts more highly than I should.

(Morning)
I offer this prayer with thanksgiving for all those who serve you faithfully.
(Prayers of Intercession)

(Evening)
God, I offer this prayer with thanksgiving for those
who fulfill thankless duties for you.
(Prayers of Intercession)

Thank you, God, for the gift of faith.

(Morning)
Prepare me this day, O God, for
another day of meeting the needs of
persons on your behalf and in your
name. Amen.

(Evening)
I want to hear you say one day, "Well
done, good and faithful servant."
Amen.

MONDAY, OCTOBER 5
(Read Psalm 66:1–7)

(Morning)
O Holy One, I rise and greet a fresh new day with a song of praise on my lips,
"To God be the glory, for the great things God has done!"

(Evening)
O Holy One, I join a world that worships your acts of faith in human history.
Thank you for your living presence this day.

I live in a world that mocks the miraculous, a world that celebrates the mediocre and the mundane. God, human wizardry in the form of high technology has become a substitute for your mighty deeds. Today I will open my heart, my mind, my eyes to sense and see your mighty hand at work in the world. Today my words and deeds will be a response to your miraculous presence in my life and my world. I will see your hand in the birth of each new baby and in the tentative steps toward peace among nations too long at war. Thank you for all of creation and for my small part in your plan for the earth.

(Morning)
Let me begin this day inhaling your creation and
exhaling your will for my life in your world.
(Prayers of Intercession)

(Evening)
Living God, you have been faithful to me throughout this day.
You know when my actions have betrayed your presence.
Be near me now as I labor to put this day to rest.
(Prayers of Intercession)

**Where my vision fails, give me hope
that the world sees your wondrous deeds and mighty works.**

(Morning)
My life shall be a song and dance in
praise and worship of your name.
Amen.

(Evening)
I rest from the work of the world to
find peace in the silence of your night.
Amen.

TUESDAY, OCTOBER 6
(Read Psalm 66:8–12)

(Morning)
Loving God, so ordinary seems the new day that greets me, yet so wondrously made. New and mysterious are the possibilities that lie ahead. Thank you, God of creation!

(Evening)
Loving God, I thank you for today and welcome the coming of night. Let me stay near you, so that in the hours that remain, my life will reflect your truth.

Am I up to the challenge today? Am I prepared to face myself, my family and friends, and my work in this community and world? Each brings challenges that I do not always see as opportunities; each brings burdens I am not confident I can bear. God, I know and believe you are with me, in every breath, in each moment. Help my unbelief. This day, give me confidence to accept the reality that, in each encounter, a piece of your truth awaits me and your strength supports me. Help me to understand that my struggle is a strand in the fabric of a world seeking your mind in the affairs of humanity. Grant me your blessing.

(Morning)
O God, my sure defender, give me the courage to face the trials of the day and to trust that in my weakness your strength is made perfect.
(Prayers of Intercession)

(Evening)
God of eternity, the day is not too long for you, the burden not too heavy. You are God of all time and every situation. Grant me patience and endurance.
(Prayers of Intercession)

"We know that all things work together for the good of those who love God, who are called according to God's purpose."

(Morning)
When I stumble and fall, you reach out your hand to me, you bind my wounds, and guide me on my way. Amen.

(Evening)
Watch me soar on winds of your spirit. And if I grow weary, renew me, for I am yours; you are my strength. Amen.

WEDNESDAY, OCTOBER 7
(Read Jeremiah 29:1, 4–7)

(Morning)
God of silence and sound, I am wholly yours and welcome the gift of this day
and the gifts this day will bring.

(Evening)
God of silence and sound, today speak to me in these moments of prayer as
I reflect upon the ways you have visited me in the people and the places
I have known.

I thank you, God, that I have a place to call home, for shelter over my head,
and for daily bread. I am keenly aware that shelter and daily bread are not
provided for everyone. I want to help find solutions. I thank you that home
is more than houses and land; it is the extended human family in your dominion. From all the lands on earth, you have called people to this land.
We are all strangers to this land and to one another, and yet it belongs to us
all and we belong to one another. I thank you that each of us can call this
place home. Remind me, God of all, that none of us lives alone, that the
welfare of any one depends upon the welfare of all.

(Morning)
Let the familiar faces I see in my town today remind me that even the faces of
strangers, here and in distant lands, bear your image.
(Prayers of Intercession)

(Evening)
I rejoice that the miracle of birth confirms your promises.
Our increase is your plan and delight.
(Prayers of Intercession)

Cities and towns come in every size; the Savior came for them all.

(Morning)
I will pray for the welfare of my town
as though my life depended upon it.
Amen.

(Evening)
Like Jesus, I weep over my town: tears
of sadness, for I know what makes for
peace; and tears of joy, for I know
what promise it holds. Amen.

THURSDAY, OCTOBER 8
(Read 2 Kings 5:1–15c)

(Morning)
Gracious God, the promise of this morning invites me to live trusting in your
grace for my life today. Even as my eyes open, the light of day reminds me of
your faithfulness to me and all creation.

(Evening)
Gracious God, both the great and the small declare your presence and convey
your truth. Open my eyes, that I may not be deceived by outward dimensions.
Let me see your face in the shapes and shadows of each day and each night.

Triumph and tragedy, truth and falsehood, power and weakness belong to
all, regardless of station or status in life. I claim no special merit in your
heart because of wealth, rank, genealogy, prowess, or religion. I cannot
demand abundance in life by any virtue I possess or to which I aspire.
Neither you, O God, nor humanity is in my debt because of any great
achievement or grand philanthropy. Justice and mercy, healing and wholeness are your gifts of grace, which come to us all, often in simple, surprising, and unexpected ways. Not my way, your will be done, O my God and
God of all.

(Morning)
May I grow in strength today as I acknowledge my frailties and weakness. May
I give even as I acknowledge my need to receive.
(Prayers of Intercession)

(Evening)
As evening casts a cooling shadow on this day, accept my thanks for joys
received and challenges met; forgive me for moments
I did not hear your voice and heed your Word.
(Prayers of Intercession)

Thank God for healing, refreshing, cleansing water.

(Morning)
I will not let my greatness stand in the
way of your grace. Amen.

(Evening)
Thank you for your truth revealed this
day, and with the night bring rest and
renewal. Amen.

FRIDAY, OCTOBER 9
(Read 2 Timothy 2:8–15)

(Morning)
God our Creator, you spoke and there was light and life.
Today is a word you speak to humanity.
I embrace it as your gift and rise to meet the revelations that await me.

(Evening)
God our Creator, "The word became flesh and dwelt among us . . .
full of grace and truth." Thank you for that Word dwelling among us today.
Thank you for the grace and the truth that I have witnessed in my life today.

Words, words, words. The Word is our salvation. Our words threaten our very lives. God, discipline my speech. Save me from talking so much and saying so little. Save me from my need to tell what I know. Save me from the fallacy of thinking that if I could just get the words right, get the doctrine just so, package the truth in precise language, all would be well. All is not well. I am overwhelmed by the aimless bantering of a noisy world and the ceaseless stream of words which flows from my troubled conscience. Silence the noise. Let me hear, let me know your Word. "One word frees us of all the weight and pain of life; that word is love" (Sophocles, *Oedipus at Colonus*).

(Morning)
Be still, my soul. Come to me, living God, in the deep places within me where
that peace beyond understanding resides.
(Prayers of Intercession)

(Evening)
Christ is alive for me today. God, your Word is free to transform the world.
My vocation is clear.
(Prayers of Intercession)

**As I seek to walk in the footsteps of Christ,
my words will follow straight and true.**

(Morning)
I will stay focused on your Word. I will not be distracted by the din of traffic, beeping computers, destructive gossip, or ruinous argument. Amen.

(Evening)
I welcome the peace evening can bring, the rest promised by each night. I have tried my best to be the person you want me to be. Tomorrow I will try again. Amen.

SATURDAY, OCTOBER 10
(Read Psalm 111)

(Morning)
God of all being, I thank you for your world-creating work, which fills this day with promise and bids me enter it with joy and hope.

(Evening)
God of all being, your presence has blessed my work today. Continue to mold and shape my witness and my work, that all I do and say will praise your name.

God, it is so easy for me to look at the world and complain, to blame and judge. I am horrified by its violence and destruction, by the pain and despair that are so commonplace, by the active practice of evil near to home and in nations far away. In the midst of disquieting realities, why is it so hard for me to be filled with gratitude when I see evidence of your wondrous and abiding presence in my life and in the world? You live above and within our history. The world is your breath of life, and from it I draw my sustenance. You were patient and faithful to the Hebrew people, and you look with kindness upon my hesitant steps. Grant me humility before your holy and awesome being. Grant me the wisdom to accept your redemption and live in covenant with you.

(Morning)
Teach me wisdom as I practice living in wondrous awe of your creation and your covenant faithfulness.
(Prayers of Intercession)

(Evening)
The work of your creation sustains me when I grow weary as evening comes. Hear my prayer for what has passed and what is yet to come.
(Prayers of Intercession)

Every day proclaims the greatness of God and invites our praise.

(Morning)
Today I will live fully and love freely, as if my life depended upon it, as if I believed that the abundant life you promised and Christ lived is available to me. Amen.

(Evening)
Let me sleep comforted by your peace. Let your Spirit keep me company in the silence of the night. Amen.

SUNDAY, OCTOBER 11
(Read Luke 17:11–19)

(Morning)
Loving God, come with me into the life of this day. Speak to my heart so that
my thoughts, my words, and my actions may glorify your name.

(Evening)
Loving God, I thank you for every sign of your presence today:
chance encounters, meaningful work, your created world,
family and friends who know me and love me still.

Let me confess my need for mercy. Let me be like the one who came running and "praising God with a loud voice." Let me be found today prostrate before Jesus, who calls me friend. Let me be like a Samaritan who is persuaded that healing and wholeness know no boundaries of race, clan, or creed. Let me be made whole by my faith, trusting in the power of love which flows so freely from Jesus, who gave his life for us all. Let me be graceful to those whose voices are silent when by your hand they have been healed. Touch their hearts, so that their living may be transformed. Help me to know when I am in their number.

(Morning)
Come, God, visit my soul with joy and gladness.
Hear me shout, "Thank you for today!"
(Prayers of Intercession)

(Evening)
O God, the night is a gift, just as is the day. Stay with me now as darkness
comes, bringing with it new promises of your faithfulness.
(Prayers of Intercession)

**There are no aliens in the household of God,
we are all brothers and sisters in Christ.**

(Morning)	(Evening)
Today I will be alert to my needs, and I will name them. I will care about the needs of others. And I will thank you now for the mercy you grant us all. Amen.	Let the night bring rest and renewal, that I may greet the gift of tomorrow with energy and with thanksgiving for the priceless gift of another day. Amen.

MONDAY, OCTOBER 12
(Read Psalm 119:97–104)

(Morning)
God of all life, you have called me into a direct and living relationship with you. As I begin this day, I pray you will go ahead of me into each new experience to prepare the next place for me.

(Evening)
God of all life, your living presence has surrounded me this day, even when I forgot or did not feel it. Now as I prepare for sleep, enfold me in your love, breathe into me your breath of life and peace.

Great Shepherd, your love is my living law and a lamp for my feet. You have called me directly into your presence, and your living Word is spoken directly into my heart. As I rest and quiet myself, let me hear, feel, understand what you are saying to me and showing me. And even when I cannot clearly sense your presence and guidance, let me rest in the knowledge of your love, and trust that new clarity and understanding will come to me.

(Morning)
As I prepare to pray for the needs of others, let me inwardly see them enfolded in your loving, healing light, you who have come through the healer,
Jesus Christ.
(Prayers of Intercession)

(Evening)
I release those for whom I pray trustfully into your hands, for your care and love for them is far greater than mine.
(Prayers of Intercession)

Lead me beyond words and ideas directly into your presence.

(Morning)
When I feel confused, help me to pause and wait for your inner guiding love.
Amen.

(Evening)
Eternal, unsleeping Love, into your hands I commit my body and spirit.
Amen.

TUESDAY, OCTOBER 13
(Read Jeremiah 31:27–34)

(Morning)
God of love, when I wake to this new day, I wake also to a new covenant with you, a new way of loving, a new way of living with you as the center of my heart. You are my great central sun, shining within all that I am and do.

(Evening)
God of love, sometimes I have forgotten my new freedom today, and have fallen into old traps and prisons of the spirit. Though often I have forgotten you, you never have forgotten me.

You who shine on me through the face of Jesus Christ, this very day you take me by the hand to lead me out of my inner prisons. You have opened your heart to me, and you call me to open my heart to you. You have put your arms around my mistakes and failures, and at this very moment your deep, radical love transforms me.

(Morning)
May all those for whom I pray and all whom I will meet this day be healed and released from their past pain and inner prisons.
(Prayers of Intercession)

(Evening)
Each day may I become more released into your life than the day before, and may those for whom I pray be released more deeply into your love.
(Prayers of Intercession)

Liberating God, when we bond with you we are released from all bondage.

(Morning)
May each moment of this day be transformed and glorified by your radiance. In Jesus' name. Amen.

(Evening)
As I move into the depth and darkness of sleep, your shining love wraps me in radiance. Amen.

WEDNESDAY, OCTOBER 14
(Read Genesis 32:22–31)

(Morning)
Faithful God, today there will be difficulties, anxieties, challenges to face. Help me to discover your angel, your own living presence, coming to meet and strengthen me in every conflict.

(Evening)
Faithful God, even as your people so long ago were led out of captivity by your mighty presence, so you have led me this day, and will lead me through the night by the strong light of Jesus Christ within me.

Living God, I am so often in inner conflict; so often I mistrust and resist love, seeing a threat instead of a gift. So often I strive against your presence, resisting your help, release, and empowerment. So often I meet my angel as my enemy, seeing only the painful shadow and not the glowing presence. Thus I exhaust and hurt myself. But you have never abandoned me. You hold me close during my night of inner wars. May I recognize your offered blessing and receive your gift of healing of my self-inflicted pain.

(Morning)
May those for whom I pray feel now the majesty, faithfulness, and tenderness of your presence, even in the midst of their conflict, fear, and pain.
(Prayers of Intercession)

(Evening)
All that we suffer, all that we feel, you have shared with us. In all our inner striving and wrestling, you are there to offer your blessing.
(Prayers of Intercession)

"If I take the wings of the morning and settle at the farthest limits of the sea, even there . . . your firm hand shall hold me fast."

(Morning)	(Evening)
Through the challenges of this day, may I receive your blessing and bring it to others. Amen.	Beloved God, you have embraced my hurts, pain, and resistance. Your blessing fills me. Amen.

THURSDAY, OCTOBER 15
(Read Psalm 121)

(Morning)
God, let my first thought this morning be the thought of you, the central light of my life. Nothing can overwhelm me. You are my source, my shelter, my strength, my sustenance.

(Evening)
God, as a full circle joins the end and the beginning, so the end of this day joins with its beginning, within your heart. As I breathed your breath of morning with all its challenge, so now I breathe your breath of evening with all its peace.

So often I have forgotten, Unsleeping Love, the mighty strength with which you surround and fill us. We need no lesser strength or source. You are the ultimate mystery. There is so much we cannot understand. But this we know, this we are told, the central life of all creation is your heart, which holds us forever. When we enter into communion with your heart, then our choices, our actions, our powers and gifts are blessed, guided, and transformed.

(Morning)
May the fears and doubts of those for whom I pray be healed, melted by your strong and limitless mercy.
(Prayers of Intercession)

(Evening)
As those for whom I pray face the end of the day, help them to sleep in trust, knowing that you keep them tenderly through the night.
(Prayers of Intercession)

**Living Christ, strong vine of our life,
help me abide in you as your fruitful branch.**

(Morning)
Let my feet be moved only by your guidance. When I go out, prepare the way for me. When I return, welcome and restore me, through Jesus the shepherd. Amen.

(Evening)
Light of all light, you are more merciful than the sun by day and gentler than the moon by night. Amen.

FRIDAY, OCTOBER 16
(Read Timothy 3:14–17)

(Morning)
Infinite Mercy, this day I take your offered hand, leading me into wholeness and completeness, and a life drenched in love. I turn to your living Word, shining on me through Scripture and in the faces and memories of those who have loved, helped, and guided me in your way.

(Evening)
Infinite Mercy, though so often I am fragmented, not aware of the wholeness you offer me, I know you believe in it for me and see it in me. As I enter into sleep, I rest on your tender faith in me.

Not what we learn, but of whom we learn is our source of life, living Christ. You have become for us the living Word, the Spirit of the Scripture unfolding in our hearts. When bonded to you, when abiding in you, Living Vine, we are transformed and made complete. It is your expanding life in us that equips us for a life of truth, strength, and love. Unfold for me today new light and meaning from your eternal Word.

(Morning)
I think of those who did not know of your love in childhood
and were not taught of your light and guidance.
May special help be given them and loving guides sent them.
(Prayers of Intercession)

(Evening)
Come personally, living Christ, to those for whom I pray. Help all of us to know that it is not a principle but a person who is our spring of life.
(Prayers of Intercession)

Living Christ, with you our *there* is *here*.

(Morning)
Keep my faith steadfast this day, and keep me centered in Jesus the Christ. Amen.

(Evening)
Living Christ, breathe on me the healing of your peace and fire of your Spirit. Amen.

SATURDAY, OCTOBER 17
(Read 2 Timothy 4:1–5)

(Morning)
Beloved God, let your Holy Spirit awaken within me. This day, sometimes there
will be need to witness to your love and truth: through words, compassionate
silence, action, joy, and laughter, and through a look or touch of healing love.

(Evening)
Beloved God, there were times today when I was absent in spirit, but you were
always present. Gather up my absences, my dimness, my flickering flame into
your hands and heart, and let them be transformed into new empowered life.

It is not always easy, living God, to be aflame with your love when we so
often feel surrounded by the indifference, doubt, and resistance of others.
May the sense of your glowing presence waken me when I spiritually sleep,
enflame me when I am dim and cold, strengthen me where I am weakest,
heal me where I am wounded, and restore me when I am fragmented. Protect me when I feel challenged, and above all, empower me with your fire
of love.

(Morning)
So many feel their faith and hope crushed or chilled. Lead them into new hope,
strength, and freedom, so they do not fall back into spiritual captivity.
(Prayers of Intercession)

(Evening)
I pray for everyone who longs to know his or her special gifts and calling, and
for the joyful strength to fulfill them.
(Prayers of Intercession)

Help me to build my inner altar, so your flame may descend upon it.

(Morning)	(Evening)
This day may I see and understand and fulfill the special ministry to which you call me. Through the light of Jesus. Amen.	Even in sleep I am in the presence of God and Jesus Christ. Blessed be God! Amen.

SUNDAY, OCTOBER 18
(Read Luke 18:1–8)

(Morning)
Faithful God, there will be times today when I do not feel your nearness, when my prayers seem unanswered. At these times, help me to know that your love is forever with me and that you heard me before I even spoke to you.

(Evening)
Faithful God, often today I have been like a locked and shuttered house, closed to your loving light poured upon me. Often you knocked and I did not hear you or open my door. As I sleep, open the deep, closed places of my heart.

When I experience the delay of my hopes, when prayer seems unanswered, when justice seems withheld, help me to trust in your unsleeping love and justice, God of my life. You have told us that you have heard us before we cry to you. Eternal Mercy, we do not need to plead with you. Eternal Wisdom, we do not need to inform you. Your longing to give is far greater than our longing to receive. The clouds that seem to block your love are not of your making. From everlasting to everlasting, you are faithful. Enlarge me, so that I may receive all that you long to give me.

(Morning)
May those who feel unloved and unheard find some sign today that you have been with them forever.
(Prayers of Intercession)

(Evening)
May those for whom I pray be led to you, where all answers are. Your presence *is* our answer, our way, truth, and life.
(Prayers of Intercession)

"We love because God first loved us."

(Morning)
As I awaken to this day, may I open all the cells of my body and the choices of my heart to your love, which seeks and guides me. In the strong name of Jesus Christ. Amen.

(Evening)
Even as you welcomed me into morning, you welcome me into sleep. But my deep spirit is forever awake, dancing in your joy. Amen.

MONDAY, OCTOBER 19
(Read Joel 2:23–32)

(Morning)
Eternal and life-giving Spirit, as I greet this new day I give thanks for the gift of life. As you have renewed the day, I ask that you renew your Spirit within me.

(Evening)
Eternal and life-giving Spirit, as this day spins to a close, may this night bring rest to all your beloved creatures. May my dreams be filled with your loving and caring Spirit.

Pour out, O God, your Spirit upon all your creation. Grant me the vision to see clearly what you have in mind for me today. Open my eyes to see the needs of those around me who cannot see with their eyes. Help me to be their eyes. May I feel the emptiness of those whose vision of a new world has dimmed. Use me as you will to change emptiness to fulfillment. May your renewing Spirit fill us afresh with life and hope.

(Morning)
O God of the sunrise, let your light spread through me. Help me to see the needs of others and your Holy Spirit at work within each of us.
(Prayers of Intercession)

(Evening)
O God, bless all those who labor to keep me safe and secure this night: those who provide power and light, food and water, protection, and those who stand ready to help when disaster strikes.
(Prayers of Intercession)

"I will pour out my spirit on all flesh."

(Morning)
Help me see beyond myself and become a word of hope for the farmers and farmworkers who face another day of hardship. Amen.

(Evening)
As I welcome a time of sleep, may I know that you are with us through the night that follows day, and in all the joys and sorrows of our lives. Amen.

TUESDAY, OCTOBER 20
(Read Psalm 64)

(Morning)
God of mighty works, because of your steadfast care for all your children, I greet this new day with peace and confidence.

(Evening)
God of mighty works, as you have watched over me this day, keep me in your everlasting arms tonight, that I may rise to serve you again tomorrow.

Sometimes I feel I am surrounded by those who would do me ill, O God. Sometimes I wonder at the evil that we do to one another. Grant me wisdom, courage, and serenity to make peace with those I distrust, dislike, and hate. Out of our conflict bring peace; out of hatred, love.

(Morning)
O God, let me hear the cries of those who suffer at the hands of others. May I use this day to put an end to the suffering and the sickness of soul that cause it.
(Prayers of Intercession)

(Evening)
As this day ends, may I hear your words of comfort and hope.
Although the sounds of suffering remain with me,
may I know that your reign of love will triumph.
(Prayers of Intercession)

**"They will tell what God has brought about
and ponder at what God has done."**

(Morning)
Each day I rise from a bed of privilege and go into a world that is safe for me but not for most people. Use me to work for a world where no one's comfort means hardship for others. Amen.

(Evening)
In this quiet hour, when I block out the noise of the day, fix my mind again on the wonders of all that you do in our lives. May this night be safer for all your children because of something done today. Amen.

WEDNESDAY, OCTOBER 21

(Read Jeremiah 14:7–10)

(Morning)
Ever-present God of action, this day may I walk in the certain hope that in spite of all my shortcomings, you are with me to show me how to live as one called by your name.

(Evening)
Ever-present God, I give thanks for your care and guidance this day. May I rest easy this night knowing I did my best for you and others.

Prone to wander, God, I feel it. Like those of whom Jeremiah spoke, I often want to follow an easier way offered by false leaders. There are times, too, that I think I know better than you what is right for me. But no matter what, you are always here for me. And for this I give you thanks.

(Morning)
It is you who made this day, O God. May I be truly thankful for this wonderful gift and the opportunities for growth and joy that it brings.
(Prayers of Intercession)

(Evening)
Some days are full of trouble. Some days go so well that they end too quickly. Most days are a mixture of both. Dear God, accept my offering of both.
(Prayers of Intercession)

"We are called by your name; do not forsake us!"

(Morning)
As I arise this morning, I place my hand in yours. Lead me. Guide me. Take my hand and show me how to live this day as one of your children. Amen.

(Evening)
Ever-watchful God, as the evening shadows close around me, I turn the cares and worries of this day over to you. As you lift them from my shoulders, I rejoice in the knowledge that you will never forsake one of your own. Amen.

THURSDAY, OCTOBER 22
(Read Jeremiah 14:19–22)

(Morning)
Gracious God, give me a restless heart this day. May I search for the peace
which you alone can give. May I share your peace with another.

(Evening)
Gracious God, throughout the ages and throughout this day, you have remembered your promises to all your creatures. Thank you, O Faithful One, for your
healing presence all day and all night long.

Where, O God, do I look for peace? In possessions, in power, in escape
from the harsh world? Help me seek peace in the right places: among the
hungry, the sick, the prisoners, and the homeless. You have shown us what
is good: to do justice, to love mercy, and to walk humbly with you. Grant
me, O God, the grace to do what is good.

(Morning)
Today I remember the many people who wait patiently for rain to nourish their
parched lands. You alone bring the rains and refresh the earth. Praise be to you.
(Prayers of Intercession)

(Evening)
As the long-awaited rain refreshes the land, as your love heals the injuries of the
day, let your mysterious gift of sleep heal and refresh my soul this night.
(Prayers of Intercession)

"We set our hope on you, for it is you who do all this."

(Morning)	(Evening)
Show me the way of peace and good-ness. This day I will follow you in the paths of peace. Thank you for the miracles of healing and peace. Amen.	Let me end this day as I began it: singing your praise and giving thanks for your mighty works of peace and healing. Amen.

FRIDAY, OCTOBER 23
(Read Psalm 84:1–7)

(Morning)
God, as the dawn breaks through the shadows of night,
let a song of joy swell in my heart. You are the giver of light, song, and joy.
Thank you for sharing your home with us.

(Evening)
God, wherever I may be, I know that you are there. You dwell with all people in
all places. And because of this, I greet the night with a happy heart.

God, whose eye is on the sparrow and who makes a home for the swallow
in your sanctuary, let me always know that you have a home for me. Sometimes I may feel that there is no place for me in the world. Sometimes I feel
like a stranger in my own town. Please take away my self-pity. Move me
out of myself. Bring me to your dwelling place—a place not made with
hands, but a house built of your love for all people.

(Morning)
Open my eyes, that I may see the loveliness of your dwelling place in the world
you create and in the lives of the people I encounter today.
(Prayers of Intercession)

(Evening)
As the swallow and the sparrow find a nesting place in you, may my body,
mind, and spirit rest securely in your love this night.
(Prayers of Intercession)

"Happy are those who live in your house."

(Morning)	(Evening)
God grant me a sense of joy and strength that only you can give. Let me live this day knowing that my footsteps can never leave your home. Amen.	Thank you, God, for your everlasting care for all your creatures: the birds; the animals; the fish; the insects; all humanity, including me. In your arms we find rest for our weary souls. Amen.

SATURDAY, OCTOBER 24
(Read 2 Timothy 4:6–8, 16–18)

(Morning)
God, I am surrounded by many who have fought the good fight and have kept
the faith. Grant me an open mind and a receptive heart to honor those who have
gone on before me.

(Evening)
God, shadows fall as the sunset. With the setting sun come the quiet and the
calm. Tonight and throughout my life, may I receive your gifts with thanks.

God of arrivals and departures, God of struggle and repose, God of racing
and waiting, grant that in all of these, I may keep my mind fixed on you.
Help me to remember that I am called first to be faithful. Remind me of
those persons who have seen the difference between "success" and faithfulness and have chosen to be faithful to you.

(Morning)
Thank you for those teachers, ministers, and dear friends who,
over the years, have shown me the way of faithfulness.
Grant me the strength to live faithfully today.
(Prayers of Intercession)

(Evening)
Tonight I rest in the knowledge that you gave me the strength to fight the good
fight, run the race, and keep my faith in you, dear God.
(Prayers of Intercession)

"God stood by me and gave me strength."

(Morning)	(Evening)
"Now faith is the assurance of things hoped for, the conviction of things not seen." I rejoice and begin this day certain that you work in and through me in many unseen ways. Amen.	If I feel totally drained tonight. I know your loving Spirit will refill my soul with new life and hope for tomorrow. Thank you, God, for your never-ending streams of mercy. Amen.

SUNDAY, OCTOBER 25
(Read Luke 18:9–14)

(Morning)
O God, on this day of rest and gladness, may I find rest and gladness in you.

(Evening)
O God, take what I have heard. Take the songs I have sung. Take all that I have done this day, and use them as you will.

Church can be a dangerous place for me, dear God. It's so easy to see the shortcomings, sins, and faults of everyone else. It's so easy to feel superior to others. Save me, O God, from the sins of the Pharisee. Take away my pride and let me worship you in spirit and in truth.

(Morning)
As I get ready for church this morning, help me remember those who, because of illness, infirmity, work, or indifference, cannot gather for worship today.
(Prayers of Intercession)

(Evening)
So often Sunday night comes as a letdown. The weekend is over, and now it's time to start worrying about tomorrow. Please bless these hours. Remind me that the cares of tomorrow are nothing compared to the joy of today.
(Prayers of Intercession)

**"For all who exalt themselves will be humbled,
but all who humble themselves will be exalted."**

(Morning)
Bless, O God, all who gather to sing your praises and learn your ways. We will meet in many places, speak many languages, and understand your Word differently. But you are above and beyond, in and through us all. Help me remember that in you we are one. Amen.

(Evening)
Dear God, I thank you that in your great mercy you have given me this holy day. Watch over me this night and let me remember that tomorrow is also a holy day. Amen.

MONDAY, OCTOBER 26
(Read Luke 19:1–10)

(Morning)
Accepting and loving God, awaken in me an awareness of the joy waiting for
me this day as I encounter the people around me.

(Evening)
Accepting and loving God, accepting challenges is hard, and yet when I give my
whole being to you, I find peace and strength. I give you thanks.

God of enlightenment, Spirit of peace, there is a surge of peace that quiets
my being as I reflect on the wisdom of the choices Jesus Christ made as an
example for me. There are times when I seek to reject the person like the
tax collector Zacchaeus, and I judge the outside behavior. As I grumble, I
am reminded that love and acceptance change lives. Give me the courage
to reach out to those I am prone to reject, to be intentional in my concern
for their well-being, to encourage them. For it is in giving love to those I
find unlovable that I feel your grace and your peace. Thanks for that gift!

(Morning)
O God, help me to love the heart of each person I meet, even in disagreement
and differences, knowing that your grace holds each one of us.
(Prayers of Intercession)

(Evening)
God of strength, remind me of your continual presence and help me
to prepare myself with the wisdom for looking inward and
then reaching out with your love.
(Prayers of Intercession)

**Accepting the challenges and disappointments of relationships with those
we find oppressive and offensive seems too hard in our own weakness.
Yet we find a new surge of energy when the awareness
of God's Spirit gently touches us.**

(Morning)	(Evening)
For the example of Jesus Christ's acceptance of those he called "lost," I give you thanks. May I, too, find and give acceptance. Amen.	I give thanks for the presence of your Spirit as I close the day. May my wisdom be enhanced, my acceptance of others expanded, and my knowledge of your grace give me peace. Amen.

TUESDAY, OCTOBER 27
(Read Habakkuk 1:1–4)

(Morning)
O God, this day as I read from the prophet, I realize how close to each other he and I seem. I thank you for the opportunity to look at some of the corruption around me, to seek understanding, and to practice patience as I long for your presence and guidance. Faith is at work here.

(Evening)
O God, grant me patience as I close this day without answers, without solutions, with wonderment for the future. My faith is tested.

God of all times and all places, help me to understand the mystery of your timing. Sometimes I cry out for you, wait for an answer, give up, and try to control the uncontrollable. I wonder why there is so much violence, and I have to see it; why there is so much illness and death, and I have to experience the pain of it; why there are so many people in positions of leadership with little ethical and moral fiber, and I have to suffer the consequences of their actions. Teach me, even just for one day, to have the patience to listen for you, to let go and empty myself to be ready to receive.

(Morning)
Give me strength this day to let go of what is not mine, and trust that whatever is a mystery now will become clearer to me as my faith allows me to wait.
(Prayers of Intercession)

(Evening)
Loving God, as I close my day, grant me the peace that comes with trust as I rest and wait. Your grace, given freely, is the astonishing gift that keeps my faith alive.
(Prayers of Intercession)

Being of little faith and waiting for an answer to prayer is the greatest stress we can place on ourselves.

(Morning)
Today I will look for ways to enhance my faith, knowing that you are with me always. Amen.

(Evening)
Give me the faith and courage to let go of unnecessary worry, to relax, and to move into tomorrow, trusting your time, not mine. Amen.

WEDNESDAY, OCTOBER 28
(Read Habakkuk 2:14)

(Morning)
Creator God, thank you for another day. My faith is strong, my being is ready—emptied from the wait and rested from being at peace. Give me courage to face the answers to the questions of a new day.

(Evening)
Creator God, you are with me just as you promised. Take what you have given to me and make me an instrument of your love in the world.

Spirit of God, after shrinking from believing, I am guided now by faith to be reliable, confident, and trusting. Breathe into me a restlessness to live the vision of your love, to make it plain to the world, and to be the truth in every way. Keep me honest, tender enough to heal, and tough enough to be healed of my own hypocrisies. Help me never to forget that you are with me through all adversity. I have only to ask and trust. With your love surrounding me, help me to remember the grace that abounds with all mystery.

(Morning)
Challenging God, help me as I teeter on the edge of my vulnerability and excitement for this new day, knowing the possibility of creating and sharing a vision of your love with another. Keep me strong and confident.
(Prayers of Intercession)

(Evening)
In the silence of these few moments, God, you are my strength and my hope. Grant me peace of mind, courage of conviction, and fruition of faith as I close this day to all the joys and struggles of its many hours.
(Prayers of Intercession)

**If we but wait, God is here. If we but ask, God is here.
If we but trust, God is as faithful as God expects us to be.**

(Morning)
It is easy to lose sight of your vision and to be weak in faith. I thank you for your patience and grace, God of love and peace. Amen.

(Evening)
Renewal comes, great and loving God, as I listen, trust, work, and love in your grace. Thank you for trusting me to be here for you. Amen.

THURSDAY, OCTOBER 29
(Read Psalm 119:137–44)

(Morning)
Tender and compassionate God, you are the source of my life, and I trust you to show me what is best for me. In this new day, form me to be a rich source of your love in all that I do.

(Evening)
Tender and compassionate God, I have never known a richer gift than your love. Slow me down to lose the frenzy of a busy day, to absorb your peaceful Spirit of rest and renewal.

With your love you seek me, O God. You know all about me, my imperfections, my shortcomings, my failures. Yet your love remains constant for me to embrace. I am excited and challenged to receive the outpouring of your grace, and I prepare to act out of that love today. With your love surrounding me, no matter what trouble I may encounter, you will be there. Help me to capture a new vision each day. Help me to feel your gentle guidance in the unfolding of life, that I may take the joy of wholeness to your people everywhere.

(Morning)
As I accept the new challenges of the day, give me strength to accomplish them. Bring courage to fear, faith to doubt, and hope to the hopeless,
O God of all vision.
(Prayers of Intercession)

(Evening)
Be with me as I seek to understand more clearly my call to be loving, just, and fully human. I put my faith in your words and your love, O God.
(Prayers of Intercession)

"Give me understanding that I may live."

(Morning)
I seek understanding, O God, because like a loving parent, I know you are fair and just. Thank you for your truth. Amen.

(Evening)
As I capture visions of the future, help me to be reminded that I must truly reflect your constant love. I live fully because I have sought your understanding. Amen.

FRIDAY, OCTOBER 30
(Read Isaiah 1:10–18)

(Morning)
All-knowing God, as I awaken to the morning, fresh from resting and at peace with the world, touch me with the awareness of all that is outside waiting for me. Help me to take off the blinders and prepare myself for today.

(Evening)
All-knowing God, you have filled me with love and care for the world. Help me to face another day by bringing peace and restoration to my soul.

Holy and loving God, you have touched me with your presence and filled me with love and courage. Enlighten me, so that I may enlighten others. Set before me images of what it means to be your servant, so that I may mirror those images in all that I do. If I grow apathetic and indifferent, shake me into being fully present and fully alive. Where there is desolation, help me to bring hope, where there is ignorance, knowledge. And most of all, help me to keep close to your Spirit, the source of all gifts and strength in times of trouble.

(Morning)
God, help me, each day, to believe in new beginnings and to make a new start;
to be a new start.
(Prayers of Intercession)

(Evening)
Spirit of the loving God, I have gone to my limits today. Calm the chaos of my hurried mind and body. Bring peace to that chaos and order to the clutter, that I may rest in your love.
(Prayers of Intercession)

Create in us a resting place. Keep renewing us to make our community a place of love, acceptance, understanding, and an ordered life.

(Morning)
We don't seem to be aware, yet we are, of all that is falling apart around us. O God, give us light to open our eyes and courage to lead into newness of life.
Amen.

(Evening)
By your grace, Sustainer God, keep me from taking myself too seriously, prod me to question what I do not understand, to live my convictions, and to hear with openness and love.
Amen.

SATURDAY, OCTOBER 31
(Read Psalm 32:1–7)

(Morning)
God, you know I have fallen short, yet you continue to forgive. Thank you for the grace-filled life you promise and give me. I seek to love you as you love me.

(Evening)
God, I can rest knowing that when I recognize and admit my own failures, seek change, and laugh a little, I feel much better. Your forgiveness is without a doubt the strongest aid to my rest. Thank you from the bottom of my heart.

O ingenious God, your Spirit touches me so deeply that I am able to find a sense of myself, even in the pain of falling short of my goals. I am grateful that, in my simplicity, I can love without hesitation because I know your love will hold me. Help me to sort the essential from the trivial and grant me enthusiasm in empty and full places. I ask that you give me courage to face life as it is and to live passionately, knowing that it is a safe place with you to tell you of my imperfections. Deepen my wisdom and gift me with your healing touch to give to people struggling with the health of their souls. Thanks and praise to you, God.

(Morning)
As you touch me with your wholeness, God of love, my heart overflows with gratitude. Help me to reach out constantly to touch another as I have been touched by your forgiveness and love.
(Prayers of Intercession)

(Evening)
There is joy in forgiveness, God, and you have given me that joy in this hour. As I rest, may I be reminded that peace begins in being right with oneself. It is in your love that I rejoice in the freedom to be honest about myself.
(Prayers of Intercession)

True abundance comes from a gift given by God.
Thanks be to God for that gift.

(Morning)	(Evening)
Remind me, God, each day I awaken, that I am forgiven and loved, forgiven and loved. Amen.	I rejoice and give thanks for all that I am and all that I can become through your love and your care. Amen.

SUNDAY, NOVEMBER 1
(Read 2 Thessalonians 1:1–4, 11–12)

(Morning)
O God, it is good to give thanks for those who work so hard in the community
of faith. Thanks come so easily, and love is so important.
May I always treat other justly and lovingly.

(Evening)
O God, at the close of this day I feel enriched by the knowledge of others who
seek to follow you. It gives me peace as I close the day to give you thanks for
lives so faithful.

God of ancient times and of this November morning, your Spirit fills my heart
as I remember the community of faith around the world. I am reminded of your
love by the saints who have gone before me, the preciousness of their lives,
and the beauty of their memory in my heart. Your love reminds me of faithful
people living the example of loving one another like hands and hearts reaching
around the world to embrace. I rejoice and give thanks for all that the people of
God around the world can be and all that we can become because of your love
and the steadfast work of your people.

(Morning)
Loving God, help me to encourage those who are faithfully sharing themselves
with the world because of the love you give them and
because of their love for you.
(Prayers of Intercession)

(Evening)
As the day comes to a close, give me the wisdom to move out of
self-centeredness; to move toward others; to give strength
in weakness, joy in celebration, peace and quiet in chaos.
Help us to know your love, so that we may love.
(Prayers of Intercession)

Love and encouragement are never given away in a vacuum.
They go right to the heart of the receiver and bring healing and peace.

(Morning)	(Evening)
O God of all love, just as Paul encour-aged the people of the early church, help me to encourage those working in today's world to pass on your love by loving one another. Amen.	I hear whispers of peace in the stillness of the evening, fresh breezes of promise for those feeling loved and appreciated. I rejoice in that love. Amen.

MONDAY, NOVEMBER 2
(Read 2 Thessalonians 2:1–5)

(Morning)
Holy One, I thank you for the promise of this new day,
and I await the advent of your new day.

(Evening)
Holy One, I am weary from my labors. Grant me rest and renewal.

Holy One, I am anxious for your time. I am anxious for the day when you will establish your order on earth, when your justice will be manifest in this world, and for the coming of your dominion. Many voices clamor for my attention. Teach me to discern your voice above the clamorers. Make me vigilant, that I may not be deceived by pretenders to your glory. Help me to be patient as I wait for that foretold time when your Child will gather your family together in righteous peace.

(Morning)
Holy One, prepare me for this day by making me sensitive
to the needs of others.
(Prayers of Intercession)

(Evening)
Holy One, prepare me for your day, when there will be no more need.
(Prayers of Intercession)

Holy One, my divided world longs to be gathered, united together in you.
(Pray the Prayer of Our Savior.)

(Morning)
Holy One, in my rising hours and in
these trying times, may I work
on behalf of others. Amen.

(Evening)
Holy One, as I sleep I look forward to
your dawn. Amen.

TUESDAY, NOVEMBER 3
(Read Haggai 1:15b–2:9)

(Morning)
Holy One, may your Word come to me today as to your prophet Haggai.

(Evening)
Holy One, may your Word work on me as I reflect on my day's labors.

Holy One, I look at my nation as Haggai looked at your temple. Is it not as nothing in your sight? Communities are in shambles, lives are broken, all is in need of repair. Then comes your Word, a charge to rebuild. But I am afraid. The task is so much larger than I. But you speak again: "Take courage . . . do not fear." Help me to see that though the cost to rebuild is great, the silver and the gold are yours. Help me to see that you will provide the prosperity, O God. Thank you for your grace.

(Morning)
Holy One, I am mindful of those of us with broken lives;
we stand in need of repair.
(Prayers of Intercession)

(Evening)
Holy One, as I prepare to sleep in peace,
I remember those of us who will tumble tonight in turmoil.
(Prayers of Intercession)

With God no task is too big, no challenge too great; all things are possible.
(Pray the Prayer of Our Savior.)

(Morning)	(Evening)
Holy One, may I mend the fractures I encounter in my world today. Amen.	Holy One, mend the fracture you find in me tonight. Amen.

WEDNESDAY, NOVEMBER 4
(Read Psalm 145:17–21)

(Morning)
Holy One, be near to me today!

(Evening)
Holy One, thank you for being a refuge for the weary.

Most Holy One, I praise you for all your wondrous deeds. You are worthy to be praised. For you are just to those who repay with iniquity. You show kindness to those who are callused by hatred. You incline your ear to those who call out to you. You bless those who revere your holy name. You protect those whose hearts embrace you. For this we all are thankful: "My mouth will speak the praise of the Sovereign, and all flesh will bless God's holy name forever and ever."

(Morning)
Holy One, I pray for those who do not know to praise you.
(Prayers of Intercession)

(Evening)
Holy One, I pray that others may see your goodness and extol you.
(Prayers of Intercession)

The thought of your majesty consumes me. I am in awe of you.
(Pray the Prayer of Our Savior.)

(Morning)	(Evening)
Let your glory shine through me. Amen.	Be near me as I slumber, my refuge as I sleep. Amen.

THURSDAY, NOVEMBER 5
(Read Psalm 98)

(Morning)
Holy One, I awake with a "new song" in my mouth in anticipation of your marvelous blessings.

(Evening)
Holy One, I am spent, and I retreat to the sanctity of your steadfast love.

Holy One, my soul rejoices in your victories. You have won great battles in my life. You have brought me relief in the midst of my struggles. You have lifted me up when I was downcast. You have been present with me when I have felt most alone. For these things I will praise you with the essence of my being. I will make myself an instrument of your praise. I will exalt you with my tongue, my hands, my feet, my soul, my life.

(Morning)
Holy One, knowing that you are able, I remember the needs of . . .
(Prayers of Intercession)

(Evening)
Holy One, I thank you now for what you have done and will do in the lives of those I have remembered.
(Prayers of Intercession)

Make me always mindful of your many blessings!
(Pray the Prayer of Our Savior.)

(Morning)
Holy One, help me to see others as you do, with righteousness in my eyes and equity in my heart. Amen.

(Evening)
Holy One, as I retire, my spirit smiles because of the wonder of you. Amen.

FRIDAY, NOVEMBER 6
(Read Job 19:23–27a)

(Morning)
Holy One, I awake confident that you are the living God.

(Evening)
Holy One, my eyes have rejoiced to see your redemption today.

Holy One, in a world that often is cold and cruel, in a time that is filled with distress and fear, it is good to know "that my Redeemer lives." As Job cried out from a sea of woes, my soul cries confidently amid my storms, "I know that my Redeemer lives." When all my friends have become foes as Job's did, you are there; you are "on my side"; to this I testify. And confidently I will take my stand against all that will assail, knowing that I have a powerful ally. Let it be written across my life for all the world to see, the surety with which I say, "I know that my Redeemer lives."

(Morning)
Holy One, I remember those in need of a Redeemer in their lives as you have been in mine.
(Prayers of Intercession)

(Evening)
Holy One, I am mindful of those who do not know that you are on their side.
(Prayers of Intercession)

I thank you for the victories your presence assures.
(Pray the Prayer of Our Savior.)

(Morning)
Holy One, no matter what comes my way today, I am thankful that you are on my side. Amen.

(Evening)
Holy One, I thank you that my Christ lives and that I will one day see my Savior face to face. Amen.

SATURDAY, NOVEMBER 7
(Read Psalm 17:1–9)

(Morning)
Holy One, I seek to hold fast to your paths.

(Evening)
Holy One, forgive me if my feet have slipped as I have walked along your way.

Holy One, I strive to do right in your eyes. I have worked to keep my inner being pure, my heart and soul as your habitation. I have sought to honor you with my mouth and to keep my lips from sin. I have shunned the ways of the wicked. I have vowed to live in peace, meeting violence with compassion. Still I often have fallen short of the goals I set. Forgive me and cleanse my heart. Renew me and make me whole. Restore me by your grace to communion with you. Holy One, attend to my cry.

(Morning)
Holy One, I remember now those of us who need a hiding place.
(Prayers of Intercession)

(Evening)
Holy One, I remember those of us who are struggling to hold fast to your path.
(Prayers of Intercession)

**When I am greatly shaken, I will run to you and
I will hide in the shadow of your wings.**
(Pray the Prayer of Our Savior.)

(Morning)
Holy One, "guard me as the apple of your eye." Amen.

(Evening)
Holy One, as you visit me tonight, try my heart and make me whole where I am broken. Amen.

SUNDAY, NOVEMBER 8
(Read Luke 20:27–38)

(Morning)
Holy One, as I awake this morning,
let me follow Jesus to your house of worship.

(Evening)
Holy One, make me "worthy of a place in that age."

Holy One, when your Child was challenged, you provided the answer. Strengthen me to be able when the trials come. Help me to overcome the snares of the crafty by a knowledge of your Word. Make me worthy of a place in that age and ready for the resurrection. Let me never fear death, because you have made me like an angel and a child of God through your resurrection power.

(Morning)
Holy One, I remember those whose faith will be tried today.
(Prayers of Intercession)

(Evening)
Holy One, I thank you for being the God who answers prayer.
Consider the needs of these your people . . .
(Prayers of Intercession)

**God cannot be tempted nor the children of God
dismayed by the wisdom of humanity.**

(Morning)
Holy One, make me equal to the
challenge of those who would try me
today. Amen.

(Evening)
Holy One, when the evening of my life
draws near, make me, like Abraham,
Isaac, and Jacob, alive to you. Amen.

MONDAY, NOVEMBER 9
(Read Luke 21:5–11)

(Morning)
O Great Spirit, I see the beauty you have created and feel hope.
I will not let evil frighten me, nor will I be deceived,
for you are the good news. You are my defender.

(Evening)
O Great Spirit, the sun sets and the heavens come alive with light.
All the universe holds beauty. Thank you for the gift of life,
so that I may behold all these things.

Jesus, you said the time would come when the stones of our temples would be thrown down. The signs are present today. Many of our temples are no longer adorned with beautiful stones. They have been burned by those who hate, or they have been neglected and abandoned. Yet hope prevails. The faith and hope you have given us through words and signs over centuries churn within us, and so we defy. We rebuild. I cannot think of anything more promising, more exciting, than to be a Christian and to know you. Praise the Creator!

(Morning)
Creator of my life, with my mind and with my heart, I absorb the sins of the world, the sins of the people, and give them to you.
(Prayers of Intercession)

(Evening)
Gracious and forgiving Spirit, thank you for what has been good and for being the keeper of my fears.
(Prayers of Intercession)

"Fear defeats purpose, and so, with purpose, I strive for faith."

(Morning)
Great Spirit, please put faith in my heart where remnants of fear may lie, so that my day will be filled with good. Amen.

(Evening)
For the gift of life, the gift of knowledge, and the gift of forgiveness, thank you, O Great Spirit. Amen.

TUESDAY, NOVEMBER 10
(Read Luke 21:12–19)

(Morning)
Creator God, you surround me with beauty today. My soul yearns to seek it, so that all may know you and your powers. I will wait for your words of wisdom.

(Evening)
Creator God, this day was all that you promised. Not a hair on my head was harmed, and you kept all of my worries so that I might do your work with a glad heart. Thank you.

Jesus, you said that not a hair on our head would perish if we followed you. What a gift to have in our lives, to know that days filled with strife need not be burdensome if we truly believe that you will protect us. We know that we will hear sad news—another child killed, or someone, somewhere, put to death because of their religious beliefs. Sadly, this has always been so. Yet when our hearts are filled with the Holy Spirit, we continue our faith journey, and we seek justice because we have to.

(Morning)
As I begin this day with a clear mind, waiting to be filled with your wisdom, be with me and those I love.
(Prayers of Intercession)

(Evening)
As I end this day in contentment, having done my best to seek your will, I ask that you bring contentment to all others in my circle.
(Prayers of Intercession)

"Though people may betray people, God never betrays."

(Morning)
Creator God, as the day breaks and the sun shines warm into my heart, help me shine warmth into my home and my community. Amen.

(Evening)
God, my loving protector. I cannot live without you in a world full of strife and turmoil. This world needs you! Amen.

WEDNESDAY, NOVEMBER 11
(Read Isaiah 65:17–25)

(Morning)
Holy, holy, holy. All around me is holy. I am holy. Creator God, there is no ugliness in your creation, only in the minds of evildoers. Help me remember my holiness and that of those with whom I associate, so that the New Jerusalem you have promised can begin here and now.

(Evening)
Holy, holy, holy. Great Spirit of all who are spiritual in mind and heart, the awe of the morning Scripture stayed with me all day. Thank you for lifting me and setting my mind on all that can be made new.

Living, breathing Spirit of God, your words in Isaiah bring so much hope: a new earth, new heavens, and a New Jerusalem; a place where there will be pure joy, long lives, and no more tears. Though I have felt pain and sadness and cried many tears, you have always been there for me. And because you have been there for me, I believe in you and this promise. The longer I linger on this message, the more excited I am to have been created just for this time.

(Morning)
Eternal and Great Spirit, lift me to sacred and holy grounds,
that I might be spiritually cleansed.
(Prayers of Intercession)

(Evening)
Eternal and Great Spirit, the magnitude of your work has been manifested with the promise of a New Jerusalem. I pray for your continuing guidance
to live out this glory.
(Prayers of Intercession)

"The serpent cannot survive on dust, so feed dust to the serpent."

(Morning)
The New Jerusalem beckons, O God. Make my walk pure. Keep the vision of a New Jerusalem before me so I can do my part. Amen.

(Evening)
I take from this day what has been good and leave the rest behind. Thank you, Great Spirit, for my lessons today. Amen.

THURSDAY, NOVEMBER 12
(Read Isaiah 12)

(Morning)
Praise to you, O Great Spirit, Creator of heaven and earth. Sanctify me.
Wash me clean. I hold my arms out to you; draw me close.
Take me to a place where I can breathe in your strength and your Spirit.

(Evening)
Praise to you, O Great Spirit, Creator of heaven and earth.
If I have angered you in any way, I know that I have been forgiven already.
With joy this evening, I receive the comfort of my Savior.

Sometimes my weaknesses overcome me. They grow like my shadow in the twilight. Confusing thoughts swirl about in my mind. I get too big. No room for you, dear God. I forget to exalt you. How can I not praise you, the One who has comforted me time and again? Scriptures like Isaiah remind me to remain humble and grateful. It is you, God, who promises us a New Jerusalem. It is you who promises salvation and provides a way for us to draw water from the wells of salvation, through your Child, Jesus Christ.

(Morning)
Creator God, how great is the One who can answer all prayers.
I pray for peace and serenity in a world of pain and turmoil.
(Prayers of Intercession)

(Evening)
A restful sleep is necessary for the peace of mind needed to do your work.
In this world there are many who do not have a place to rest.
God bless all those who are meek and without rest.
(Prayers of Intercession)

"God's anger is never very long, God's comfort is forever."

(Morning)
Today I will sing praises to the Most High, for glorious things have been done. Thank you, God. Amen.

(Evening)
For all that has been good today, I thank you, Great Spirit. For those who have helped me, I thank you. Amen.

FRIDAY, NOVEMBER 13
(Read Malachi 4:1–2a)

(Morning)
Dearest Jesus, some days you walk beside me, some days you carry me,
and some days you have to drag me; but you never, never give up on me.
Just knowing you are with me today is enough.

(Evening)
Dearest Jesus, you were with me today, and I felt you. I needed you. I always
need you. Thank you for this very special day and for your special presence.

Prophets like Malachi encourage our faith. God, he reminds us of your
anger, wrath, and love. We leap from our idleness with conviction and begin the process of restoration when strong-willed purpose is thrust on us.
We need your love exposed to us time and again. Scripture reminds us that
"the sun of righteousness will rise with healing in its wings," if we respond
to the call. I want to respond to your call. I want healing. Am I prepared?
Am I helping you to build a New Jerusalem today?

(Morning)
Holy Spirit of God, I want to respond to your call.
I want healing, and so I ask for healing.
(Prayers of Intercession)

(Evening)
My soul rests in you after a long and busy day.
I am so grateful to have you in my life.
(Prayers of Intercession)

"Despondency gets you nowhere. Respond, instead."

(Morning)
Holy and Great Spirit, I welcome this
new day. May your warm winds of
heaven blow softly on me and bring
sunrise into my heart. Amen.
(Cherokee blessing)

(Evening)
Great Spirit, make me always ready
to come to you with clean hands and
straight eyes so when life fades, as
the fading sunset, my spirit may come
to you without shame. Amen.
(American Indian prayer)

SATURDAY, NOVEMBER 14
(Read Psalms 98)

(Morning)
Dear God, your mighty creation trembles. Mother Earth seems to be shrinking with fear and trauma. We are cruel. We forget the sacredness of life. Today teach me kindness and respect for all that you have made.

(Evening)
Dear God, your mighty creation trembles. We forget the sacredness of life. Continue to teach me kindness and respect.

God, you are so good. Your Child, Jesus the Christ, is so good. Your Holy Spirit is so good. I give praise to the triumph over evil that I have been given through your Word. I praise you for all those blessed, tormented, committed, and loyal people who wrote down your words. I can seek justice, peace, and especially guidance from those age-old stories and words. Let us sing, let us make a joyful noise, let us bless all of Mother Earth's living creations. Let us prepare ourselves for the New Jerusalem.

(Morning)
You have done marvelous things for us. Thank you, God.
I praise you today and ask you to reveal your righteousness to the nations.
(Prayers of Intercession)

(Evening)
Holy Spirit, I end this day with hope and yet with some trepidation.
Salvation is needed for me, for us, here and now.
(Prayers of Intercession)

"If we do not sing, we miss the joy of praising God mightily."

(Morning)
God, thank you for those inspired, faithful old songs and hymns. I have a song in my heart this morning that tells me to keep "my mind stayed on Jesus." Amen.

(Evening)
Holy and Great Spirit, as shadows lengthen across the sky, I wait for the stars to light up the heavens, for all these things tell me how mighty you are. Thank you for another blessed day. Amen.

SUNDAY, NOVEMBER 15
(Read 2 Thessalonians 3:6–13)

(Morning)
Great Spirit and Creator of all, you rested on the seventh day. Some of us rest every day. Remove from me the idleness and complacency that sometimes set in. Provide me with the spiritual nourishment to do your work today.

(Evening)
Great Spirit and Creator of all, provide me with
the spiritual nourishment needed to continue your work.

God, Paul tells the church to keep away from those who are idle. He reminds us that he and others became models for us to follow. He also reminds us that we cannot wait for Christ's return in order to set the world right. There are things we must do here and now! I have found that a structured and directed life is easier to live. Most important, it detracts us from associating with people who are not as spiritually inclined as we are. Paul says to stay away from those kinds of people, to detach from them. I must get busy and prepare for Jesus, now.

(Morning)
Dear God, you have taught me so much through all of your prophets and disciples. I ask you to help me become a model for others.
(Prayers of Intercession)

(Evening)
Great Spirit and Creator of us all, idleness and evil are everywhere. Help me to stay on the path you have determined is mine, so I may witness for others.
(Prayers of Intercession)

"Idleness breeds anxiety and defeat. Prepare yourselves daily."

(Morning)
Great Spirit, I face all directions this morning with hope and with the spirit of willingness. Amen.

(Evening)
Holy, holy, holy God. You've kept me from evil, you've given me a glad heart to do you work, you've guided me. Thank you. Amen.

MONDAY, NOVEMBER 16
(Read Luke 1:68–79)

(Morning)
God of the prophets, thank you for remembering me today. Shine your light on
me, fill me with joy, and give me the words to praise you with today.

(Evening)
God of the prophets, thank you for remembering me today.

Creator God, I praise you for all you have done for me, your servant. You
haven't forgotten me; you haven't left me to wallow in my troubles or to be
trapped by those who attack me. You have fulfilled your promise of sending a leader. I will serve Jesus by proclaiming his mercy and righteousness,
and I will enjoy the light of God which has been given to me.

(Morning)
May your praise burst forth from me today,
proclaiming the fulfillment of your will in my life.
(Prayers of Intercession)

(Evening)
God of the ages, thank you for leading me through another day. If I failed to
share with others the story of what you've done for me, forgive me.
(Prayers of Intercession)

**Thank you for the opportunities to tell of the ways
in which you move in my life.**

(Morning)
I will serve you today and follow your
paths. Amen.

(Evening)
May I be ready to follow you wherever
you might lead. Amen.

TUESDAY, NOVEMBER 17
(Read Jeremiah 23:1–3)

(Morning)
Almighty God, thank you for stories of your action and intervention in the lives
of your people. I read these words today with a renewed sense of hope
and trust in your guiding hand.

(Evening)
Almighty God, thank you for stories of your action and
intervention in the lives of your people.

Dear God, there are people who are abusing positions of leadership and
authority. Their idolatry has led those of us under their charge to be removed from your way. Their false instruction has driven us apart and forced
us away from our paths. Here our cry, God of wisdom, and bring us back
into community with one another. Heal us and let our endeavors develop as
you would have them do.

(Morning)
May I live this day wary of false voices and those who misuse their position.
(Prayers of Intercession)

(Evening)
God who knows all things, grant me a night of renewal and regeneration.
If I have followed today the stray path of false leaders, forgive me.
(Prayers of Intercession)

**Thank you for your Spirit which guides us
away from evil and brings us together.**

(Morning)	(Evening)
I commit myself to following only your way, my God. Amen.	May I be ready tomorrow to walk in the path which you have chosen for me. Amen.

WEDNESDAY, NOVEMBER 18
(Read Jeremiah 23:4–6)

(Morning)
God of righteousness, thank you for the assurance that you will nurture leaders to walk with your people. As I begin this morning, fill me with confidence in your guiding hand.

(Evening)
God of righteousness, thank you for the nurturing of leaders.

I know, Creator God, that you are able to touch me and bring to life my talents and abilities. Develop my capabilities, that I might provide leadership to your people in whatever form you would have me do so. Enable me to help your people face new challenges with courage and unity. Make me like a "righteous branch," and give me the discernment to make wise decisions and proper moves in the execution of today's responsibilities.

(Morning)
May I enter this day with the conviction that you will give me a spirit of leadership when you would have me lead.
(Prayers of Intercession)

(Evening)
Righteous God, who has inspired me this day,
grant me a night of peaceful rest. Forgive me if I failed
to take up the mantle of leadership when you called me to do so.
(Prayers of Intercession)

Thank you for providing me with a spirit of leadership this day.

(Morning)
I enter this day looking for areas in which you call me to lead. Amen.

(Evening)
May I face tomorrow with enthusiasm for heeding any call to leadership you may give. Amen.

THURSDAY, NOVEMBER 19
(Read Psalm 46)

(Morning)
Protecting God, I face this day with confidence, knowing that you are with me as I go through today's experiences. Thank you for hymns and poems of praise that express my faith in your guidance.

(Evening)
Protecting God, thank you for hymns and poems of praise
that express my faith in your guidance.

God of strength, you are our shelter amidst the trials of our life. When problems and difficult situations threaten to engulf us, you protect us and give us what we need to weather the storm. You are with us in the community, making your presence known even through the troubles of our times. We must slow down enough to experience your calming presence in all aspects of life and to witness how you move in this world.

(Morning)
May I be still enough today to experience your company
in all the areas of my life.
(Prayers of Intercession)

(Evening)
Sustaining God, who has been my sanctuary today,
provide me tonight with rest and the comfort of your guarding hand.
Forgive me if I failed to trust your presence this day.
(Prayers of Intercession)

Thank you for sending your guiding and protecting Spirit this day.

(Morning)	(Evening)
I will draw strength from you today and allow you to be my retreat. Amen.	I look forward to experiencing your presence tomorrow and increasing my faith in your direction and protection. Amen.

FRIDAY, NOVEMBER 20
(Read Colossians 1:11–14)

(Morning)
Eternal God, who gives us energy to live, thank you for the witness of your
servants, who endured tribulation with long-suffering and praise on their lips to
you. As I begin a new day, let that same thanksgiving spring forth from me.

(Evening)
Eternal God, thank you for the witness of your servants' endurance
and thanksgiving.

My vigor comes from your wonderful, awesome might, Creator God. You
let me tap into your power in order to survive and be strong in whatever
situation I find myself in; you give me a spirit of perseverance. It's amazing how you empower me to sing your praises with joy and enthusiasm,
even while I go through the difficulties of life. I know that I walk through
the same trials that your servants have endured throughout history, and I'm
excited to know that, like them, I will receive your blessings! Through
your mercy, you have allowed me to dwell in the world of the Christ.

(Morning)
May I live this day in a spirit of perseverance and praise to you.
(Prayers of Intercession)

(Evening)
Everlasting God, your presence has enabled me to make it through the trials of
the day. Grant me rest along my journey, and forgive me if there were times
when my heart withheld thanksgiving from you.
(Prayers of Intercession)

**Thank you for the strength to live this day
with energy provided through the Savior.**

(Morning)
I receive your power this day, in order
to live with vigor and with praise to
you. Amen.

(Evening)
May I continue to draw upon your
energy tomorrow, giving all thanks to
you. Amen.

SATURDAY, NOVEMBER 21
(Read Colossians 1:15–20)

(Morning)
Everlasting God, whose presence is in all the universe, thank you for the way in which your servants have praised you over the ages. As I begin this day, fill me with the peace and completeness that come from you through the Christ.

(Evening)
Everlasting God, fill me this evening with the peace and completeness that come from you through the Christ.

I am brought to you, Creator God, by the One who is your manifestation. Through the Christ I can begin to see your wonders and the dynamic way in which you move in the universe and in my life. I know that the eternal Christ is my leader, and the One who brings together my brothers and sisters in the faith. I come to you, Creator, through the sacrifice of Jesus; now I am brought back to you, and I am able to experience the abundance of your love and will for my life.

(Morning)
May I experience this day the completeness that you offer through the Christ.
(Prayers of Intercession)

(Evening)
Endless God, you have filled me today with the peace that comes through the Christ experience. Restore me tonight as I rest. Pardon me for any times that I was not in harmony with you.
(Prayers of Intercession)

Thank you for the boundless reconciliation I have with you through Christ.

(Morning)
I go forward this day in the peace of the Creator, expressed through the Christ experience. Amen.

(Evening)
May I awake tomorrow knowing that you, Creator, will present yourself to me through my experience with the Christ. Amen.

SUNDAY, NOVEMBER 22
(Read Luke 23:33–43)

(Morning)
Loving God, you have given us the opportunity to read the story of those precious moments on the cross, to understand what you have done for me through Jesus' sacrifice. As I feel the love you demonstrated in the midst of your pain, my heart cries, "Thank you, merciful God, thank you."

(Evening)
Loving God, you have given us the story of your sacrifice on the cross.
Thank you, merciful God.

Somehow, my God, you forgive me. When I crucify you with my thoughts, my actions, my unfaithfulness, you forgive me. When I gamble away and waste the resources and talents you have provided me, you forgive me. When I taunt you and play games with your love, you still forgive me. Let me not pretend that I deserve your mercy; enable me to receive your blessings with thanksgiving for your amazing and all-encompassing love, your paradise, your dominion.

(Morning)
May I live this day ever mindful of the love you demonstrated for me.
(Prayers of Intercession)

(Evening)
Caring God, whose love for me is more than I could sufficiently praise you for, grant me a restful night. Forgive me if I have lived today without forgiving others and reflecting toward them the caring you show me.
(Prayers of Intercession)

**Remember me, Savior, as I endeavor today
to live a life worthy of your dominion.**

(Morning)
I commit myself to embrace the experience of the cross by showing love to others. Amen.

(Evening)
May I love and forgive tomorrow, as you have done for me. Amen.

MONDAY, NOVEMBER 23
(Read Isaiah 2:1–3)

(Morning)
God, I open my eyes this morning to a glimpse of your mountain. The dreary clouds of November have shifted to reveal your house on the rock, and I see that it is stable and strong. May I start this new week on a path which leads to your house; may I follow the winding road up to your mountain.

(Evening)
God, I give thanks to you for a day of learning, a day of risks. Your strength and wisdom nourish me and guide me on the road. Have I inched closer to you by the day's end? Am I nearer than I was at sunrise? I pray for you to answer, "Yes." For you to say, "Come closer still."

Eternal God, I hear the ancient call which beckons, "Let us go up to the mountain of God, to the house of the God of Jacob." I yearn to share your home with you, to be with you always. But how scary to make that climb. What awaits me at the peak? Will I find stability? Or will I need, also, to face my fear of falling from the cliff? Loving you, dear God, is risky.

(Morning)
God, you are always within reach. Help me to be aware of your presence. Remind me today to stay focused and intent on my journey toward you.
(Prayers of Intercession)

(Evening)
You ask that I follow your way, O God. Provide me with ears to hear your Word, with the vision to see your path. May Christ be with me this evening as my teacher and my guide.
(Prayers of Intercession)

Come, let us go up to the mountain of God.

(Morning)
Thank you, loving and forgiving God, for this new opportunity to be with you. Each day you grant me yet another invitation to visit your house on the mountain. Your faith in me does not waver. Help me to have that same faith in you. Amen.

(Evening)
Ever-present God, I know that our time together does not end when I sleep. Thank you for being with me always. May I wake tomorrow with the knowledge of your presence. Amen.

TUESDAY, NOVEMBER 24
(Read Matthew 24:36–39)

(Morning)
Powerful God, I am thankful for your presence in my life. This morning I seek to be especially mindful of your Spirit as it works in me, through me, and reveals your beauty in the people I encounter.

(Evening)
Powerful God, may I be awake to your call and stirred by your voice, each day and every hour.

God, you surprise me again and again. When it seems that I have forgotten you, you rush, like a flood, back into my life. You were never really gone. I was the one who was absent. When I become distracted and busy with the details of this crazy world, you and your Child come to me, unannounced, and demand that I turn and look. Help me to remember that daily life has more meaning when I invite you to be a part of it. It is crucial for me to remember you, not only in crisis, but in all times.

(Morning)
All-knowing God, grant me the ability to hear your voice above the noise of life. Grant me the wisdom to respond.
(Prayers of Intercession)

(Evening)
I pray for, and with, all of my sisters and brothers who need you in their lives. We all need you. Please answer our cries. Be with us now. Help us to welcome you. Help us to work together in peace.
(Prayers of Intercession)

And they knew nothing until the flood came and swept them all away.

(Morning)
I pray that today will be nothing like yesterday. I ask for tomorrow to be new and fresh. I will strive to notice you in all of the beauty and in all of the struggle of your creation. Amen.

(Evening)
God, it takes energy and effort for me to be in this relationship with you. Help me to stay on your path. May tonight's rest be fuel for tomorrow's journey. Amen.

WEDNESDAY, NOVEMBER 25
(Read Matthew 24:40–42)

(Morning)
Creator God, you have caused the sun to rise once again. What a beautiful reminder of new birth and resurrection! The rising sun is one unchanging element in this ever-changing world. I praise you and the new light you bring to the world each day.

(Evening)
Creator God, thank you for guiding me through another day. I am grateful for your forgiveness when I refuse to pay attention to your coming. You still have not left me behind!

Maker of both darkness and light, I know that each day you will reveal yourself in a new sunrise. I have yet to find a morning where the sun refuses to rise or an evening without a sunset in the west. Thank you for giving me some things that are certain. Help me to respond quickly to those things that are unexpected, to be like the woman grinding meal who stopped her work to go with you. I fear that you will come to me when I am asleep and inattentive. I will attempt to follow the words of Scripture. I will strive to keep awake.

(Morning)
God, I pray today for the gift of your presence.
Please, make yourself visible to me. As I work, celebrate, breathe, and live, give me the power to know you when you come.
(Prayers of Intercession)

(Evening)
Forgive me, God, if my eyes were closed to you today.
Forgive me if I did not hear you speak. Help me live out my desire to know you. Help me respond to your call.
(Prayers of Intercession)

One will be taken, and one will be left.

(Morning)
God of us all, today I am willing to see your light break through in life's most mundane moments. I will try to be awake to your unexpected grace.
Amen.

(Evening)
I have participated in another day. I have been present for another sunset. I pray that I will see more vividly the colors of your sun and feel more deeply the warmth of its light. Amen.

THURSDAY, NOVEMBER 26
(Read Psalm 122)

(Morning)
God, as my spirit makes the journey to your house once again,
I pray that you will also come to my house.
Be with me and my loved ones as we celebrate Thanksgiving.

(Evening)
God, another holiday has passed. You are so generous. You provide me with
all I need. Grant me the goodness of heart to pass this generosity on to others.

Sustainer of Life, forgive me when I do not recognize the ways in which
you care for me. Teach me to live in a spirit of thanksgiving, not for one
day each year, but every day. Help me to measure my blessings in love,
peace, good health, and family, rather than by the world's material stan-
dards. On this Thanksgiving Day, may I focus on the themes of Psalm 122:
thanks and peace. If I become more aware of the gifts you send me, perhaps I will be able to give more to others, and perhaps peace will be easier
to achieve.

(Morning)
God of all nations, I pray for the strength to say, "Peace be within you," to
whomever I meet. I pray for my immediate family, and for families around the
world who need you. Touch their lives as you have touched mine.
(Prayers of Intercession)

(Evening)
Generous God, I seek to understand more about your peace.
I pray for the places where war and conflict continue to wage.
Help turn my prayers of peace into action.
(Prayers of Intercession)

For the sake of my relatives and friends, I will say, "Peace be within you."

(Morning)
Whether I spend my holiday surrounded by loved ones, in an intimate
circle of two or three, or alone with
my God, bring to my heart a true
sense of thanksgiving. Amen.

(Evening)
May this new holiday season be a time
of honest reflection and renewal of
purpose. Help me to finally understand
the messages of goodwill and peace on
earth. Amen.

FRIDAY, NOVEMBER 27

(Read Isaiah 2:4–5)

(Morning)
Mother God, I arise and give thanks for your peace, which extends beyond all human understanding. Show me today how I can become a more effective witness for peace in your world.

(Evening)
Mother God, as another day ends, I celebrate the moments when I acted in peace. I praise you for showing me the way.

You speak to us, God, in your powerful voice about the ways of your peace. But my sisters and brothers and I still choose war. I continue to live in turmoil instead of reconciliation. How did we learn to make war against ourselves and against you? You created us to live in peace, and we have turned away from your love for us. Guide me back to you, O God. Guide me back to your peace.

(Morning)
I pray that your prophecies may come to fruition, that our guns may be beaten into tools of knowledge and our bombs into creativity's power.
(Prayers of Intercession)

(Evening)
God of wisdom, remind me to let you be the judge. Only you have the power to judge the nations. Only you have the power to judge my neighbor. Help me to remove the plank from my own eye before I bother to notice the sawdust in my neighbor's.
(Prayers of Intercession)

Neither shall they learn war any more.

(Morning)
Strengthen me, God, with the memory of peacemakers who have come before me. May I learn from the strides that have already been made and be inspired to put down my own sword and shield. Amen.

(Evening)
As I sleep tonight, may I dream of peace. Wake me in the morning, dear God, with the unquenchable desire to transform the dreams into reality and truth. Amen.

SATURDAY, NOVEMBER 28
(Read Matthew 24:43–44)

(Morning)
God of love, I drift out of sleep, thankful that you are present both in
my dreams and as I wake. You are always ready to protect me and love me.
For this, I am grateful.

(Evening)
God of love, this evening grant me the ability to stay awake. You may come like
a thief in the night; but unlike the thief, you come to repair, not to destroy. No
matter how unexpected, I will celebrate your coming.

God of paradox, you are right in front of me, but I am blinded by your
light. Though you have never left, you must reenter my life again and again.
You come like a flood, like a thief, like manna from heaven. And I, like so
many of your people, am stubborn and not ready for you. But God, you
keep trying. You have even sent your Child Jesus to us. This time, may
Jesus help me to welcome you in. May I be forced to wake up!

(Morning)
Strengthen my heart and energize my spirit, so that I may serve you and your
people today. Open me to opportunities for sharing Christ's love.
(Prayers of Intercession)

(Evening)
Gracious God, help me to distinguish between your Word and those of
impostors. Grant me the wisdom to know the difference between your coming
and that of false prophets.
(Prayers of Intercession)

You must be ready.

(Morning)
This morning I commit myself once
again to walk along the road to your
house. I know that I will stumble
many times before I reach the
mountaintop, but I have faith that you
will lead me home. Amen.

(Evening)
Tomorrow the season of Advent
begins. Christmas will soon be here.
God of understanding and mercy, I
pray that I will awaken to hear your
call, see your face, touch your Spirit,
and say your name. Amen.

SUNDAY, NOVEMBER 29
(Read Romans 13:11–14)

(Morning)
Praise God! Soon your Savior will be born again into our world.
The time of waiting has begun. On this first day of the Advent season,
I sit in joyful anticipation.

(Evening)
Praise God! Thank you for your salvation, for rescuing me again. Now is the
moment for me to sleep. Now is the time for me to accept your gift.

God Emmanuel, each year you provide me with another chance to grasp
the meaning of Christ's birth. Each year you give me a new armor of light
for protection and strength. But I am stubborn and refuse to wear it. When
will I learn to choose the light? You are so patient with me, Savior God.
Help me to be patient, too, as I anticipate the power of your coming. Now
is the time for me to wake from sleep! You have warned me to be ready.

(Morning)
Guide me, O God, from the depths of this sleep into the reality
of Jesus Christ's coming.
(Prayers of Intercession)

(Evening)
During this time of sacred and holy days, lead me to the light of your star.
Open my ears to the voices of your angels.
(Prayers of Intercession)

For salvation is nearer to us now than when we became believers.

(Morning)	(Evening)
May I live and work honorably in this day. As the night ends and the time of Advent begins, I will sit with the knowledge that a new day is near. Amen.	Help me as I sleep not to be afraid of the shadows. Your light is always available to me if I choose to see it. You ask that I be patient as I wait for answers, but I have faith that when the waiting is over, there will be joy and peace. Amen.

342

MONDAY, NOVEMBER 30
(Read Isaiah 11:1–5)

(Morning)
Sovereign God, grant that I begin this day with wisdom to honor you and
to bear others with understanding. Remind me to treat the poor and
the needy with fairness and justice.

(Evening)
Sovereign God, endow me with understanding, that I may help the cause of
justice to flow as a river that never runs dry.

When we gaze upon the world of nature—the moon, the stars, the trees,
and the bright morning light—we see that it truly portrays your harmoni-
ous handiwork. However, with the human beings whom you created infe-
rior only to yourself, there is madness, confusion, and greed. Help me,
God, to resolve the complex nature of my being and to assert that love
overcomes all forms of division and hatred.

(Morning)
Loving God, forgive me where I failed in what I have said and done.
Help me to be fair, honest, and sensitive to the needs of others.
(Prayers of Intercession)

(Evening)
Thank you, God, for your love, which enables me to do the best I can.
Grant me the provisions of a blessed sleep.
(Prayers of Intercession)

"With justice Christ will give decisions for the poor of the earth!"

(Morning)	(Evening)
Like them who heard the gracious call of Jesus, let me rise and follow you, God. Amen.	God, let me cast my burdens and go to sleep with a renewed confidence in you for tomorrow. Amen.

TUESDAY, DECEMBER 1
(Read Isaiah 11:6–10)

(Morning)
Gracious God, give me courage to stand on what is right. Let the Spirit of truth
dwell in me to transform the worst within. At the beginning of this day,
help me to overcome all forms of hatred and to share instead the peace which
surpasses all understanding.

(Evening)
Gracious God, whose redeeming power renews my life,
let me at the end of this day rejoice and be grateful.

Sovereign and gracious God, it is marvelous to behold a small child leading animals formerly ferocious and wild. Provide me this feeling of bliss to
assure that no one is beyond redemption in your Child Jesus, the Christ.
Make me gratefully aware of this transforming power which makes beautiful even one's ugliest nature. Let it be said that in my community of faith,
the wolf dwells with the lamb.

(Morning)
Eternal God, grant me the spirit of insight, that I may begin this day to be
attentively mindful of your transforming influence all around me.
(Prayers of Intercession)

(Evening)
Gracious God, whose unmerited grace has molded and moved me to act
my faith throughout this day, receive my heartfelt thanks and grant me
a night of peaceful rest.
(Prayers of Intercession)

See how lovely it is to live together in peace and unity.

(Morning)	(Evening)
God of grace, let me begin this day	Gracious God, give me a good night's
with the full knowledge	rest and let righteousness
of your abiding presence. Amen.	be the order of the next day. Amen.

WEDNESDAY, DECEMBER 2
(Read Psalm 72:1–7)

(Morning)
God of mercy, thank you for bringing me safe to the beginning of this day. Let the Spirit of fairness and honesty remind me of my obligation to the well-being of others and to find delight in peace and justice.

(Evening)
God of mercy, accept my grateful praise for the season of Advent, which celebrates the prophetic fulfillment of peace and goodness on earth.

Thanks be to you, God, for your transforming power in today's reading from the book of Psalms. It is reassuring to hear the wise counsel of the people of faith to cling to the splendid hope for justice despite the unjust situation of their day. Help me, O God, to be as faithful, even when life seems unfair and uncertain. Grant that in my daily actions friends will not be unduly favored nor enemies unfairly treated, but that I will remain fair and honest with all.

(Morning)
Create in me, O God, a lovingly caring heart, that I may love the unlovely and care for the children of the needy.
(Prayers of Intercession)

(Evening)
Thank you, God, for your gentle and wise influence in making my day. Grant me now a good night's rest and the strength to reflect your loving care tomorrow.
(Prayers of Intercession)

Pray that righteousness will flourish and prosperity abound for everyone.

(Morning)
God, with deep commitment, let me become a faithful partner in the service of caring. Amen.

(Evening)
May I meet the challenges of tomorrow with a new resolve to uphold the rights of the poor and the oppressed. Amen.

THURSDAY, DECEMBER 3
(Read Psalm 72:18–19)

(Morning)
O God, in the brightness of a new day, let me praise your holy name. Help me to know more about you and make me ready for your revelation in Jesus Christ.

(Evening)
O God, at the close of day receive my grateful praise.
Help me to gain understanding of your marvelous deeds and
let me feel the influence of your presence.

Let the people praise you, O God, and may the whole earth be filled with your glory. God, open my heart, that I may burst into joyful songs of praise. Where once there was some dismal shadow, now the bright light of a new life of love and holiness has come. Keep me singing and praising your glorious name. Let all the nations be blessed.

(Morning)
Thank you, God, for the gifts of home and friendship and for
the spiritual influences of living. Grant that in the midst of uncertainties
I shall always feel your guiding hand.
(Prayers of Intercession)

(Evening)
O God of hope, hear my humble prayer for the afflicted people of the earth!
Remove from my life hatred and prejudice and
replace them with love and kindness.
(Prayers of Intercession)

Let the glory of God be seen everywhere on earth.

(Morning)
God, the morning sun reminds me of the goodness of your creation. Let me live in the light of your love. Amen.

(Evening)
God, let me go to bed with singing. Grant me a refreshing sleep, and in the morning awaken in me a joyful heart. Amen.

FRIDAY, DECEMBER 4
(Read Romans 15:4–6)

(Morning)
O God, have patience with me at the beginning of this day. Open my mind, that
I may apply the teachings of the Scriptures in my daily life.

(Evening)
O God, thank you for the many illustrations of the power of patience among
people of faith recorded in the Scriptures.

In today's reading from the letter to the Romans, Paul alluded that the Scriptures were written for instruction and improvement. They are not to be regarded as a charm, and a mere possession of them would not do any good. Teach me, God, how to internalize and use the Scriptures with my intellectual and moral capabilities, so that I may endure and persevere in achieving the unity of faith. Remind me how patient you have been in waiting for an appropriate time to send your Child Jesus to set your people free.

(Morning)
May I begin to emulate the good examples of the power of patience among
people of faith.
(Prayers of Intercession)

(Evening)
Forgive me, God, for failing to recognize that the wider the variety of gifts, the
stronger the unity of our faith.
(Prayers of Intercession)

**Unity is not merely in outward association,
but more so in the spirit of mutual love and common adoration.**

(Morning)
God, let me find rest in Jesus, who
came to set your people free. Amen.

(Evening)
God, reassure me of your promise of
guidance and the blessings of a better
tomorrow as I go to sleep. Amen.

SATURDAY, DECEMBER 5
(Read Romans 15:7–13)

(Morning)
God, thank you for the gift of sustaining light of the new day.
Let me begin this day with the new resolve that the true foundation of peace
is in the heart of the Eternal.

(Evening)
God, meet me at the close of this day and grant me strength of mind, body, and
spirit at the dawn of the new day.

God, at the height of contention between the Jewish and Gentile Christians, Paul asserts that the purpose of Jesus' ministry is to fulfill your promises for the children of Israel and to extend these covenant mercies to the Gentiles. This was in keeping with Isaiah's prophecy of the Messiah's reign over the Gentiles as well as the Jews. Save me, God, from this age-old controversy, and grant me the Spirit to be considerate, patient, and forbearing with others, that I may light the lamp of hope along the path of life.

(Morning)
Help me, God, to be considerate and helpful to all, regardless of background.
(Prayers of Intercession)

(Evening)
Make me, God, an instrument of your peace.
(Prayers of Intercession)

Welcome one another just as Christ has welcomed you.

(Morning)
God, help me to believe that the promise of a Messiah finds its fulfillment in Jesus Christ. Amen.

(Evening)
God, cast all my doubts and let me rise tomorrow with a new vigor of my faith in Jesus Christ. Amen.

SUNDAY, DECEMBER 6
(Read Matthew 3:1–12)

(Morning)
Almighty God, whose promise of the Messiah the world awaits,
grant that my heart is ready for the exciting wonder of Jesus' coming.

(Evening)
Almighty God, whose wonderful grace replaces gloom with a bright hope of
life, grant me the readiness to clear the way of Christ.

John the Baptist, in a clear and convincing testimony, declares that your
Child Jesus is the Christ who takes away the sins of the world. While the
Advent season should gladden our hearts, it also makes us sad to think how
little we have done to prepare the way of Christ. Gracious God, let your
goodness lead me to repentance and set me in motion as an active partici-
pant in the reconciling work of Christ.

(Morning)
Help me, God, to face the challenge of the day, and make me mindful of the
inherent power of a consecrated life.
(Prayers of Intercession)

(Evening)
Strengthen me, O God, to proclaim the glorious hope of Advent.
(Prayers of Intercession)

The Scripture is replete with the series of God's consoling intervention.

(Morning)
God, with a deep sense of commitment, let me rise up and work, that
others may see what you have done to
save to world. Amen.

(Evening)
God, forgive my indifference which
hinders the program of your dominion,
and let the new day bring me new
strength. Amen.

MONDAY, DECEMBER 7
(Read Isaiah 35:1–7)

(Morning)
Loving and healing God, strength for my fearful heart,
I open the door of my attention to you this day.

(Evening)
Loving and healing God, at the close of this day I look to you.
Thank you for being present with loving attention to me and to this world,
even when we are unaware.

God, in this season of Advent waiting, I lose sight of you. I look at all that needs to be done, and I feel anxious. I look at what others are doing in preparation for the season, and I feel driven. The holy way of your coming loses its fragrance, and my heart becomes a dry wilderness when propelled to rush. But you come to where I am in my fatigue and fear, and invite me to look to you. When I gaze at you, my eyes are opened; I see my anxious ways for what they are; and you pour springs of water on the parched ground of my being.

(Morning)
Healing God, you who come to save, open my eyes to see you in this day,
in this season of Advent waiting.
(Prayers of Intercession)

(Evening)
Dear God, as I reflect over the day, help me to see where crocuses have
blossomed, to notice the springs of water you are giving.
I rest beside the pool of your presence this night.
(Prayers of Intercession)

In the presence of your love, I pray.
(Pray the Prayer of Our Savior.)

(Morning)
As I move into this day, God, you are here. Shape the desires of my heart and the work of my hands, so that I co-labor with you in the wilderness of this world, for Jesus' sake. Amen.

(Evening)
I rest in you this night, O God, giver of streams in the desert and joy on the way. In Jesus' name. Amen.

TUESDAY, DECEMBER 8
(Read Psalm 146:5–10)

(Morning)
Loving God of Jacob, Yahweh; you made heaven and earth, the sea,
and all that is. I look to you for help.

(Evening)
Loving God, I come to you, thanking you for watching over all of creation
today and for caring for this tired world.

God, Jacob ran from home in fear. When we lose trust and run, you run
with us. You wait to meet us when we pause for weariness and sleep. As I
open my heart to receive your help, I discover you are faithful. You help
me see your creating and sustaining presence beneath and around heaven
and earth, and your faithful love beneath and around those who are fearful,
lost, oppressed, lonely, and abandoned. You meet us and lift us up as a
tender parent holding a lost and lonely child.

(Morning)
Loving and gracious God, help me to notice your goodness in this day, and help
me to see others—the lost, the unwanted, and the overlooked—as you see them.
(Prayers of Intercession)

(Evening)
God of all Jacobs, as I reflect on this day, help me to see the people I encoun-
tered as you see them. For Jesus' sake.
(Prayers of Intercession)

Humbly I pray.
(Pray the Prayer of Our Savior.)

(Morning)
Jesus, I thank you that as I once again
wait in the Advent of your coming,
your Holy Spirit meets me and lifts
me, and opens my eyes to see your
presence and care. Amen.

(Evening)
Dear God, you watch over all this
night with loving, tender care. Thank
you. In Jesus' name. Amen.

WEDNESDAY, DECEMBER 9
(Read Luke 1:47–55)

(Morning)
God, my Savior, I praise you this day. In you I find the source of all my joy.

(Evening)
God, my Savior, help me to notice where you have been the source
of my joy this day.

God of might and mercy, I listen to Mary's song today. As she sings, her song opens a door and allows me to see her heart—that inner continent where we both hide from you and long for your presence. Now you are present in her body, for she carries Jesus. Mary sings, even while she is at risk: Joseph is fearful of this scandal; Herod is violent in his opposition. Embracing the Christchild means being embraced by you. You give joy, for you, God, are ever present.

(Morning)
Mighty One, you come to us in the womb of our lives in Jesus. Grow within me.
Scatter those proud thoughts that are against you, and bring down the powers
that wage war against you within me.
(Prayers of Intercession)

(Evening)
Savior God, you are at work even as I sleep this night. Help me
to lean into your ways, your coming; to embrace the Christchild within me;
and to risk the security of your embrace.
(Prayers of Intercession)

In thanksgiving I pray.
(Pray the Prayer of Our Savior.)

(Morning)
Just as Mary sang in the house of Elizabeth, help me to discover persons who acknowledge your presence and work within me and this world. In Jesus' name. Amen.

(Evening)
With Mary, I sing to you, Mighty One, in thankfulness for your help and goodness this day. In Jesus' name. Amen.

THURSDAY, DECEMBER 10
(Read Isaiah 35:3–6 and Matthew 11:2–11)

(Morning)
Loving and healing God, I look for you this day. I wait for your coming.

(Evening)
Loving and healing God, as I look back over this day, help me to see you in new ways, with the loving eyes of Jesus.

Saving God, you don't come the way I sometimes wish you would. You don't come with vengeance, stomping on abusers and war-makers, thieves and murderers, throwing out selfish rulers, and putting yourself in charge of governments. Maybe that is why John wavered and wondered, "Jesus, are you really the One to come?" Today the world barely notices you. But you still come to us one by one, healing, giving, restoring life, and speaking good news to us who are poor. Help me to see you today as you are.

(Morning)
Loving God, help me to notice you this Advent. And help me to keep you at the center. May others notice your kindness, and believe.
(Prayers of Intercession)

(Evening)
Saving and Healing One, be with your servants this night who are tired and fearful, who sometimes doubt your presence and care.
(Prayers of Intercession)

In confidence I pray.
(Pray the Prayer of Our Savior.)

(Morning)
This day, loving Jesus, open my eyes and my ears to see and to hear your presence. In your love. Amen.

(Evening)
As I rest this night, I thank you that you come to be with us in gentle, healing ways. In your name, Jesus. Amen.

FRIDAY, DECEMBER 11
(Read Matthew 11:2–11 and James 5:7–10)

(Morning)
Present and coming God, as I awake this day, I look to you and for your coming.

(Evening)
Present and coming God, forgive me for forgetting you and complaining against others. I thank you for not forgetting me.

Holy One, help me to live in the expectancy of your coming again. My heart grows impatient, turns to other things, forgets the age in which I live: the Advent of your coming. Gentle me into the fruitful rhythm of seedtime and harvest, for you are the owner of the field of this world. Like seed, your loving dominion is planted—oft-hidden, sometimes seen.

(Morning)
Coming God, I am not patient in suffering. Help me sit with John the Baptist today and contemplate the signs of your coming.
(Prayers of Intercession)

(Evening)
This night, strengthen and encourage those who speak in your name and suffer for your sake.
(Prayers of Intercession)

Patiently I pray.
(Pray the Prayer of Our Savior.

(Morning)
As I move into this day, dear God, help me to look for seedlings that are sprouting, signs of your presence. In Jesus' name. Amen.

(Evening)
Your coming is near, Mighty One. Your presence brings healing, gentle Jesus. Gentle us into trusting sleep, renewing rest this night. For our sake and in your great love. Amen.

SATURDAY, DECEMBER 12
(Read Psalm 146:5–10 and Matthew 11:2–11)

(Morning)
Yahweh, I look to you this day. I am your servant.
You are my help and my hope.

(Evening)
Yahweh, as this day comes to a close, I open my heart to you.

Merciful and holy God, I ask your help as I look back over this week to see
as you see. For what am I grateful? . . . (*Pause to reflect.*) In what ways
have I noticed your presence? . . .Where have I doubted your presence? run
from your love? . . .Where have I responded in trusting faith to your presence? . . . How have I shown your love to others, especially those who are
alone, in need, fearful? . . .

(Morning)
Freeing God, forgive me for times when I have forgotten you,
for times when I have avoided loving others as you love them and me.
Healing God, open my eyes and ears to see and hear you.
(Prayers of Intercession)

Evening
Gentle us now into your healing presence.
Bring healing and hope to all who are prisoners of impaired sight,
those who are bowed down, alienated, orphaned, and alone.
(Prayers of Intercession)

In gladness I pray.
(Pray the Prayer of Our Savior.)

(Morning)
We cannot love you without your
help, or see you without your giving
us sight, or hear you without your
giving us ears to hear with the heart.
Be our healer and help this day. For
Jesus' sake. Amen.

(Evening)
Gentle me now into your healing
presence, O God, who upholds the
orphan and the widow. Hold all that is
orphaned and alone within me in your
love this night. In Jesus' name. Amen.

SUNDAY, DECEMBER 13
(Read Isaiah 35:1–10 and Luke 1:47–55)

(Morning)
O mighty God, my soul magnifies you, and my spirit rejoices in you. For you have done great things, and holy is your name.

(Evening)
O mighty God, your mercy comes like streams in the desert; your favor creates pools in the burning sand. I rest with joy, and my heart is glad as I look to you at the end of this day.

God of goodness, Giver of joy, I thank you for making a way, a holy way for us to walk. Thank you for your mercy for all that is lowly; you do not let us go astray. Thank you for your protection from what is wild and destructive. Thank you for lifting sorrow and sighing from our heart and mind. And thank you for your gift of song and everlasting joy as we walk with you.

(Morning)
My soul sings, and my spirit rejoices. Help me to hear the song you give within my heart, and to walk in joy and gladness this day.
(Prayers of Intercession)

(Evening)
As this day comes to a close, I thank you for your great strength on behalf of all in need this day. How kind you are! I rejoice in your care.
(Prayers of Intercession)

In your mercy I pray.
(Pray the Prayer of Our Savior.)

(Morning)
Great God, joy that lasts for all time comes only from you. I rejoice with gladness and singing this day. In Jesus' name. Amen.

(Evening)
This day, Mighty One, you have lifted those who are low, filled those who are hungry, and helped those who serve you. Thank you for remembering. I praise you for your faithful, loving care.
In Jesus' name. Amen.

MONDAY, DECEMBER 14
(Read Psalm 80:1–3)

(Morning)
Merciful God, as I prepare to face this new day, remind me of your saving
power. Enable me to know that there is nothing that can separate me
from your love through Christ Jesus our Savior.

(Evening)
Merciful God, forgive me for those moments today when I failed to glorify you
in thought, word, and deed. Cleanse and restore me, saving God,
and empower me to be the person you called me to be.

Despite all the manifestations of your saving power, I confess that there
are times when it appears you have abandoned us. Then you remind me
that I am part of a human community that has lost its way. As I look at the
systems of oppression and injustice in the world today, I am aware of my
own participation in the evil I condemn. Save us from attitudes and behavior that do not reflect your will for humanity. Deliver us from self-righteousness and hypocrisy, and awaken within us a renewed sense of community. Restore us to right relationship with you and with one another, and
grant us your peace.

(Morning)
Help me to trust the guidance of your Spirit,
and teach me to acknowledge you in all my ways.
Empower me to be a faithful disciple, so that your name will be glorified.
(Prayers of Intercession)

(Evening)
Merciful God, thank you for reassuring me of your love for me.
Thank you for the manifestation of your presence and power in my life today.
(Prayers of Intercession)

Thank you for your saving grace and power in difficult times.

(Morning)
May I live today with the confidence
of knowing that your love for me is
everlasting. Amen.

(Evening)
Grant me a peaceful rest from the
burdens of the day, and renew me to
face the challenges of tomorrow.
Amen.

TUESDAY, DECEMBER 15
(Read Psalm 80:4–7 and Isaiah 7:10–13)

(Morning)
God of mercy and compassion, thank you for your steadfast love,
even when I turn away from you. Teach me to walk in your ways for your
name's sake, and save me from decisions and actions
that are inconsistent with your will for my life.

(Evening)
God of mercy and compassion, thank you for the gift of mercy and
grace which restores me to right relationship with you.

Sometimes the pressures of life seem too difficult to bear. The burdens and
sorrow I experience from time to time cause me to cry out to you from the
depths of my soul, "How long?" I realize, O God, that some of my problems
are the consequences of my own poor decisions and reluctance to
follow your guidance. I regret my disobedience, and I ask you to correct
me when I go astray. Be patient with me and sustain me in the midst of my
sorrows. Continue to keep me and grant me your peace. Reassure me of
your presence as I cling to you in faith.

(Morning)
May I begin this day mindful of your ever-present Spirit.
Teach me to live in a way that pleases you.
(Prayers of Intercession)

(Evening)
Your Spirit comforted and sustained me throughout the day.
Thank you for hearing my prayers, even when they seem to go unanswered.
Teach me to wait patiently for you.
(Prayers of Intercession)

God is an ever-present help in times of trouble.

(Morning)
Grant me the grace to follow the
guidance of your Spirit. Restore to me
the joy of your salvation and give me
your peace. Amen.

(Evening)
Grant me a sweet and peaceful rest
from the worries of the day. May I
have another opportunity tomorrow to
glorify you in thought, word, and
deed. Amen.

WEDNESDAY, DECEMBER 16
(Read Isaiah 7:10–16)

(Morning)
Merciful God, thank you for not abandoning me, even when I fail to obey you.
I begin this day aware of your mercy and grace, and pray for a sensitive spirit
to discern your presence throughout the day. Thank you, loving God,
for standing with me and never leaving me alone.

(Evening)
Merciful God, thank you for demonstrating your love by comforting me in
moments of despair. Your grace amazes me and shows me how blessed I am
to be in relationship with you.

Throughout my life, you have demonstrated your profound love for me.
You have delivered me from dangers seen and unseen, and so you instruct
me to trust and obey your voice. In the midst of my fear and confusion, you
promise to be with me, and you always keep your word. Despite your faithfulness to me, I, like Ahaz, often try to solve my problems in ways that
reveal my failure to trust you. Forgive me, merciful God, and teach me to
trust you more each day. Teach me to rely on your promises, and thank you
for standing by my side, even when I foolishly turn away from you.

(Morning)
Sharpen my spiritual ears and eyes,
that I may hear and see your presence in my life today.
(Prayers of Intercession)

(Evening)
Thank you for revealing your Spirit to me throughout the day. As I close my
eyes to sleep this night, continue to be merciful and gracious to me.
(Prayers of Intercession)

Thank you for teaching me to love and trust you more each day.

(Morning)
I will listen and look for your presence in and around me on this day
you have given me. Amen.

(Evening)
May I sleep now and begin again
tomorrow with a spirit that yearns to
trust and follow you more fully. Amen.

THURSDAY, DECEMBER 17
(Read Psalm 80:17–19 and Matthew 1:21)

(Morning)
Creator God, I face the new day praising you for life and for the privilege of calling on your name. Thank you for another day; help me to live today in a way that pleases you, for your name's sake.

(Evening)
Creator God, your Spirit revived my weary soul at moments throughout the day. Thank you for answering my call for help and comforting me with your presence.

As I look back on my life, I see your saving grace more clearly. You have been with me through moments of exultation and despair, and you have delivered me from situations and circumstances that threatened to destroy me. And so I must praise you because you have demonstrated your love for me in more ways than I can count. Thank you for the promise that you will never leave or forsake me. Thank you for salvation and restoration.

(Morning)
I thank you, merciful God, for a mind and spirit that desire to praise you. Continue to cultivate in me a spirit of praise and thanksgiving for the many blessings you have given me.
(Prayers of Intercession)

(Evening)
I praise you for the gift of this day. Thank you for the joy and peace your Spirit imparted to me. May I prepare to rest now with the same blessed assurance of your presence.
(Prayers of Intercession)

Salvation is from you, O God. Teach me to call upon your name at all times.

(Morning)	(Evening)
This is the day you have made; I will rejoice and be glad in it. I will call upon your name as long as I have breath. Amen.	Grant your child a peaceful rest and strengthen me where I am weak, so that I may worship you and serve your people tomorrow. Amen.

FRIDAY, DECEMBER 18
(Read Matthew 1:18–21 and Romans 1:1–4)

(Morning)
God of salvation and deliverance, I begin this day with a renewed and thankful spirit. Thank you for the gift of Jesus Christ and the story of his wondrous birth. Help me to discern your creative Spirit at work in me and in the world.

(Evening)
God of salvation and deliverance, you sustained my body and spirit throughout the day. Thank you for protecting and saving me from danger seen and unseen; I praise you and humbly acknowledge my dependence on you.

Creating and loving God, your plan of salvation inspires within me a spirit of profound wonder and gratitude. Your ways and your thoughts are infinitely beyond my own; and yet by the gracious gift of Jesus Christ—a Savior who knows the experience of being fully human—I am reconciled to you through faith in Christ's name. The story of Jesus' birth reminds me that no human predicament is beyond the realm of your saving power. For you, the appearance of scandal and controversy is an opportunity to demonstrate your wisdom and saving grace. Thank you, merciful God, for Jesus the Savior and the good news of his birth.

(Morning)
Thank you, O God, for making me a vessel for your Spirit. May my words, thoughts, and deeds glorify you.
(Prayers of Intercession)

(Evening)
Thank you for my journey this day. As I prepare to close my eyes in rest, allow me to meditate on your mercy and grace made known to us in the birth, life, and teachings of Jesus Christ.
(Prayers of Intercession)

Thank you for salvation and the gift of Jesus Christ.

(Morning)
Thank you for a Savior who knew human limitations and whose resurrected Spirit enables me to be in relationship with you. Teach me to accept the grace you have shown me in Christ Jesus. Amen.

(Evening)
Forgive me for those moments when I failed to glorify you in my words, thoughts, and actions. Grant me a peaceful rest, that I may begin afresh tomorrow more sensitive to the guidance of your Spirit. Amen.

SATURDAY, DECEMBER 19
(Read Matthew 1:22–23 and Romans 1:1–2)

(Morning)
God of yesterday, today, and tomorrow, you fulfill all of your promises and are always faithful to your Word. Thank you for waking me this morning.

(Evening)
God of yesterday, today, and tomorrow, thank you for teaching me to love and trust you a little more each day. Thank you for revealing your Spirit in my life.

God of time and God of faith, your Word has creative power that transcends anything known to the human mind. You speak things into existence, and have called me to be in relationship with you. You teach me that without faith in the word of your promise, it is impossible to please you; help me where my faith falls short, and grant me a more trusting spirit. You spoke through the ancient Hebrew prophets about the birth of Jesus centuries before it occurred. Teach me, therefore, to trust your promises even before they are fulfilled. Equip me with all that I need to share the gospel with those who have not yet come to know you.

(Morning)
Inspire me to study the Scriptures more diligently and to have faith in the promises of your Word.
(Prayers of Intercession)

(Evening)
Merciful God, your steadfast love has been demonstrated faithfully throughout the ages. Grant your weary servant a restful sleep, that I may glorify you throughout tomorrow's journey.
(Prayers of Intercession)

**Thank you for fulfilling your promises to me
through Christ Jesus our Savior.**

(Morning)
I am prepared to face the day because of the strength and faith you have given me. Thank you in advance for fulfilling your will in my life. Amen.

(Evening)
God of life, thank you for the experiences of this day. Continue to unfold your will for my life in my thoughts and dreams this night. Amen.

SUNDAY, DECEMBER 20
(Read Matthew 1:24–25 and Romans 1:5–7)

(Morning)
Merciful God, thank you for calling me to belong to Jesus Christ.
Your gracious Spirit caused me to have faith in you,
and you have called me to share the good news about Jesus Christ with others.
Grant me the grace I need to accomplish this sacred mission.

(Evening)
God of faith and grace, thank you for leading and guiding my thoughts,
words, and actions today.

Your grace called me, and I heard your voice deep in my spirit. You made it possible for me to have faith and empowered me to respond to your call. I have no strength that does not come from you, and when I obey your command it is only because you enable me to do so. Thank you, loving God, for calling me to be a partner with you in the work of sharing the gospel. Fulfill your purpose for me, and continue to equip me with the faith that leads to acts of obedience. Enable me to identify your voice and to follow where you lead me, for Jesus' sake.

(Morning)
Loving God, help me to be a faithful instrument of your will. Help me to listen
for your voice, and guide me in the direction you would have me go.
(Prayers of Intercession)

(Evening)
Thank you for the guidance of your Spirit throughout the day's journey. Forgive
me if my thoughts and actions were inconsistent with your will, and grant me
more faith to follow where you lead me tomorrow.
(Prayers of Intercession)

Fulfill your purpose in my life and mold me after your will.

(Morning)	(Evening)
I commit myself to being a faithful vessel for your will through Jesus Christ. Amen.	Grant your child a much-needed rest from the challenges of the day. Renew and strengthen me to face tomorrow with more faith than I had today, for Jesus' sake. Amen.

MONDAY, DECEMBER 21
(Read Psalm 148:1–6)

(Morning)
God, now Christmas week begins. Let me not be so caught up in the
trivialities of holiday preparation that I fail to hear the music of the spheres.
All creation is singing praises to you.

(Evening)
God, as I close my eyes, fill me with thanksgiving that I have been included
in your creation, to love, protect, and enjoy it forever. Help me, God,
to be worthy of this gift of life by acting as your steward on this earth.

Creator God, help me to fathom the wonders of your work. All nature celebrates. Even the trees clap their hands. Let us make this week a time of
praise and thanksgiving for your whole creation and especially for the gift
of Jesus, Emmanuel, God-with-us.

(Morning)
Loving God, sustain within me the understanding that I am vitally connected to
all your creation. Help me to live all my life with that awareness within me.
(Prayers of Intercession)

(Evening)
Be with me, Gracious One. Fill me with your presence this night
and throughout my days.
(Prayers of Intercession)

Praise our God from the highest heavens and even to our inmost being.

(Morning)
God, I praise the new day and give
thanks for all the opportunities ahead
to serve and honor you. Amen.

(Evening)
As I close my eyes, may I know even
in my dreams the majesty of the
wonders wrought by you, the God of
us all. Amen.

TUESDAY, DECEMBER 22
(Read Psalm 148:7–14)

(Morning)
Creator God, in wonder we perceive the changing seasons.
Today the solstice occurs and winter begins.
With this shortest day and longest night, make us aware of those
who depend on your sun's rays for warmth and light.

(Evening)
Creator God, give us peace and rest this night.
Restore our energies to do your will when the new day arrives.

Young men and women, children and old ones praise you, everlasting God. Help us to fathom our part in the vast unending nature of your creation. As Christmas nears, we sing of these wonders. We rejoice that in the midst of our longest night, Jesus, the true light, was born for us all.

(Morning)
Emmanuel, surely this day you are with me.
Help me to strive to be your true disciple,
for it is you who showed me the way.
(Prayers of Intercession)

(Evening)
On this longest night, fill us with your Holy Spirit,
giving us new hope amidst the sorrows and injustices of our world.
Ease the pain of all who suffer and let them feel your presence.
(Prayers of Intercession)

Sing praises to our God through all our days.

(Morning)
Let not this day be wasted; it is
precious in your sight. Let me live it
doing your will. Amen.

(Evening)
Carry me into a peaceful sleep,
knowing that when I awake, I shall be
renewed to journey ahead in God's
way. Amen.

WEDNESDAY, DECEMBER 23
(Read Isaiah 63:7–9)

(Morning)
O God, as I start this day, clear my mind. Help me grasp the meaning of your
presence with us. May I know the strength of your redeeming love.

(Evening)
O God, I was carried this day in the knowledge of your goodness.
Now, as I close my eyes, I pray that all people may know your love and mercy.

Our world awaits your coming through Jesus Christ, our Savior. Give to
your people thankful hearts, that we may be carried by a steadfast faith and
lifted to do your will. May these not be idle words but convictions which
direct our lives.

(Morning)
Merciful God who knows the suffering of your children,
be with us this day as we seek to be your instruments in healing.
(Prayers of Intercession)

(Evening)
Through all our days and nights, be with us. Break into our lives.
Help us in our striving to be the people you sought to create in your own image.
(Prayers of Intercession)

**"In all their affliction God was afflicted,
and the angel of God's presence saved them."**

(Morning)
Jesus Christ, who brings light into our
world, help us to show forth the love
and compassion manifest in your life.
Amen.

(Evening)
O God, Giver of all good gifts, we
thank you this night for the abundance you have showered upon us.
We ask for renewed strength to use
these gifts in your service. Amen.

THURSDAY, DECEMBER 24
(Read Hebrews 2:10–13)

(Morning)
Loving God, help me this day to prepare myself to accept your most gracious
gift. Jesus enters into our lives.

(Evening)
Loving God, on this holy night, we look to the manger where
Mary gave birth to our Savior. May we ponder anew
the wonder of this gift and sing our hallelujahs.

We thank you, God, that you make yourself incarnate through Jesus the
Christ, the pioneer of our faith. You share in the suffering of all your children. Help us to be renewed during this holy season as we receive Jesus.

(Morning)
God, our parent, forgive us our failure to know and accept the fact that we
are your children and that Jesus, your perfect Child, is our brother.
Let us live this day in trust close to you.
(Prayers of Intercession)

(Evening)
On this Christmas Eve, may we be filled with your glory
as the gift of Jesus comes into our world.
(Prayers of Intercession)

**The one whose name is Emmanuel, God-with-us, is born this night.
Thanks be to God.**

(Morning)
May the glad tidings which are about
to break forth fill us with peace and
joy this day. Make us heralds of the
good news. Amen.

(Evening)
O holy night. Buena noche. May all
the nations hear in their own tongues
that your love, God, fills the whole
earth with peace and joy. Amen.

FRIDAY, DECEMBER 25 (CHRISTMAS DAY)
(Read Hebrews 2:14–18)

(Morning)
Emmanuel, God-with-us, at the beginning of this Christmas Day,
before the bustle and the distractions begin,
center my prayers in gratitude for your birth in Jesus.

(Evening)
Emmanuel, God-with-us, now and forever we thank you for family
and friends gathered, for the loving care and preparation which made this
a joyous day, and above all for your presence among us.

"For because he himself has suffered and been tempted he is able to help those who are tempted." We are ever grateful to you, God, that because you came into our lives in mortal flesh through Jesus the Christ, we have been given a mediator and a faithful high priest.

(Morning)
Give me a warm and open heart this day, O God, that I may truly celebrate the heights and depths of your unfathomable love in the gift of Jesus, your Child.
(Prayers of Intercession)

(Evening)
I rejoice that I have been part of this wondrous day.
Help me to be worthy of your blessings.
(Prayers of Intercession)

**Gracious God, grant that we may learn to live
in your holy presence and carry out your will.**

(Morning)
Use me, God, in your service and give me a voice to sing songs of praise on this Christmas Day. Amen.

(Evening)
Now the day is over. May we never be weary of praising you and singing, "Glory to God in the Highest," for the gift of Jesus given to us this day and for ever more. Amen.

SATURDAY, DECEMBER 26
(Read Matthew 2:13–18)

(Morning)
God, as I awaken, I remember the joy and exultation of yesterday and give thanks that so precious a gift has been given.

(Evening)
God, protect your people from the evil caused by jealousy and rage. Console those who suffer loss. To those like Rachel, weeping for her children, who find no consolation, give of your peace and love.

Help us to deal with the wicked, knowing that you, O God, will ultimately be victorious. In suffering, give us a sure knowledge of your presence and abiding love. Help us not to lose courage and stamina to fight against the Herods of this world.

(Morning)
Loving God, sustain me this day in the light brought forth by the birth of Jesus.
(Prayers of Intercession)

(Evening)
Protect me this night from the evil so rampant in our world. Give me rest to strengthen my resolve to combat those who oppose your will.
(Prayers of Intercession)

**Almighty God, the world is new with the coming of Jesus
and the Holy Spirit.**

(Morning)
Save me from temptations this day. Let me not waste your marvelous gifts, given that we might live this life abundantly. Amen.

(Evening)
Through these long nights, may I be mindful of all the Rachels who are weeping. Help me to be some small instrument in saving your suffering children. Amen.

SUNDAY, DECEMBER 27
(Read Matthew 2:19–23)

(Morning)
O God, as I awaken from the dreams of night, allow me to be aware
of the angels who would warn me of wrong directions.
May I live this Sabbath day attuned to your words.

(Evening)
O God, guide me with your wisdom as I review this past year.
I give thanks for all the blessings and ask forgiveness
for the ways I have failed to follow your path.

Let us remember Mary and Joseph, who by heeding the warnings of danger
protected the precious Child by carrying him to Nazareth. There he grew to
be the pioneer of our faith. May we also listen to the signs of evildoing
around us. Help us to be among the protectors of your children throughout
the world.

(Morning)
Help us to act this day against evil. Protect us from the dangers inherent in the
principalities and powers of our world.
(Prayers of Intercession)

(Evening)
As we close each day, may we read the Bible
and grow from the study of its wisdom.
(Prayers of Intercession)

**The leader and provider of our faith, Jesus Christ,
be our guide throughout our days.**

(Morning)
In the morning light, we raise our
voices with hymns of praise for the
living presence of your Child Jesus
Christ in our lives. Amen.

(Evening)
This Sabbath day comes to a close as
we seek the rest which will give us
strength to be disciples tomorrow and
throughout the new year ahead.
Amen.

MONDAY, DECEMBER 28
(Read Solomon 10:15–21 and John 1:1–9)

(Morning)
Holy Wisdom, as you bring me again into the morning light,
inspire me to live this day as one in love with you and your creation.

(Evening)
Holy Wisdom, I am grateful to have spent another day with you.

You are the source of goodness, mystery, and blessing. Though I cannot
see all that you are, or comprehend fully what you do around or within me,
I trust your movement in history, in nature, and in my own life, from age to
age. May I be led along your marvelous way, providing shelter to those in
need. May my life be a beacon through which, like a starry flame, you
brighten the night sky.

(Morning)
May I be vulnerable to your desire that I love the world you have made
and all human, and other, creatures in it.
(Prayers of Intercession)

(Evening)
Now I lay me down to sleep with you, my God and my shelter.
(Prayers of Intercession)

Thank you, sweet Sophia, for the gift of yourself in friendship.

(Morning)
I will do my best to live this day as
your sister (brother), come what may.
Amen.

(Evening)
Strengthen with rest my body, my soul,
my self, so that I can awake confidently in your Spirit. Amen.

TUESDAY, DECEMBER 29
(Read Sirach 24:1–7 and John 1:10–18)

(Morning)
Brother Jesus, we often do not recognize you.
Open my eyes to see who you are among us today.

(Evening)
As the day fades, so too may all my doubts that you are with me in every
waking moment and in my sleep. Thank you, O God, for never leaving us.

Walking in the depths of the abyss, you seek a resting place. May you find
it among those who love you and your creation. May I rest with you in this
place. May I offer you companionship and comfort through my desire to
struggle for justice, compassion, and mercy. May you take heart in my
turning over to you all that is ragged or broken, wrong or simply unfin-
ished, at the end of the day.

(Morning)
May I remember that you, too, need rest and that I can help
create a place for you this day.
(Prayers of Intercession)

(Evening)
Eternal resource of peace, I am grateful to you for accompanying me today.
I am touched that you choose to be with me.
(Prayers of Intercession)

You are my resting place. May we be yours.

(Morning)
May I accept the things I cannot
change today and change the things I
can. Will you show me the difference?
Amen.

(Evening)
May you, O God, be nourished with
me through this time of rest tonight.
Amen.

WEDNESDAY, DECEMBER 30
(Read Sirach 24:8–12 and Ephesians 1:3–14)

(Morning)
Dear Jesus, may I realize today how precious I am to you
as a brother (sister) in this world at this time.

(Evening)
Dear Jesus, I am grateful to have lived another day as a chosen one.

From the beginning, your Sophia, O God, has chosen us all—every nation, tribe, and person—to love one another as you love us. We, not you, have narrowed the way, puffing ourselves up with false notions of being closer than others to you. As we prepare to begin a new year in the common era of Western history, make us aware of how truly *one* we are in your Spirit. May we embody and value our differences as many magnificent windows into your movement, purpose, and love.

(Morning)
You have "made known to us in all wisdom and insight the mystery of your will" (Eph. 1:9a). Thank you for giving us the power of your Spirit,
not only to know your will but to do it.
(Prayers of Intercession)

(Evening)
Knowing your tenderness, may I let go of whatever I did today that I ought not to have done, and of whatever I did not do that I ought to have done. Rock me to sleep, O God, and wake me into a new day in which amends can be made.
(Prayers of Intercession)

I need you, O God, and I know you need me.

(Morning)
I am grateful to be chosen to help make your love incarnate by doing what I can today on behalf of justice and compassion. Amen.

(Evening)
May I accept my own limits and be ever ready to make amends, to forgive and be forgiven, and begin each day, again, with you. Amen.

THURSDAY, DECEMBER 31
(Read Psalm 147:12–20 and Jeremiah 31:7–14)

(Morning)
For this new day, praise God! For breath and dreams and friends, praise God!
For food and laughter, work and hope, praise God! For the year that has passed
and the one to come, praise God! O my heart, sing praise today!

(Evening)
For this new night, praise God! With the passing of this day, I am grateful for
the opportunity to participate in the unfolding of your purpose.

You turn mourning into joy and bring gladness out of sorrow. Through
whatever loss and grief, sadness and disappointment I have known this
year, you have labored faithfully to secure my confidence in you, Sophia,
and in myself with you. I believe that all will be well as long as I am with
you, and I know also that you are intimately involved with all creation,
making us friends of God, transforming our tears into streams of living
water, wellsprings of hope for the world. May we end this year and begin
the next in renewed commitment to live as your people, one day at a time.

(Morning)
For friendly, furry creatures, praise God! For the voices and lives of prophets,
praise God! For snow, cider, and the winter hearth, praise God!
For the manifold blessings bestowed upon us and for those that lie ahead,
praise God! O my soul, sing praise today!
(Prayers of Intercession)

(Evening)
With the passing of the year, I am grateful for the opportunity to participate
in your movement, in history, in this world.
(Prayers of Intercession)

**Looking to the new year, may I keep my sights upon God—
and my neighbor as myself.**

(Morning)
Whatever may come, may I experience
your presence, Sophia, my rock and my
salvation. Amen.

(Evening)
Walk with me, Jesus. Talk with me,
and be my resting place in the year to
come. May I be yours as well. Amen.

Contributors

Kathleen Crockford Ackley is the associate editor for curriculum resources, United Church Press, United Church of Christ.

Douglas B. Bailey is a retired United Church of Christ minister. He is the former training program administrator for the Franklin County Children Services.

Palmer H. Bell III is the vice president of EnTel Communications. He is a member of the United Church of Christ.

Ronald S. Bonner Sr. is the assistant to the president for affirmative action/equal employment opportunity, United Church of Christ.

Paul F. Bosch is a retired campus pastor and professor of worship. He is a member of the Lutheran Church.

Kenneth R. Brown II is an educator. He is a member of the United Church of Christ.

Joan Brown Campbell is the general secretary of the National Council of the Churches of Christ in the United States of America.

Michael C. Carson is the senior pastor of historic Wayman Chapel African Methodist Episcopal Church in Kokomo, Indiana.

Mark L. Chapman teaches at Fordham University in Bronx, New York. He is a member of the United Church of Christ.

Sonya H. Chung is a public policy advocate in the Office of Church in Society, United Church of Christ.

Laurie Ruth Colton is a teacher in transition. She is a member of the United Church of Christ.

Arthur Lawrence Cribbs Jr. is the executive director of the Office of Communications, United Church of Christ.

Barbara R. Cunningham is an ordained minister in the United Church of Christ.

Tom T. Fujita is a pastor in the United Church of Christ.

J. Dorcas Gordon is a college professor in Toronto, Canada. She is a member of the Presbyterian Church in Canada.

Michael Leon Guerrero is a community organizer. He is a member of the Roman Catholic Church.

Cynthia L. Hale is the senior pastor of Ray of Hope Christian Church (Disciples of Christ) in Decatur, Georgia.

Mary Ruth Harris is an ordained minister in the United Church of Christ.

Juanita J. Helphrey is the minister for racial justice programs, Division of American Missionary Association, United Church Board for Homeland Ministries, United Church of Christ.

Carter Heyward is a professor of theology at the Episcopal Divinity School in Cambridge, Massachusetts, and a feminist theologian. She is a priest in the Episcopal Church.

Linda H. Hollies is the outreach field director for the West Michigan Conference of the United Methodist Church.

Darryl Farrar James is rector of Messiah and Saint Bartholomew Episcopal Church in Chicago, Illinois.

Ben Junasa is a retired minister in the United Church of Christ.

Virginia Kreyer is a retired minister in the United Church of Christ.

Andrew G. Lang is a writer in the Office of Communications, United Church of Christ.

Deborah Chu-Lan Lee is an educator living in Berkeley, California.

Michael E. Livingston is the campus pastor and director of the chapel at Princeton Theological Seminary. He is a member of the Presbyterian Church USA.

Vilma M. Machín is the minister for education on pluralism, United Church Board for Homeland Ministries, United Church of Christ.

Madeline McClenney-Sadler is an ordained minister in the Baptist Church. She is a doctoral student at Duke University.

Gay Holthaus McCormick is an advocate for teachers, a writer, and a speaker on disability rights. She is a member of the United Church of Christ.

Marcus Meckstroth is an ordained United Church of Christ minister and the assistant director for admissions at Pennsylvania State University.

Wendy J. Miller is a campus pastor and faculty member of the Eastern Mennonite Seminary.

Deborah Alberswerth Payden is the associate pastor of First Congregational United Church of Christ in South Milwaukee, Wisconsin.

Thomas N. Payden is pastor of First Congregational United Church of Christ in South Milwaukee, Wisconsin.

Morris D. Pike is a retired United Church of Christ minister.

Tyrone Reinhardt is an ordained minister in the United Church of Christ living in Hawaii.

Ferdinand "Fred" M. Rico is an engineering technician. He is a member of the United Church of Christ.

Lillian Valentín de Rico is a freelance writer and an ordained United Church of Christ minister.

Sarah Daniels Roncolato is an ordained minister in the United Methodist Church.

Paul H. Sadler Sr. is the minister of evangelism for African American and Native American Indian church development, United Church Board for Homeland Ministries, United Church of Christ.

Rodney Steven Sadler Jr. is an ordained minister in the Baptist Church. He is a doctoral student at Duke University.

Armin L. Schmidt is the executive director of the United Church of Christ Council for American Indian Ministry.

Joan Solomon is a retired teacher and a freelance writer. She is a member of the Roman Catholic Church.

Kikue K. Takagi is retired. She is a member of the United Church of Christ.

Daisybelle Thomas-Quinney is the religion and minority student adviser at Thiel College in Greenville, Pennsylvania. She is a member of the Church of Christ.

Ansley Coe Throckmorton is the president of Bangor Theological Seminary in Bangor, Maine. She is a member of the United Church of Christ.

Hamilton Coe Throckmorton is the pastor of Barrington Congregational Church in Barrington, Rhode Island.

Helen B. Webber is retired. She is a member of the United Church of Christ.

Roger Wharton is an environmentalist. He is a priest in the Episcopal Church.

Albert L. Williams is a teacher and minister in the United Church of Christ.

Rebekah Woodworth is a member service representative for Vantage Healthcare Network, Inc. She is a member of the Associated Reformed Presbyterian Church.

Flora Slosson Wuellner is an ordained United Church of Christ minister, an author, and a retreat leader.